THREE CLICKS AWAY

THREE CLICKS AWAY

Advice from the Trenches of eCommerce

MICHAEL DRAPKIN
JON LOWY
DANIEL MAROVITZ

John Wiley & Sons, Inc.

New York ➤ Chichester ➤ Weinheim ➤ Brisbane ➤ Singapore ➤ Toronto

Published by John Wiley & Sons, Inc.
Published simultaneously in Canada.

This publication is designed to provide accurate and authoritative information in regard to the subject matter covered. It is sold with the understanding that the publisher is not engaged in rendering legal, accounting, or other professional services. If legal advice or other expert assistance is required, the services of a competent professional person should be sought.

Library of Congress Cataloging-in-Publication Data:

Drapkin, Michael.
   Three clicks away : advice from the trenches of ecommerce /
Michael Drapkin, Jon Lowy, and Daniel Marovitz.
   p. cm.
Includes bibliographical references and index.
ISBN 0-471-39682-6 (cloth : alk. paper)
   1. Electronic commerce—Management. 2. Internet. I. Title: Three
clicks away : advice from the trenches of ecommerce.
II. Title: Advice from the trenches of ecommerce. III. Lowy, Jon,
1972– IV. Marovitz, Daniel, 1972– V. Title.

HF5548.32.D73 2001
658.8′4—dc21

               00-061963

Printed in the United States of America.

10 9 8 7 6 5 4 3 2 1

MLD—To my mentors, Bonnie Powell,
D. Stanley Hasty, and Dr. Robert Freeman, my
soulmate Suzy Drapkin, and my lifelong friend and
boi, John Bruce Yeh.

JL—For Harrold, Lorraine, Ernest, Lilly, Thomas,
Beth, David, and Rachel.

DJM—To The Alpaca, Bill, Margaret, Caroline,
Brendan, and the memory of Ronnie.

Contents

Section III   Project Management

Foreword

Three Clicks Away appears at a time when the market is reevaluating the wisdom of sticking an "e" in front of everything and calling it a runaway success. Frankly, it couldn't come at a better time.

The world of e-commerce emerged and grew up during a period where (at the time this was written) the economy has experienced 40 straight quarters of growth. While this tremendous period of growth has helped to nurture the new economy, the true test of business is surviving the lean times.

How do you create entrepreneurial-minded organizations with long-term strategic competitive advantage? That I believe is the biggest challenge for most organizations today.

This book addresses that question. It recognizes that while the Internet represents the business opportunity of a lifetime, there are core principles and steps to follow when operating a solid new economy business.

My firm, BroadVision, is a leading worldwide supplier of personalized ebusiness applications. BroadVision's end-to-end solutions enable companies and governments to rapidly deploy and cost-effectively operate secure, scalable, intelligent, and flexible ebusiness applications for e-commerce, financial services and knowledge management.

But before managers can make the best use of our technology, they must first achieve the steps laid out in this book. They need to understand the Web landscape in order to gain an appreciation of the types of business models being used today for formulating effective online strategies. Next, a firm needs to build a world-class organization to meet the challenges inherent in a fast-moving industry. Finally, the challenge is to execute and exceed expectations, and keep your customers happy. If you can do all of that, you will be unstoppable.

Three Clicks Away is full of insights that will help you do that. Each critical area needed for structuring, organizing, and running your endeavor is discussed. It is extremely important to be the first mover of the industry. The information in this book can help you to achieve this goal.

Over the next few years, e-commerce will become fully integrated into our everyday lives. With multiple touch points like cellular telephones and other hand-held devices, people around the world will have seamless access to content and transactions instantly, anytime, anywhere. New e-commerce systems will ensure that the information received—regardless of the access device—is relevant, as it will be personalized to the individual.

Consumers now have the choice of turning to traditional retailers for product information and/or directly to the suppliers themselves, who, through the Web, can establish dialogue and community for the first time directly with the end consumer of their products. Suppliers are in a much-improved situation with such a direct feedback loop. Retailers also have the opportunity to strengthen their relationships with their customers through value-added services such as "one-stop" shopping and bundled products and services.

More and more companies, both mainstream players and small firms alike, will continue to embrace the Web as a new channel to save money or to generate new revenue. If a company's web site successfully attracts thousands, or even millions, of visitors to its new site, and these prospective customers don't have a positive experience because the site is slow or offline, they don't come back. On the Web, like everywhere else, you only get one chance to make a first impression.

What kind of impression do you want to make on your company, on your start up or on the business world? Use the information in this book to help you be ahead of the curve rather than behind the curve. Use this information if you want to create a business not just for tomorrow or even the day after, but for the long-term.

DR. PEHONG CHEN
President and CEO
BroadVision, Inc.

Introduction

Many years from now, our grandchildren will ask us to tell them stories about the time, at the turn of the millennium, when the web emerged and changed our society and economy forever. Unfortunately, this somewhat invisible revolution is hidden in cables and humming metal boxes, but its implications are just as large as the dawn of the airplane age. We live in a time when the World Wide Web and e-commerce are turning the fabric of business and society inside out.

The Internet is the most significant change in the structure of how business is transacted since the invention of the telephone. It is a market maker, a market destroyer, and an inverter of traditional models. This radical change has put enormous pressure on today's firms to present their products, services, and brands online. Managers and executives are suddenly faced with the responsibility of leading electronic commerce initiatives, but they do not have the tools or education needed to respond effectively, and this gap is becoming increasingly critical. Many traditionally safe businesses are being cannibalized by "dot-coms."

Part of the impetus to write this book came from our explaining the same things, over and over, to seasoned businesspeople. How e-commerce actually gets done hadn't ever been packaged for overworked businesspeople in a digestible way. In our search for materials on the subject, it became clear that e-commerce resources were few and far between.

We decided to pool our knowledge. Our insights into the web—perceptions honed from long hours and missed vacations spent building and nursemaiding the birth of websites—were collected for the benefit of others. We have had our share of successes and, probably more important, we have learned from fantastic web disasters.

The result of this collective knowledge and experience is what you're holding in your hands.

Over the past two years, business on the Internet has increasingly been called *electronic commerce* or *e-commerce,* defined as business transactions that are conducted over the Internet, such as purchasing a product, obtaining a price quote, moving funds in a bank account, or changing a mailing address for a magazine subscription. E-commerce is complex because it entails the convergence of graphics and design, marketing, and merchandising, as well as a wide array of sophisticated technologies.

To be successful, today's business leaders quickly need to grasp the fundamentals of e-commerce. We felt that there were all too few places to go. The information available on electronic commerce has focused almost exclusively on two areas: visionary futurology and technological nuts-and-bolts explanations.

This book does not attempt to supplant traditional works on how to manage projects, marketing, or technology. Rather, it addresses the core issues of how to develop an e-commerce-specific strategy for an organization; what web companies and web people do; how to find the resources needed to recruit, develop, and manage personnel in the e-commerce arena; and the basics of evaluating and delivering e-commerce projects. Meeting these challenges is what it takes to succeed in e-commerce.

If you are a leader of an organization, *Three Clicks Away* will provide you with the twenty-first century tools you need to navigate the multidisciplinary world of e-commerce. All of the issues are presented from the perspective of business management: *How can you effectively manage e-commerce in a rapidly changing, critical, technical, and complex environment?*

We believe that the book will prove useful to a wide audience of corporate strategy managers, students, retailers, executives, and anyone else who manages or wants to manage e-commerce to achieve better technology, marketing, sales, administration, and operations.

One point we would like to make. You will find perhaps a surprising number of references to Gateway, the San Diego-based computer maker and its website, gateway.com. The reason is simple—we worked there. We worked there during some of the fastest growing, wild west years of e-commerce, when in order to go in any direction you had to blaze new trails. The lessons learned during those formative years heavily influence how we think about building businesses on the web.

We would like to acknowledge the following people, some of whom worked directly with us on this book:

Carter Adamson, William Appling, Brad Briggs, Zeev Chared, Paul Cuthbertson, Murat Dulger, Matt Epstein, Tom Fisher, Chuck Geiger, Ian Gheogeghan, Jason Grosfeld, Tom Grueskin, Surie Hecht, Maurice Henry, David Hock, Adam Hurwitz, Vadim Iasenik, Jim Kirsch, Dennis LaRock, Gaven Mandelbaum, Damian Manning, Marcus Miholich, Ralph Pastore, Laurie Pick, Arthur Roses, Jordan Rubin, Steve Ruegnitz, David Steigelfest, Suresh Subramanian, Sandra Thomson, Roman Trakhtenberg, David Turnbull, Ted Waitt, Howard Wiener, Etta Wilson.

In well-designed websites, surfers are never more than three clicks away from what they want. Use this book as your pan and pickax for mining the Internet. By wisely using the knowledge it contains, you may be only "Three Clicks Away" from internet success. Good luck!

MICHAEL DRAPKIN
(mdrapkin@drapkintechnology.com)

JON LOWY
(jon@lowy.net)

DANIEL MAROVITZ
(dan@marovitz.com)

Section I
Strategy

Strategy is a much-abused term. It is often used in juxtaposition with "tactic," or in its place. For example, "What's our strategy for killing this email backlog in the tech support inbox?" Another vague business term is "approach": not quite a strategy, not quite a tactic, not even a plan. If you are ever given an "approach document," run, or at least dismiss the management consultant who billed your firm for producing it. Let's outline our definitions of these terms.

Strategy involves orchestrating a unique combination of core business factors. To use a musical metaphor, a strategy is the conductor's concept for the performance of a piece of music. It normally begins with an interpretation of the composer's work, but must then take into consideration the musicians, the venue, the audience, and the management of the orchestra. A strategist analyzes a business's unique internal and external assets and liabilities, defines the firm's goals, and plots a course to achieve them by altering and harmonizing these factors. In any industry, this type of thinking requires a special understanding of the business and its supporting technology.

E-commerce strategy is not the old corporate strategy that has long been the domain of scholars, analysts, and management consultants. We have seen millions of dollars literally thrown away by old-guard strategists who were arrogant enough to think that their (debatable) analytic techniques would translate successfully to e-commerce. In general, they don't translate. In the current global business environment, if you take the time to develop a strategy "the old-fashioned" way, the world will have changed enough to invalidate your conclusions.

1

In a mature industry, analysts and strategists have a list of statistics and formulas that can be counted on to inform them of status and to project quantitative and qualitative outcomes. For example, in a retail business, there is a bricks-and-mortar equation: the site itself (floor space, volume, climate control, displays, interior design) plus location (average income, population density, city infrastructure, economic growth/decline), supply chain, shipping, staffing levels, current retail consumption and competitor presence, point of sale, accounting systems, and advertising costs—to name just a few factors that can be readily analyzed.

With an e-commerce business, you still have to consider many of the traditional factors along with new technologies and market forces that resist quantitative analysis because of the pace of change. The other enormous difficulty, of course, is that there is so little historical precedent to guide your path. The short history of the online business world is, in many ways, not likely to be predictive of the future. It is still involved in an erratic, "noisy" beginning; it has not yet developed the patterns of a mature system. Because of this lack of history, many entrepreneurs got caught—in the second quarter of 2000. They assumed that the market would continue to absorb endless overvalued IPOs (initial public offerings). The ebusiness world will eventually rationalize and become more predictable.

In this section, we categorize the different types of e-commerce business models:

➤ Pure internet businesses (like Yahoo!);
➤ Companies that sell physical products online but have no legacy bricks-and-mortar channels (like Amazon);
➤ Bricks-and-mortar firms that are projecting their businesses onto the Internet (like Gateway).

We also discuss auctions, portals, stores, b2b, b2c, mobile commerce, and other elements that comprise the web landscape.

Chapter 1

Formulating an Online Strategy

When your boss pats you on the back and says, "Congratulations! You are now head of our icommerce—I mean, e-commerce—initiative. I know how you love that PC thing on your desk," this is where you turn. This chapter will help you break down the rather ominous task of starting to drive your company's e-commerce effort: how to get an initiative going, how to avoid boiling the ocean the first time out, how to have a big strategic vision but shoot for tactical achievement.

■ GET A STRATEGY

Epanic. That is what we call it. Epanic takes over when an organization suddenly realizes that it is up the proverbial creek without the proverbial paddle, and the proverbial spring deluge of e-commerce competition is coming downstream with the force of a Godzilla-induced tsunami. The urge is to get online—fast! Build. Get "something" up. Converts are always the most zealous practitioners of their newfound faith, and in no case is that more true than with executives who have seen the "dot-com" light. They tend to become evangelists for e-commerce.

The ensuing epanic usually introduces an expensive consulting firm that doesn't know much, an e-commerce czar who is ill-prepared for the task, and vocal senior people who spend a lot of time disagreeing on how the company's website should "look."

It is best to avoid all the above, and it is not monumentally hard to do so. Even if the people in your organization are not familiar with the Internet, there are ways to address your move into the online world without generating lots of unnecessary effort and disappearing dollars. But move fast and keep your chin up. Large organizations in particular have huge momentum toward the scenario outlined above. It is not the scenario you want to experience firsthand.

Let's first examine the three basic stages that businesses pass through on their way to e-commerce nirvana—or at least to having a meaningful, commercially sound web presence:

1. Process improvement.
2. Electrification.
3. New paradigms.

■ PROCESS IMPROVEMENT

It is best to start with the easy stuff. Process improvements—ways to get your company's feet wet by using the new technologies—will make existing business processes work better, without trying to go too far too fast. Sophisticated transactional websites are not inexpensive, easy, or quick to build. In almost every business, there will eventually be a need to do more sophisticated things, but, for several reasons, we advise starting small. If you are just starting out, you probably don't have access to an in-house web development staff. Instead, you plan to outsource the development of whatever you aim to do. As we continually repeat throughout this book, *outsourcers must be managed.* Generally, good business practices and skills will get you somewhere, but, at the end of the day, you need to understand something about what your contractors are doing if you hope to get the best work out of them.

The same goes for managing employees. It sounds like an obvious statement but people often forget it when the Internet is involved. There is a sense that "practitioners" of the Internet (a.k.a. techies—those strange, highly paid twenty-somethings) are some form of modern-day alchemists. They manage an arcane art—making websites—and you need to just let them do what they do and not worry about it. Be glad you have one (or more) in your organization.

As is true in every other part of your business, knowledge is power, and knowing more will help you ensure success. Being non-technical is OK to a point, but understanding the fundamental principles of how technology operates and how programming works is an unfortunate prerequisite for managing websites effectively.

There is an inescapable Catch-22 for businesspeople who are new to the Internet and need to formulate an online strategy. Success on the Internet demands that you strategize and plan before you start building. (Reverse that order and disastrous results always follow.) Yet, to formulate a comprehensive strategy, you need to understand the realm of the possible and the implications of development. The best way to learn what is really deliverable and manageable in the web space is to manage the construction of a site. The best way to ensure the success of a development project is to have a strong strategic vision . . . you get the idea. This leads us to a critical point about formulating strategic and organizational formulas for successful management of websites: Technologists need to sit in at strategy meetings.

If technologists are ordered to execute a business vision without having been included in its formulation, opportunities will invariably be missed. If you are very new to the Internet, try to connect yourself to a strong technology person when you are deciding what you want to attempt online. The issue is that, like you, people who are beginning an e-commerce career often make incorrect assumptions about the time, cost, and difficulty of doing things online. Some things that might appear very sexy and out of your league may be technically rather trivial to implement. Conversely—and unfortunately, far more likely—the functions that you see on big consumer sites are difficult to achieve and beyond your organization's resources.

Online strategy and development is a process of give and take. Sometimes the "business" side drives a vision and the technologists are pushed to make it a reality. At other times that are rather different from the flow of traditional business, technologists will have an insight or an innovation that enables business functionality, or even whole businesses that were not possible before. We will discuss this concept, and the roles and structures that help promote these idea exchanges, in later sections.

The best strategic advice is to take as much time as your competitive environment will allow. Learn and grow your skills, comfort, and experience with web technology before you lock your strategy. It is particularly important that you cut your teeth on smaller projects before engaging a major "info builder" (what some consulting firms are calling themselves these days) for a $25-million project. "Process improvement" is a great way to add real value to your organization. The projects are less expensive because they are internally focused; the environment is more controlled; and there is an added benefit of touching more groups and more people and getting the overall organization focused on the magic "e."

There are lots of ways that internet technology and the principles of e-commerce can add value to your organization without trying to go from the Wright Brothers to the Space Shuttle in one day. Begin by looking for the ways in which your organization distributes and utilizes internal information. Huge cost savings and improvements in service quality and sales efficiency can come with a simple corporate intranet.

For a few thousand dollars, a simple intranet website can be produced in a couple of weeks. If your resources are modest, start with information that is relatively static. You won't need to spend consulting dollars, and you can use internal people to make updates. Good candidates in this category can usually be found in the Human Resources (HR) department. Employee handbooks; vacation days, travel, and expense policies; honor code documents; employee assistance programs; and similar documents can be expensive to print because they may be long (like an employee handbook) and they tend to change only minimally over time.

Process improvement is the first step in the chain, and it can become quite sophisticated. Within the HR intranet realm in particular, companies are doing interesting things. Common transactional HR sites allow employees to change their benefit elections, check their 401(k) investments, exercise stock options, request vacation time, and so on. Often, these types of services (in particular, investment-related services) are outsourced to financial services providers. They create a private-label website that lets employees of a firm like Gateway think they are on a Gateway site when they exercise their stock options, for example. In fact, they are living completely within the Salomon Smith Barney environment. It is the bane of the administrators of internal networks, but companies are also providing computer-based training (CBT) at their employees' desks, with sophisticated applications that use animation, video, and sound.

Even if you are part of a steering committee, or an executive strategy team looking at a sophisticated business-to-business e-commerce website, it is valuable to dig into a simple intranet site. If the Internet is new to you, even as a user, let alone a builder, the intranet environment is usually a safe and pretty simple environment in which to learn. The bottom line is: The more you understand about how a web server works, and the level of skills (or lack thereof) necessary to write a page of HTML, the more comfort and power you will have.

■ ELECTRIFICATION

This is the second step. This very broad category essentially involves taking your existing business online. The vast majority of companies around the world—even those that have been investing heavily in internet projects for years—are still essentially at this stage of development. Within this category, there are two main types of activities:

1. Online assist.
2. Transition.

An easy example of online assist would be a local grocery store's website, providing information about products, specials, and maybe even coupons that you can download and print out from your computer. This area doesn't get much air time but is arguably the largest factor in the new economy's commerce. Because it is difficult to track, it doesn't get as much respect as its massive impact deserves. Lots of people never, or rarely, buy anything online, but they use the Internet to research and compare products before making all major purchases. Even if you can't go for a true transactional site where people are selecting and paying for goods online, the web can be a powerful contributor to educating your customers and helping new customers find you via traditional purchasing mechanisms.

A business transition model refers to a site where you can actually buy groceries online and have them delivered directly to your door. The bulk of the high-profile etailers fits into this category.

The road to the electrification of your business onto the Internet can be as extensive, expensive, disruptive, and time-consuming as the deployment of the electric power grid was to our cities and towns, so be prepared for a fundamental change in how you do business, and a long-term commitment.

■ NEW PARADIGMS

This is the most interesting and, in most cases, the most difficult category of site to conceive of and to execute. eBay, the enormously powerful online auction, is an example of a new paradigm site. There is no practical way—using paper, TV, or telephone—for a company to remotely and economically administrate tens of thousands of simultaneous auctions in hundreds of categories where customers get to individually tailor the parameters of their sale. Building an eBay would simply be impossible without the web. eBay is a business that exists solely because of the marriage of fantastic ingenuity and new technology.

Even the mighty Amazon.com is, to some extent, a site concerned with bringing an old model online. Amazon is really a cataloger. Its catalog is so enormous and offers so many categories that printing all the information available on the site would be cost-prohibitive, but the basics of its business *could* exist without the web. eBay, however, is a pure product of the information economy.

It is difficult to give advice on creating a "new paradigm" business. There are, however, new-paradigm features that you can consider in your strategic planning: community elements, auctions and exchanges, users' reviews and rankings, personalization, and so on. To be successful online, you do not need to tear your business apart to the foundation. Just be aware that there is a new tool set for serving and communicating with your customers. Chapter 2 will help you become more familiar with the array of models, businesses, and technologies that characterize the fabric of e-commerce.

When you are planning a web strategy, it is critical to keep these stages of ebusiness growth in mind and to start as small as possible. Part of how aggressive you are will obviously be determined by what is happening competitively online and offline in your category, but take the time if you can. Set yourself up for success by setting clearly definable and achievable steps, given your resources, culture, and know-how. Don't try to reinvent your entire world in a day.

■ GENERATE VALUE

Thinking about web development in these three strategic phases is useful, but what it really comes down to is how you *make money* or *save money* by using the Internet in your business. It goes almost without saying that if you aren't able to do either, or both, don't spend your dollars or time on developing internet strategies. There are and will continue to be companies that will not substantially benefit from building a website, or that can be served by a modest internet offering. If that is what your research concludes, count yourself lucky and don't be uncomfortable with the decision.

All e-commerce businesses can be broken down into three categories: (1) convenience plays, (2) cost savers, and (3) money makers. If the venture you are considering doesn't fit one, or, in the case of the most successful business models—all of these—you need to rethink your needs.

➤ Convenience Plays

Time is the real currency of the new economy. A great way to build customer loyalty is to make your site convenient and easy. The return-on-investment (ROI) math is a little more complex when the goal of your site is to build a strong brand and increase the loyalty of your customers, rather than to decrease the direct cost of sales or increase overall revenue, but it will pay a dividend over time. Strong brands achieve better marketing efficiency and make customers more likely to hang in, even if they have occasional bad experiences.

➤ Cost Savers

Eliminate salespeople. Eliminate paper catalogs. Consolidate warehousing and distribution, and you have *value*.

➤ Money Makers

These come in three basic flavors:

1. *Advertising.* Sites that monetize traffic by selling ads to visitors. Not an easy model to make click.
2. *Shopping.* Sites that sell stuff.
3. *Assisting or supporting.* Sites that don't sell directly or present ads that drive customers into traditional channels. Be careful with this flavor. Evaluating the strength of your e-commerce

strategy by the number of customers that walk into your physical retail store may not be the best long-term strategy, but it can be valid in the right situation.

When you have your strategy in place, you will need to build your plans on how to achieve your goal. We discuss project planning and project management in later sections, but there is one key concept that you should grasp early on. Internet projects that extend longer than about six months become unwieldy very quickly. Technological change, rapid shifts in competitive pressure, staff turnover, and so on, make it difficult to keep a project on track for long periods of time. Still, it is useful and sometimes critical to shoot for an eventual target that is not achievable in less than six months. Manage this by knowing where you want to go, keeping the target in sight on the horizon, and not attempting to plan every stage of the journey. Take the journey in digestible pieces. After you achieve each phase, plan in detail how you will get to the next phase. Keep the goal in sight, but avoid trying to map the path all the way.

If you do this, three things will happen:

1. You will get in the habit of successfully delivering functionality, keeping customers happy with new functions and content on your site, and maintaining high morale among your staff.

2. You will avoid lengthy planning phases when you are trying to achieve overly complex goals. In the web environment, forward incremental movement is always better than high-risk distance jumps.

3. You will inevitably find that the goal you are shooting for in the distance will change over time.

Change *before* you attain it. That's OK; it's an exhilarating and frustrating feature of e-commerce development. If you are making your way forward in manageable pieces, you will never be too far off course if the goal changes. If you plan longer and more complicated segments, you may find yourself miles from the target.

Chapter 2

Understanding the Web Landscape

This chapter will help you grasp the enormous range and scope of businesses on the Internet. To evaluate the tools provided by the web, to understand the competitive climate, and to keep yourself from trying to reinvent well-trodden ground, you need to understand the lay of the virtual land. This chapter is divided into sections that explore, in some detail, the key components of web infrastructure, technology, business-to-business, and the consumer web companies that form the main features of the Internet today. The business models, technologies, and companies that are explored in this chapter will be referenced repeatedly throughout the book. Even if you are comfortable with the web, this chapter will help you get more from the chapters to come.

■ A BRIEF HISTORY OF THE INTERNET

For many years prior to the introduction of the World Wide Web (WWW), the Internet was a land of pioneers, geeks, academics, scientists, and lonely computer-lovers. Hypertext and its language, HTML, were the domain of literary pioneers who were experimenting with a new medium and using phrases like "nonlinear fiction." Around the middle of 1994, the first glimmers of commercialism began to appear on the WWW, and ecommerce arrived. With the dawning of the age of commercial sites, capitalism was suddenly injected into the Net.

The World Wide Web has advanced onto the scene with such ferocity that even those of us who have been involved in it from the early days are startled at how the world is dripping with dot-com advertisements. Casual conversations about items purchased online are overheard in restaurants; and commonplace references to websites for more information abound on TV and in print. Without a moment's hesitation, users seem to accept a new level of internet ubiquity with every passing month. The comparisons to the invention of the printing press and the telephone are a bit overplayed, but *this is* one of the most dramatic revolutions, peaceful or otherwise, in history.

So where did it come from? Who was the inventor? How did this happen? How did we wake up one day and find that a company called Yahoo! was worth 300 percent more than Coca-Cola, and 200 percent of the gross national product (GNP) of Indonesia?! The story is particularly amazing when you realize the tremendously humble beginnings of this place we now call the online world.

During World War II, then-General Dwight D. Eisenhower was impressed by the speed with which the German army was able to move people and supplies around Europe, even though horses and wagons were still doing most of the pushing. This mobility was attributed to a phenomenal road system. Years later, back in the United States, he initiated the building of the Interstate Highway System, which is still being built as we speak. One feature of the system's design was that the major highways were routed so that they would meet outside of major cities. With this pattern, if a U.S. city was destroyed or captured during a war, the major supply lines wouldn't be cut off. This became the design principle of the Internet.

The dot.com explosion has its roots in the technology that was created by the U.S. military to help maintain the defense system's command and control in the event of a nuclear attack (presumably, by the Soviet Union). The Arpanet (Advanced Research Projects Agency Network), a system begun in 1969 by military engineers in the Defense Advance Research Projects Agency (DARPA), was designed to allow America to be able to launch nuclear counterstrikes, and to generally continue to communicate electronically even if most of the country had been turned to glass after nuclear strikes on our soil. In essence, the military wanted a network that could intelligently reroute data down a different pathway—even if nuclear bombs took out a significant section of the network.

The Internet began as a series of connections between large-scale computers at the University of California at Los Angeles (UCLA),

Stanford University, the University of California at Santa Barbara (UCSB), and the University of Utah. In the next four years, Internet Protocol (a way of packaging data and delivering it across the Internet), email, File Transfer Protocol (pretty much what it sounds like), and Telnet (a way of opening a remote terminal session for controlling distant computers) were all invented by engineers connected on the Arpanet. These four structures are still central to how the Internet operates, but their inventors are more or less lost in academic and military mists. The early internet pioneers who built the systems, architectures, and languages for communicating and moving data went more or less unrewarded for building the foundation of the dot-com revolution. Today, they would be stock-option paper billionaires on the front cover of *Business Week*. In those days, they were just geeks working hard to connect themselves to other geeks.

In 1986, a rogue branch of the ever-expanding Arpanet, called NSFNET (National Science Foundation Network), was founded. The system had much higher speed than Arpanet and linked together the nation's supercomputing centers. Within a few years, most U.S. colleges and universities were connected, and expansion to overseas sites began to heat up. In 1991, the first web browser was born. The movement from the purely text-based, rather esoteric-feeling old "internet" (as NSFNET and its offshoots had begun to be called) to the friendlier, hypertext-driven world of the World Wide Web was born. The world has not been the same since. This quote drives the point home:

> The Internet's pace of adoption eclipses all other technologies that preceded it. Radio was in existence 38 years before 50 million people tuned in; TV took 13 years to reach that benchmark. Sixteen years after the first PC kit came out, 50 million people were using one. Once it was opened to the general public, the Internet crossed that line in four years.[1]

When we talk about the World Wide Web, we usually mean the Internet as a whole, but that's not exactly the original intent of the WWW or "the web." To be precise, the WWW refers to the vast interconnected matrix of websites that eventually all link up somehow, like the Kevin Bacon game.[2]

The invention of the web was simultaneous with the invention of HTML (hypertext markup language) and HTTP (hypertext transport protocol). The creation of these technologies and their realization (the first web browser and web server), and therefore of the web itself, is accredited to Tim Berners-Lee, a computer scientist. HTML and HTTP work together with browsers and web servers to let people create web pages (HTML) and download them (HTTP). What is immediately obvious and entirely remarkable about the web is that it is so like a spider web. Download a page with links, and those links point to more pages with links, which point to more pages, and so forth and so on.

The government and university support that paid for the initial infrastructure (principally, transcontinental and transoceanic data lines) is gone. The web is now in the hands of private citizens and industry. When you download a page from a website, the information may pass through several dozen different machines and different networks, all owned by different people and companies. A social consensus has created an environment in which everyone agrees to faithfully forward any information that wants to pass through them, lest someone deny their own data safe passage at some later date. The Internet is now an impossibly complex aggregation of thousands upon thousands of different networks that agree principally on a common addressing system, and a few common protocols for communicating and packaging data. All else is chaos, but these few standards are enough to allow a computer in Namibia to reach a server in Monaco via Cleveland. This grand chaos is fueling a global revolution.

Some Chinese historians believe that about three centuries must pass before we have enough distance and perspective to really grasp an event's implications. We are very close to achieving a decade of perspective on the beginning of the web boom. These past few years have brought about such rapid growth that we are, collectively, feeling somewhat breathless. The message to learn from the history of the web to date is: Prepare yourself and your organization to embrace and move with change. The "Not-invented-here" syndrome and the "We've never done it that way before" whine have no place in the online world. Heroes are made villains; the rulers of empires are reduced to beggars, the tiny and insignificant become the leaders of revolutions—sometimes in the space of weeks. Fasten your seat belt.

■ CONTENT PUBLISHING

One of the biggest deals in history, the American Online (AOL)–Time Warner merger, is all about content. Time Warner has one of the largest, if not the largest, catalogs of conventional content in the world, and AOL has the largest network of online content, and the largest number of online subscribers. The phrase "content is king" is trite, but in many ways has rung true since the early days of the web.

It's all well and good to have cool design, flashy effects, and nifty tools for navigating your site. It's also great if you have a novel and compelling way to place ads and present buying opportunities to visitors. However, if you don't have content, you are out of luck. Look at Yahoo!, the most successful site on the Internet, hands-down.[3] Arguably, it has the ugliest, dinkiest user interface (UI) ever conceived by any person or animal. Why is it so successful? Make the case that its UI is simple and easy to use, and you could half convince us. The truth is: It *is* simple, but it's not brilliant or original in any way. The key to Yahoo!'s success is *content*. It has what you want, so you go there: directory listings, articles, stock quotes, gossip—it's that simple.[4]

Content publishing is about taking content of whatever kind (usually the bad kind) and delivering it to users in an engaging and—more importantly—profitable fashion. Most content providers have the same model. They aggregate and/or create content, they drive traffic to their site, they try to learn as much as they can about their users and their behavior, and if they can attract enough eyeballs and keep them coming back, they can make money by selling advertising and sponsorship positions. They mainly sell banner ad space (see Chapter 3, "Advertising on the Web").

The interaction between magazine-like content and internet advertising is an interesting model. To drive traffic to a website, companies have to advertise; to make money, they need to sell ads. Conventional print magazines can be put on display at a newsstand. Interested consumers then shell out, for the magazines, at least enough money to cover the price of having shipped this clunky pile of paper to the newsstand. With online publications and content sites, unless you have unique or scarce content (i.e., Lexis-Nexus, Reuters, Bloomberg, TheStreet, etc.), consumers are not willing to pay anything.

The truth is, most content publishing sites do not make money. Some of the most wildly successful content sites (Yahoo!, CNet, NYTimes.com) are just beginning to show profits for the first time, and inconsistently at best. Most of these sites subsist by what amount to subsidies from their corporate sponsors, or they are owned by profitable internet companies that use the content to drive customers to more profitable opportunities. In other words, content publishing, as a business model, rarely stands on its own feet. The history of the Internet is littered with failed dot-coms that bet the ranch unsuccessfully on content.

There are many, many different kinds of content, and they run the gamut from serious to ridiculous: news sites, hypertext soap operas, sites of special interest, animated cartoon funnies, bad poetry, and really bad poetry.

One of our all-time absolute favorite content sites is the "Bert[5] is Evil" site, which was shown to us by our friend Arthur, years ago. Unless you are easily offended by irreverent humor, stop reading right now and check out http://www.bertisevil.com. You will laugh. This is what web surfers do—they surf content sites and email their friends when they find something funny.

Let's take a moment to thank the gods of the Internet for all the free funny stuff that people post. They post it not for commercial purposes, but just because they want to share their creativity with the world. It's a better World Wide Web because of them. From an ecommerce point of view, these sites usually aren't that significant, but that's OK. Anyone who wants to can put up some pages and publish them to the web. All it takes is imagination.

On the other hand, sometimes these funny sites take off like wildfire and turn into little and not so little businesses. The Hamster Dance site was listed by Media Metrix[6] as one of the top 50 sites visited during 1999. It even attracted advertisers like Visa International—the card that's "everywhere you want to be." Visa paid top dollar to advertise on the silly single-page site. You can bet that the insane kids who put this monstrosity together in college, while pulling massive four-foot bong hits, never in their wildest pipe dreams imagined that it could be so popular.

Practically speaking, no successful content sites are technically as easy to create as Hamster Dance, and perhaps none is as successful. Maintaining a deep content site like CNet's News.Com (http://www.news.com) requires a virtual organization comprised of many writers to create the content. Editors, designers, programmers, lawyers, and various other professionals are needed to manage the whole process. Finally, robust web publishing and content management systems make the whole process manageable.

When CNet got started in the early 1990s,[7] there were no products on the market to help automate the needs of a robust-content publishing site. Publishing systems have long laundry lists of requirements. The content creators, usually writers, need non-techie tools to enter their product—text—into the publishing system. They can't be expected to do the HTML coding themselves. The editors and other managers need to have a way to keep track of deadlines and review the submitted work of the writers. The designers and HTML layout people need a way to manage the web page templates so that all of the written content somehow neatly fits into the appointed places on the page. In addition, there needs to be a way to:

➤ Keep track of different versions of documents.

➤ Relate different documents to each other for navigation purposes (think of the "related articles" links on many news sites) and for organizing articles into sections, so that they can be browsed in many different ways.

➤ Plug in and rotate banner advertisements in various pre-allotted areas on the pages.

➤ Preview everything before it goes live.

➤ Coordinate everything so that, for example, when you put up the new daily stories all at once at midnight, and move yesterday's stories to the "archive area," you don't break everything.

Get the picture?

The analogs of the newspaper or magazine publishing process don't really hold up. One of our best friends, who is a graphic designer at a big international business weekly, only works in print. She said she would never move into web media because "It's never done." "When a magazine goes to press, it's done. Finished. There is no more you can do, there is nothing to fix, and you get a sense of accomplishment. With internet sites, it's never done. It's an eternal work-in-progress. It would drive me nuts!"

Welcome to our world!

The tools and systems used to manage an eternal work-in-progress need to be sophisticated *and* usable by a lot of different people in a lot of different places. Faced with this mess of requirements for its content-oriented properties, and without any off-the-shelf products to buy, CNet started to build its own web content management system, and it pretty much succeeded. Eventually, the system matured to the point where it was actually marketable. CNet licensed it to Vignette, which still sells it under the name Story Server. To this day, it is still the leading content management product.

Many content sites and corporate intranets have successfully adopted Vignette's product for managing their sites. Others have been frustrated by its lack of flexibility and extensibility. If you want to make a site that works pretty much like CNet's sites, and if you want to manage your workflow in a way that is fairly similar to the way CNet does it, then you are in pretty good shape using Vignette. But if you want to do things your own way, and you want to have rich content and navigation that can be personalized, you will need to either grow your own system or spend some significant time shopping for another product. When you are doing brand-new things in brand-new ways, you can't necessarily go out and buy a product to do them. If you are lucky, and have developed your own software, you may find others who want to do what you do, and it may make business sense to license your technology to them. But we wouldn't count on it. Stories like CNet and Vignette are very rare.

Most content publishing sites are, thankfully, not as huge as CNet, and most are more focused, so it is almost always more convenient and ultimately much more affordable to create your own system. You can use off-the-shelf products—databases, version control software, workflow management tools, and a myriad of off-the-shelf components and applications—to make your life easier. However, ultimately, you have to figure out how to manage your contributors and how you want your content site to work: where you want it to be like others and where you prefer to be different. There are never easy no-brainer solutions such as, "Let's just buy Vignette for that. They do content management." These are famous last words.

Without a well-integrated and automated system, the steps for content publishing look something like this:

1. Writers write articles in Microsoft Word (most good writers probably don't know HTML and they shouldn't have to); the articles are then sent to the editors.

2. Editors and other reviewers email the documents around. After receiving the necessary approvals, they annotate the documents so that they fit into the rest of the website. Then they pass them on to the designers and HTML people.

3. HTML specialists and graphic designers turn the articles into HTML documents, adding links and navigational elements as indicated by the editors' annotations.

4. Quality assurance (QA) people look for errors, and, inevitably, the writers, editors, or lawyers have to change something. Steps 1 through 3 are repeated until the content is good to go.

5. Technical people review each page and add any special bits of code that are needed. They then stay up all night getting ready to deploy the new stuff on the site and remove the old.

As you can see, the purpose of a content management system is to separate and coordinate the work of content creators, editors, marketers, reviewers, designers, and technologists. Without a content management system, you would have unnecessary dependencies among different groups of people. These would slow the process and very quickly render the entire enterprise unmanageable.

A lot of lessons can be learned from the content publishing world. All sites that have more than a few handcrafted pages, such as hamsterdance.com, are based on templates that permit a uniform look and feel, navigation, and display of many different kinds of messages that come from many different authors or sources of data. The challenge of orchestrating and coordinating the work of all of the people and systems that contribute to a content site is the essence of web content publishing. Successful website operators spend much of their time engaged in a never-ending search for the best and simplest ways to manage this complexity. There are no easy answers with publishing. The only advice anyone can give is the age-old business platitude, KISS: Keep It Simple, Stupid. Think Yahoo!, think Amazon, think eBay.

■ SHOPPING

Shopping is the heart and soul of the B2C (business-to-consumer) ecommerce landscape. People go to these sites to buy stuff. There are tens of thousands of websites in this category, and the granddaddy of them all is the mighty Amazon.com, with its huge market capitalization and powerful global brand.

In the early days of online shopping, it would have been wrong to say that the sites were selling. They were taking orders. Ask any experienced salesperson to explain to you the difference. Sales involves actively working with a customer, working over a customer, listening to the customer's needs (stated or not!), picking up on clues, making recommendations and suggestions, and closing the sale. Most websites still do not do much, if any, of this. They merely take orders. Order taking is what happens when you call L. L. Bean or J. Crew and the representative asks: "First item, please . . . what color, how many . . . credit card number? . . . Thanks for calling J. Crew!" This is still what most websites do today, except that they go one step further: You have to fill out all the forms yourself.[8]

The bottom line is that most online shopping sites are still basically catalogs. The web allows for a catalog that is bigger and has more information, more product views, more photos, and so on, than would be possible in paper. But at the end of the day, these are still plain old catalogs.

That having been said, the number of key functions that can be built around the basic catalog functionality make online stores a special experience. Here are four of those functions.

➤ 1. Recommendation Engines

These are being increasingly used by a host of different companies. The concept was popularized by Amazon.com, where it has been used as a powerful mechanism for cross-sell and upsell.[9] This is a critical concept and a critical technology for helping to approximate the effectiveness of a talented flesh-and-bones sales rep with an electronic selling system. One of the tools that salespeople use very well to increase the size of a ticket is a notation of the sort of things that a customer likes, such as, "Why not get one in blue as well? If you like Donna Karan, you should try some Hugo Boss." This is selling. It is not something that a paper catalog does very well, and it's not something that websites do terribly well either, particularly in these still early days of the development of ecommerce.

A recommendation engine analyzes the purchase affinities between buyers and looks for buying patterns. Perhaps everybody who buys Danielle Steele novels also buys a Shirley Maclaine self-help book; perhaps everyone who buys Sergeant Pepper also likes Miles Davis. Some of these connections would not necessarily be so obvious, but they become clear and transparent quickly when companies' databases are used to store their product catalogs and their customers' orders. Recommendation systems form a key component of the next topic: personalization.

➤ 2. Personalization

This is one of the buzzwords that haunt people building websites. Personalization is so sexy and compelling, and seems so obviously a part of the Internet promise, that everyone wants to have it on his or her site. Executives, particularly those who pay loads of unnecessary dollars to big-name consulting firms, tend to discover this notion, and they hug it to their chests like so many pinstriped Dorothys holding Totos during a twister.

What is it? Well, it is many different things. Some are relatively trivial to implement, but people have poured millions of dollars into others for years, without much success. The general principle is to customize the experience so that when any given customer comes to a website, what he or she sees is different from what other people see. The profusion of "my.[insert name of favorite website].com" portals, probably the most pervasive example of personalization on the web, really started with my.yahoo.com.

In my.yahoo.com, each customer can make a series of selections relating to the stocks that are to be tracked, the types of news that are of interest, the cities for which weather information is needed, and how all this information is to be formatted when it is delivered.

For many companies, personalization may mean a greeting to users who have registered and been to the site before: "Hello, Jimmy! Welcome back!" Or it may mean a sophisticated presentation of historical transactions with the company, personalized news, and the status of previous orders.

The issue with implementing personalization, as with all technology on the web, is to have a clearly defined business purpose for wanting to use it. If the main purpose is to post when the apple pies leave the oven in the local bakery you own and operate, you probably don't need to delve too deeply here.

➤ 3. Community

In some implementations, personalization is used in conjunction with a recommendation engine. The idea, when incorporating community and shopping, is to enrich the shopping experience so it becomes something more than just "buying stuff." This was the central idea behind iVillage.com's foray into ecommerce.

iVillage is one of the 30 largest sites on the Internet and the leading site dedicated to women. It is a media property—something like an online women's magazine with enormous scope and depth—but it is also a community. As an example, the area of iVillage that deals with parenting, childbirth, and child rearing is popular and has an enormous amount of content. In an area that discusses the decision of whether to breast feed, people can not only read articles by experts on the subject (on both sides of the issue) but also chat in real time with other iVillage members or with occasional guest experts, and post questions on an electronic bulletin board. The idea with a community site is that it is not just passive. The user is not only extracting information from the site but is also a contributor. Sites that are interactive (users participate as content creators and members) tend to be "stickier"; there are more repeat visits, longer visits, and more involved usage.

The community commerce idea creates an environment for "contextualized commerce"—commerce with camaraderie, advice, involvement, and support—but it is also a great recipe for compromising the integrity of your community and your store. Few companies have been able to blend community and commerce together in a way that is valuable enough for use by consumers and does not sully either experience. It is important to understand this concept, but, in general, it is interesting on paper and not great in execution.

➤ 4. Guided Chat

This is an interesting set of technologies that are intriguing but have yet to find their true niche. Here's what occurs: If a customer is browsing a shopping page and has a question about a product or is unable to find what he or she is looking for, a click of a button on the page will fulfill a request to "chat now." Then, assuming that a customer service agent is ready[10] to "take your call" immediately, a little chat window pops up and you can type your conversation and receive real-time replies from a customer service person.

Some more sophisticated implementations of the technology allow a customer service rep to take over a portion of your browser and "push"[11] pages to you. eBags.com, a company that sells bags of every possible description, uses this technology to good effect. If you request a chat session and tell the representative that you want to see the largest, rolling piece of leather luggage available, the rep will push you to the relevant page of the site with a photo and detailed product specs.

The issue with this technology is not whether it is good for the customer. It is clearly enormously convenient, particularly for folks who are coming into the site via a dial-up modem connection and have only one phone line in their home. The issue we have with it is that people often look to real-time chat, and to chat with push technologies, as a way to achieve cost savings. Think of it this way: Which can you do faster: tell somebody what you want, or *type* a message that tells somebody what you want? It is a customer service play, not a cost saving tactic. If you approach it that way, you'll be safe.

It is useful to examine the various types of shopping sites that exist on the web. New combinations and twists appear all the time, but a few basic structures will get you oriented.

➤ Bricks and Mortar Assist (Clicks and Mortar)

It makes sense that this is probably the largest category of shopping sites on the Internet—the new channel of sales, distribution, and marketing. All of the big companies you know and love have moved onto the Internet, and most of them have kept all of their[12] traditional assets and are simply using their website as an additional distribution mechanism.

Think about the weekly scramble, at a company like Kmart, to get a circular ad prepared for the local newspapers. You can't advertise the special sale on 10-pound bags of corn chips unless you know you have them in the store. But the printing process takes time. The decision to put corn chips in the ad has to be made several days in advance of the printing. Now, Kmart can say: "See Kmart.com for more great specials online and in your local store." It's a small point with big implications.

The problem with clicks and mortar is that it implies a level of integration between systems that is not usually achieved. Gateway launched a marketing concept based on the slogan: "Call, Click, or Come In!" The message says that Gateway offers customers a number of different mechanisms for interacting with the company. They can buy, or receive technical support, from a call center, over the web, or in a Gateway retail shop. Yet all these businesses exist on different technical platforms. If someone buys a system on the web, a sales representative in a retail shop has no easy way to tell that customer the status of his or her order.

However, from the customers' perspective, a clicks-and-mortar approach is almost always ideal. Most bank customers have become very comfortable with the idea of doing online banking. They can pay bills, move money between checking and savings accounts, and manage their credit cards. But would a first-time home buyer get a first-ever mortgage online? Probably not. Someone about to make an enormous financial commitment that is notoriously complicated and fraught with prickly legal points will probably want to discuss it face-to-face with a lender. Depending on how your business is structured, it may not be possible to offer customers a choice of multiple contacts or methods, but it is almost always preferable. If your long-term strategy is to drive customers out of your bricks and mortar and into your clicks, then it must happen organically. Short-term artificial incentives might drive people to try out your site, but, at the end of the day, the overall quality of the experience will determine the contact structure (and therefore the economics of your business!) to which your customers will gravitate.

➤ Pure Play

These shopping sites exist only on the web. There are no supporting bricks-and-mortar stores and no paper catalogs. If the term is applied stringently, companies that maintain telephone-based customer service centers would not fit the definition.

There are very few large-scale pure play sites on the web. Think about most of the shopping sites you are familiar with. Chances are they are not pure plays. There are a number of reasons for this. For starters, the Internet has been with us for only a short amount of time, and there are far more well-established traditional brands than there are internet companies. The second issue is that, for many products, customers prefer a combination of contact methods.

To some extent, what drove many companies to create pure plays (as opposed to potentially more customer-friendly clicks-and-mortar structures) was the NASDAQ—the tech-heavy stock exchange. The market applied a heavy discount to companies that had large amounts of capital tied up in "old economy" assets. There is some reasonableness to the proposition that pure new-economy companies—without expensive aging factories, for example—are better prepared for the future. At the same time, however, it is immature to believe that customers will gravitate immediately and completely to online tools just because they are more efficient for the companies these customers patronize. With the recent corrections in the NASDAQ, it seems a fair bet that the market will become a little more sophisticated about applying massive valuation multiples to pure-play companies and punishing brick-and-click firms.

The other major issue is that it is quite difficult to be a pure play. Let's examine, again, some of the history of Amazon.com. In its original Securities and Exchange Commission (SEC) filing for its initial public offering (IPO), management went to considerable lengths to describe how Amazon would not be burdened with the enormous infrastructure and physical plant overhead that burdened all other booksellers (Amazon's primary and initial product category). In addition, management spoke of the concept of "virtual inventory." Amazon was not going to hold any inventory at all. Instead, it would work within the existing book distribution infrastructure, and, when orders came in, they would be sent along to distributors. If a book wasn't in stock at a distributor, Amazon would place a special order and communicate a longer shipment lead time to the customer.

Amazon learned very quickly that in the vast majority of cases, the concept of virtual inventory is a pipe dream. Internet shopping is focused on immediacy, ease, convenience, and dependability. If the experience fails to offer any of these advantages, customers will abandon it, particularly when commodified products (such as books) are widely available in many locales. The problem is that an outsourcer doesn't own your customers. *You* own your customers, and you are responsible for the quality of their experience. An outsourcer (1) doesn't directly feel the benefit of a loyal customer who gives you repeat business, and (2) gets paid whether the order is from a new customer or an old customer. For a website manager, the economics of maintaining an old customer vs. being forced to acquire a new customer are very clear. Return visitors are good for the bottom line. Customer acquisition is a killer.

The key here is the *total* customer experience, which goes beyond the website. It includes the experience of receiving the delivery, accepting the package, opening it, unwrapping the book, browsing through it, smelling it, and so on. Amazon realized very quickly that to ensure that its products arrived on time, were beautifully packed (with the packing slip placed just so), and were wrapped in enough material to prevent damage, their own employees had to do the picking, packing, and shipping at a warehouse. Also, to maximize the efficiency for the warehouse operation and to have better control over the product procurement delivery stream, Amazon needed to own and control the whole process.

The current Amazon.com reality is very different from the original proposition. At the beginning of the year 2000, Amazon.com had more than 3.5 million square feet under lease for warehousing and distributing products. That space is equivalent to more than 200 percent of the volume of the Empire State Building, or nearly 30 Barnes & Noble bricks-and-mortar superstores. Not exactly what we'd call *virtual*.

➤ End-to-End Commerce

Some companies that are selling products on the Internet control not only the web's front end and the user interface, but also the procurement, warehousing, and pick/pack/ship operations.

➤ Front-End Only

A number of traditional distribution and product merchandising firms have emerged as partners to ebusinesses. They allow a company to create a website that sells DVDs, for example, and to be worry-free regarding buying, warehousing, and shipping DVDs. The firm builds a website that allows customers to search for the DVDs they want, buy them, and pay for them with a credit card. After an order has credit card approval, it is sent to the outsourcer for shipment, and the outsourcer takes care of the rest.

This is often a good strategy for rapid entrance into a market, although, by definition, the markets in which these types of services are available are already well represented on the Internet with the offerings of several firms. From a technical perspective, one of the parts of this outsourced model can become complex: the communication of inventory availability, particularly the "out of stock" message. Naturally, you don't want your website to commit to deliver a product to a customer overnight, if your outsource partner doesn't have it in stock. (This sequence can put you in legal jeopardy.)

➤ Private Label

In a number of categories of ebusinesses, a company will provide you with not only the back-end procurement, warehousing, and pick/pack/ship operation for a given category, but with the website as well. The private-label company will work with you to develop a customized look and feel, but 95 percent of the site will be identical to those of other companies using the service. If you use one of these services, the definition of your offering will not be very unique. Success is more likely if you are already successful in one category (probably one that you manage yourself), and you want to increase the robustness of your offering and become more of a one-stop shop.

The largest question that tends to emerge, with both the "front-end-only" and the private-label options, is: Who owns the customer experience? Your customers' experience with you will determine whether they do their repeat purchasing with you or go elsewhere. It doesn't mean that outsourced models can't work or won't be a strong base for business. But just remember Amazon's experience.

➤ Distribution Partner

In this modification of the private-label scenario, the outsource company does not do the merchandising, the selection, or the purchase of goods. It only does inventory receiving, warehouse put-away, and the pick/pack/ship function.

➤ Agents and Aggregators

This is a relatively new but expanding category of shopping sites. These companies do not make or market products themselves; they merely help consumers find companies that do. For example, if you are trying to buy fly-fishing gear, there are a number of ways to approach that purchase. You can type in the names of stores you already know; or type the name of the desired product into Yahoo! or a similar engine, or randomly type in the web address for the stores, products, and brands you seek. Agent sites try to scour the web, both electronically and manually. They look for shopping sites, aggregate them into categories, and build links to their product presentation pages. This allows customers to find a vendor for a product when they don't know where to look, and to compare prices at different sites that sell the same product.

A few new sites are actually beginning to editorialize about products rather than just presenting them. Productopia.com is a site that is trying to position itself as a concise and stylish *Consumer Reports*. But instead of trying to be comprehensive and encyclopedic in scope, Productopia.com presents just a few products in each category, such as the best quality mountain bike, the most techie mountain bike, the best deal, and so on. This is done for dozens and dozens of categories.

These sites make their money, or try to make their money (none has been terribly successful financially yet), in two major ways: (1) by selling targeted banner ads based on a category of product; and (2) by receiving a bounty or commission from the sites to which they refer their customers. If you are looking for a mountain bike and end up clicking through to one of the sites mentioned by the agent, the target site is able to track where you came from and then pays the agent site for either the referral or an eventual sale. The issue, of course, is whether either of these models has any editorial integrity to protect consumers. Many of the "Chinese walls" between editorial and advertising functions, which are hard and fast in the offline world, become dangerously hazy on the web. In our view, the same rules should and will apply, and much of the questionable "advertorial" content appearing on websites will be reduced as consumers and their lawyers get savvier and raise their voices in protest.

■ COMMUNITIES

In many ways, communities are the reason the Internet and WWW exist. The original military roots notwithstanding, the desire, among scientists, to create a common communication platform for sharing ideas, data, and analysis drove the original creation of the Internet. Before the World Wide Web, the explosion of the news group structure—tiered hierarchies of postings on every topic under the sun—formed the backbone of internet content. Famous communities such as The Well played key roles in what we consider to be the "netizen" style and philosophy of online living. Online meeting points, where people created friendships and rivalries as real and involved as in the physical world, were a major feature of the early Net. The Well, and dozens if not hundreds of other communities like it became places where people shared the birth of children, the joys and hardships of everyday life, and even their final moments before death—all online.[13]

Today, communities take several basic forms on the web. Pure communities without any commercial intent are still alive and well, or even thriving, on the Internet, but they are no longer the only game in town. Commercial and advertising-driven sites are coupled with community,[14] but not always in healthy ways, on the web. Nearly all of the leading consumer ecommerce sites have powerful community elements that provide stickiness, product review, and a sense of membership among buyers.

Aside from Usenet and the Internet Relay Chat (IRC)—which are generally only usable by techies—AOL was and has been the classic community in the commercial world. Arguably, a great deal of the attraction that has allowed AOL to grow to its gargantuan size came from its chat rooms. AOL smartly gave the people what they wanted: the ability to interact in real time through their chat rooms. AOL cleverly seeded the opportunity in two different ways: (1) a series of pre-defined general-interest rooms was created and the topics were set by AOL; (2) the "created by AOL Members" rooms dealt with every conceivable topic—from the sacred to the profane—according to the wishes of the users themselves, who created them at will. The rooms are destroyed when the last active participant leaves. AOL loosely polices all chat rooms through its users, who can report offending members for Terms Of Service (TOS) violations.

AOL couples this grass-roots user-oriented policing of its chat rooms with permission for users to create invisible "invitation-only" chat rooms. A password is needed to get in, and instant messages—one-on-one private conversations between two "consenting" members—are the draw. AOL puts the framework for policing and monitoring, along with no-holds-barred private venues, where the members can say whatever their hearts desire. This has created, within AOL, an enormously attractive culture of community that has gone a long way toward creating vast stickiness in its service, in addition to an idiot-proof "everything you could want in the Internet as long as you use our AOL desktop app" product.

These kinds of communities have had interesting societal ramifications as well. People now regularly meet on the Internet through venues like AOL-ICQ, IRC, and others. Often, these relationships cross into real life and result in "real life" friendships, romances, and, more often than not, marriages. In our high-paced, high-pressured society, these virtual communities provide an easy alternative to traditional social settings. Users can sit down at their computer, in the comfort of their home, and extend themselves socially into any electronic community of their choosing: people in their own neighborhood, strangers almost anywhere in the world, or a group of chatty individuals who simply share a common interest.

On the ecommerce side, Amazon gives powerful support of community through its user reviews. Amazon was one of the first sites to incorporate anonymous user recommendation systems as part of the buying experience. The company recognized quickly that, in the online book business, if someone searches for a book in an unknown area and comes up with several choices, he or she really has no way of making a decision. Most bookstore clerks are terribly knowledgeable about their products these days, but, in the online world, the buyer is totally alone and has millions of choices. *The New York Times Book Review* does not professionally review the vast majority of books, so users are left with nothing but the publisher's description. Amazon lets anyone (after its editors' screening for inappropriate content is completed) post a review of any book. It not only provides a useful service, albeit of radically variable quality, it allows users to make their mark in *their* store. Someone who has obscure interests—say, in twelfth-century Chinese pottery—could feel free to expound at length about the triumphs or sins of two books in the category. Unusual, slow-selling products are economically sold. Unusual, unheard views are given voice—in a commercial context.

Many of the outdoor product sites—most notably, Patagonia and REI—mix together the type of recommendation engines popularized by Amazon. You can write a review of a pair of hiking boots that you bought and include information about nature and the environment. More pure community elements come in because areas of the sites are dedicated to message boards about conservation, favorite hiking and fishing destinations, and questions and advice from members to members about how to train, how to improve your canoeing technique, and so on.

It so happens that Patagonia and REI actually do give a portion of their annual proceeds to charity. So, at least to our minds, the touchy-feely, nonprofit "feel" that comes with community seems less phony there than in other places. That doesn't stop lots of companies without an altruistic bone in their corporate bodies from trying to load up on community as well. Community features in the wrong context can actually demotivate shoppers. Touchy and soft as it may be, a successful community helps to drive one of the most powerful and elusive site attributes in the ebusiness world: stickiness.

Stickiness is a label for frequent, repeat visits that involve lots of page views. Unless you are running something like an online grocery (not necessarily recommended, given the mostly catastrophic failures of companies in this sector), chances are your customers are not going to come back to you month after month, let alone day after day. Applications like stock trackers, email, weather reports, and, yes, community are powerful stickiness drivers. Features like these are dynamic; they change. Change brings people back. People who get really involved in communities might "hang out" there weekly, or even several times a day. Each visit is an opportunity to sell them something, and selling them something is the goal of ecommerce. You came to Patagonia.com to discuss the serious environmental problems caused by hydroelectric dams, and "Oh, cool. What a great jacket . . . I mean, I know I am never going to climb Mount Everest—in fact, the treadmill in the garage has the evidence of nine generations of spiders—but that $300 Gore-Tex shell is GREAT!" Ah, the rather honorless world of community and commerce! The descent into fake, corporate bombast is easy with community.

eBay, however, is a prime example of a commercial community. The entire auction model of eBay relies on a trust-based, self-policing community. In eBay, the community is the store—an ecommerce chicken-and-egg situation, if you will. Amazon is more or less a traditional retailer using community and other mechanisms to enhance the experience of shopping in its stores. eBay is a store that has no products of its own; it is the structure on which a massive community of buyers and sellers has grown. It is a marketplace—a forum for commerce, the virtual agora. It doesn't really do any commerce itself. It just extracts what amounts to a sales tax for the commerce that occurs within its "borders."

In the eBay context, the recommendation engine is used to discuss the merits and sins of the members of the community—the buyers and sellers on eBay's auctions—not the merits of products. Anyone who buys from a given seller earns the right to review the seller via a star rating system, and to write some comments about the experience. Were the goods as described? Did they arrive in good condition? Did they arrive when promised? And so on. Any seller can earn the right to comment on a buyer. Basically, did the buyer pay appropriately and on time?

Nearly every commerce business plan that we see these days contains some community elements. When community elements are applied correctly, they can have a strong impact on traffic and, eventually, on sales. Just be honest with yourself. Certain businesses have relatively natural community affinities; others do not. Books, health, sex, environmental issues, politics, religion, and the products that surround these topics are pretty obvious candidates for community plays. If you sell steel wire (no offense to the steel wire marketers in our readership), chances are your customers are not going to be highly inclined to gab for hours about their favorite wire colors. It is important to understand the web landscape and see what has worked for other firms. Learn the complete tool set of web features. Community is an area that you should enter into carefully, and not just because your expensive management consultants think it is sexy. Happy chatting!

■ PORTALS

"Portal" is one of the most abused terms in the ecommerce industry (and this industry has been devastating in its abuse of the English language). It has gotten to the point where the words *portal* and *website* and *web portal* are often used interchangeably. Clearly not every website is a portal. So, what makes a portal a portal? We broadly define the term thus: A portal is a website that aggregates a set of capabilities in a user-friendly manner.

Some history. The original and archetypal portal is Yahoo!. What most people don't realize is that Netscape made them the giant that they are. Back in the mid-nineties, Netscape was getting hits from virtually every user on the Internet. Why? Almost everyone on the Internet used Netscape Navigator (Netscape's web browser) to surf. It followed that the default homepage for almost every user was http://www.netscape.com. Netscape senior management asked themselves, "What are we going to do with all of these eyeballs?" Netscape's website had little content to captivate the average web surfer. Unless you were interested in Netscape's products and technology resources (the authors certainly were!), there was little reason to browse there. Practically down the street from Netscape's offices in Mountain View, California, were the offices of a little web company called Yahoo! that had just left its original home at Stanford University in Palo Alto.[15] At the time, Yahoo! was nothing more than a directory of websites, organized in a few basic categories. It was probably the biggest directory of its kind, but it was essentially a routing mechanism—a way to get to somewhere else. Since Netscape had nothing better to offer, they decided to put a big link on their homepage to send all their eyeballs to Yahoo!. While we don't know the specifics of the deal, looking back with perfect hindsight, we can see that Netscape got the short end of it. As a result of all the users coming to Yahoo! again and again, Yahoo! had to answer the same question: "What do we do with all of these eyeballs?" Yahoo! took a different approach from Netscape and that has made all the difference.

Yahoo! added more and more services and content to their site with this goal in mind: Keep the users here as long as possible and always give them reasons to come back. Every time they come back show them lots of advertising. This is known in the trade as "monetizing traffic." News, stock quotes, weather, email, bulletin boards, sticky things—things you check every day was where they focused their development efforts. Needless to say Yahoo! quickly became one of the largest sites on the web and has successfully maintained its dominant position. Netscape's site, which had massive traffic opportunities, lost its place as an online destination and retreated into its software business. Microsoft rapidly eroded its software business and Netscape was swallowed whole by America Online.

If you go to Netscape.com now, you will see that their home page looks very similar to Yahoo! It has much of the same functionality that Yahoo! has. Netscape realized that they missed the portal boat a few years ago and made a mad dash to catch up with the Stanford wunderkinds but it was a simple case of too little too late. They still get lots of visitors at www.netscape.com, but they are effectively off the map of big portal sites today.

In the case of Yahoo!, search engines, and many general content/community sites, most of the revenue comes from advertising. Sites include Lycos, Excite, MSN, and Netscape Netcenter. With these, the strategy is to keep you coming back and make you stay a long time when you do. Once they get you coming back for one thing (e.g., free email is very popular), you may find there is something else you want to use. No new registration forms to fill out, since you already did it when you signed up for email. Once you find a "portal" site that you like, you tend to stay there, because all your preferences are recorded and you know how to get around. The resistance to trying new services is diminished because you are already set up as a user in the general portal system. If you go to a completely different site you will have to register and build a new profile. This stickiness makes the users increasingly valuable. As data is gathered about user's behavior across a number of services, the ability to target users with advertising and purchasing opportunities gets better and the rates advertisers will pay increase.

What is remarkable about Yahoo! is that it is in fact not a single website. It is hundreds of websites! Although all of the functionality and content is presented through a uniform look and feel, the actual websites that provide such things as stock quotes, weather and chat are quite independent from one another. Yet, wherever you go on Yahoo! the navigation is the same, your username is the same, and your personal preferences are reflected. So, this is what we mean when we say that a portal "aggregates a set of capabilities in a user-friendly manner." Portals are all about managing complexity.

Many people in the marketing industry generically refer to these advertising-funded sites as "portals." This causes some confusion because not all portals have the same functionality and business model. In fact there are as many types of portals as there are types of businesses. Let's examine a few.

There are of course a dozen or so major general portal/web directories—Yahoo!, Excite, Lycos, MSN, AOL, and so forth. They are all more or less the same. In fact many of them subcontract various pieces of the portal, stock charting, to the same companies. Portals are full of "private labeled" technology and content. Lots of disparate pieces used to fill out the user experienced integrated under the same brand and navigation structure.

There are personal finance portals like Quicken.com which allow you to enter in information about your investments, track and analyze them, learn about tax optimization structures, research and actually sign-up for a mortgage online, forecast retirement needs, and so on. Just to make things more complicated there are personal financial portals nested inside portals like Yahoo!'s Yahoo! Finance and MSN's, moneycentral.com which are both complete financial portals within the larger general portal structures of their parent sites.

There are general shopping portals, effectively what Amazon has become, and more targeted shopping portals like eLuxury.com and ashford.com (backed by Amazon), which bring together the world of luxury goods under one roof. Increasingly the portal metaphor is being used in the B2B world. Take AsiaBondPortal for example. This creatively named site brings together a number of investment banks in a consortium to create a platform for trading Asian fixed income products. Deutsche Bank and the large German software house, SAP, have established online electronic marketplaces for a wide range of products targeted at mid to large sized corporations. This allows businesses to access a portal with pooled buying power.

We are also seeing interesting movements from the content world to the commerce world and vice versa, all in the name of achieving "portal" functionality. Travelocity.com started as a way to cheaply and easily buy airline tickets. It is now trying to cast itself as a destination site (read: portal) for all a person's travel needs. Airplane, train, car, hotel, destination guides, restaurant info, and so on. Again, the point of a portal is that it allows you to aggregate lots of functions together in an easy, navigable, branded environment. This is not a simple task.

As more and more firms find themselves needing to add functionality and content to their websites in a coherent way, there are some emerging portal trends. The first is the appearance and rapid acceptance of Application Service Providers (ASPs) that host private label (or white label) web sites for companies. One popular example for large public firms is the investor relations (IR) section of the corporate website. Most of these firms don't have the facility to get real-time stock quotes and display pretty charts, so, for a monthly fee, smaller ASPs offer to host the entire IR portion of the site, ensuring that everything fits into the overall website's navigation and look and feel. In other words, when the user clicks on the IR link, she or he goes to the private label website that is hosted by the ASP, but is entirely unaware that this has happened because the look and feel is consistent. It still feels like the user is still on the same site. In general, this arrangement works out pretty well because the IR section of a website is pretty much a stand-alone section, so it isn't too hard to manage as a fully outsourced service.

Other portal ASPs are more granular in what they provide, meaning that they don't provide a whole site (or "sub-site"). They just provide elements of pages that you need. Following the same IR example, there are several companies that just provide stock quotes and charts. As mentioned above, all of the big "portal sites" use these outsource services. With a more granular offering, the ASP delivers data and images and the subscribing site incorporates them into their own web pages. The advantage of this type of portal service is that the portal owner keeps more control over the entire site (rather than outsourcing a whole section of the website). There is more upfront work required because of the complexity of integrating different pieces from different places into a single web page (i.e., your pieces and the pieces from the ASP), but long term this makes the site cheaper to manage and provides a better user experience.

So, one way of building portals is by integrating third-party functionality into your website. In some cases the third party may be a partner or yourself (when your firm owns two distinct websites and wants to tie them together). What is nice about the portal trend is that many companies have designed their websites in such a way that they can be more easily integrated into other sites. These companies see themselves as portal building blocks, but they often showcase their capabilities (not to mention creating value by attracting users) within their own branded portal. An example of this is Microstrategy, which offers analytic tools that can be plugged into any website. They also host a portal, strategy.com which uses these tools. Another example of this model is vicinity.com, which offers a range of services such as, address locators, travel directions, and maps. For a fee, these can be incorporated seamlessly into your own website.

While there are many sites that are built on a portal model, the vast majority of websites are built with a focused purpose and were not intended to fit into a larger framework. When creating a portal, the pieces that need to be integrated are generally not plug and play. To meet this challenge, portal products are flooding into the marketplace. These are products, such as Netegrity's SiteMinder, that make the job of integration easier. They include tools to pull third party content into your site, search multiple sites at the same time, and enable users to use more than one website without having to login more than once (called single sign-on or SSO).

Even with all these new tools to help, the pitfalls for of portals are numerous. When you merge two commercial websites you have to deal with the technical complexity as well as all the dimensions of an offline merger. To integrate multiple websites and lots of different functions into a coherent user experience requires a great business vision and strategy, careful and constant planning, very sophisticated technology, and a touch of genius or luck (either will do).

Most people who make the attempt end up with an unfocused site with lots of features that are poorly integrated and hard to find. We term these sites Frankensteins: A bolted-together monstrosity of ill-fitting pieces. There are far more difficult-to-navigate, confusion-creating Frankensteins on the Web than there are well thought out, useful portals. Hearing the word "portal" come out of your mouth or anyone from your firm in reference to something you are going to build should cause you to take a deep breath. We don't mean to say that if you have the time, money, and corporate will to build a serious portal you shouldn't go for it, just enter into this territory with respect. The big portals have taken literally thousands of man-years of work to achieve what they have achieved. Don't be fooled by the seeming simplicity of Yahoo! This is an absolute monster of a site, and if you have used it much, you know that even mighty Yahoo! is far from perfect.

■ B2B, B2C, B2—WHO CARES?!?

With shuffling, plodding steps and heavy sighs, we drag ourselves to this topic. "But this is critical! Everyone is always talking about B2B models, and why they are so much better than B2C! I have to sell my B2C stocks because it's an unworkable model on the web!!!!" We know what you've heard.

Slow down. Relax. Welcome to one of the worst buzzword domains of ecommerce. It has become very trendy to say "We're B2B." So what does it mean? B2B stands for Business to Business. Essentially, B2B websites are dedicated to serving the needs of *businesses* that serve consumers, not the end users themselves. Think wholesale. B2C is Business to Consumer. These sites are dedicated to selling stuff to lonely guys who have an AOL account and a maxed-out Visa card. Think retail.

An argument that has erupted is that B2C is hard to do because the marketing and discounting/promotional costs of trying to get millions of consumers to know a brand and use a particular site are unbearable. There is no way to ever have the business *turn* (the buzzword for "make a profit") because the marketing costs and the need to have special sales that destroy margins never go away. In other words, it's an endless sea of red ink. People love to point to Amazon.com as the great example of the B2C disaster: a huge brand, millions upon millions of customers all over the world. Amazon should have achieved real scale by now and should be showing profits—yet, it hasn't and it doesn't. If Amazon, mighty Amazon, can't make money B2C, how can any of the rest of us poor losers ever hope to crack the model?

➤ The Amazon Secret

Here's the reason Amazon loses money: The market allows it to. Yes, it is true that, by the second quarter of 2000, Amazon's stock had been knocked 60 or 70 percent off its high, but the valuation is still stratospheric. Mr. Jeff Bezos, the CEO of Amazon, has a clean strategy that he will continue to maintain until the market genuinely and truly punishes him by delivering a 50 to 75 percent drop in the value of the company, below its already depressed level. Bezos wants to make Amazon an absolutely dominant global brand. He will keep pouring his *hundreds of millions* of dollars into advertising, crushing his competition, buying up other great websites, improving his service, and growing overseas until the market finally demands profitability. He will then need two fiscal quarters to dial back the marketing spend and be profitable, on demand. Don't shed any tears for Amazon's red ink. It is there because Amazon wants it to be there.

On the B2B front, why has B2B been declared the "future of ecommerce" and "the only workable ecommerce model"? Because, as the logic goes, fewer customers are available to call upon. By definition, as you move up the distribution chain, fewer people need to be educated about your products and your brand, not millions. With B2B, massive amounts of marketing dollars don't need to be spent on expensive and often highly inefficient consumer advertising campaigns. You only need some targeted marketing in some not-too-terribly-expensive trade publications, and some flesh-and-blood salespeople who like expensive restaurants and know their wine.

There is some logic here, but this argument has a number of problems. The first and most basic problem is that the B2B/B2C situation is no different on the Internet than in traditional "real world" bricks-and-mortar businesses. Retailers, whether virtual or physical, still have to get the message out to many more people than, say, a clothing manufacturer who is only worried about talking to the five buyers at the five big department stores that place large orders. So, frankly, where all the new media press noise came from is a bit mysterious but is nothing new.

The second problem is that, just as in the offline world, getting one of those five department stores (in our earlier example) to buy a product is not, in principle, any easier than getting 50,000 people to come to a retail store. Those five apparel buyers are bombarded by lots of guys like you who want to sell their products in those stores. Landing a sale with the likes of Macy's ain't easy.

The bottom line is that business is difficult, any way you slice it. It comes down to a question of what type of activities you think you and your firm are good at, what your competencies are, and what connections you have. Neither model is inherently more workable than the other. It is also important to try to keep an eye out for models on the web that suggest where your company can leverage off the massive marketing spend and correlated massive traffic of, say, an Amazon or a Yahoo! And guess what? Yahoo!, AOL, and all the other big boys know that you would like to have that leverage, and that knowledge serves as the cornerstone of *their* advertising and sponsorship businesses.

Very few easy models or free rides are left on the WWW. In the real cowboy days, prior to 1998 or so, arbitrage opportunities could be had as CEOs of real companies were figuring out their ecommerce strategies. Great deals could also be cut that would garner free traffic and free exposure on a major portal site. But it doesn't take long for people to pick up all the gold nuggets just lying around; assume they have pretty much all been found. Figure out what business you want to be in—B2B, B2C, or even C2C—and execute well. Success through a lot of hard work is possible with *any* structure. There is no place in the distribution chain that guarantees success.

■ FINANCIAL SERVICES

In many ways, the perfect industry for the Internet is financial ser-vices.[16] When you think about it, it seems unlikely that so much early internet sales volume would be driven by the sale of hard goods such as books, computers, CDs, videotapes, clothing, and so on. True enough, all of these products work pretty well over the Internet, and there is definite convenience for shoppers—and, if properly exe-cuted, operational efficiency for retailers. At the end of the day, how-ever, all of these items need to be shipped. Many are nice to try on, or pick up, or feel in your hand. But they need to be moved physically: picked out of a warehouse, boxed, packed, labeled, and delivered somewhere in exchange for money.

This isn't really what the web is about. When people talk about *cyber* this, and *virtual* that, and the elimination of time and space as constraints for business, are they really talking about cardboard boxes on trucks?!? Not really. Many of the big websites that garner lots of attention in the ecommerce world are merely efficient cata-logers. They are catalogers with community and catalogers with in-conceivably large selections of products, but catalogers nonetheless.

Enter the world of financial services. The key activities in the consumer space are banking, brokerage, credit card management, loans and mortgages, insurance, and bill payment. The world of institutional financial services is more like a universe. All of these services are informationally intensive and complex, and they in-volve, most importantly, a product that is genuinely *ether.* Whether it's a wire transfer or an analyst's report, it's all just ones and zeroes. These are personal, critical, and sensitive ones and zeroes, but purely digital content all the same. In short, no FedEx drivers need apply. Financial service products can be delivered as fast as a web page can load.

This really is the perfect industry, the one that is ripe for the In-ternet revolution, and it has been experiencing just that over the past several years. Let's examine the brokerage business. What really cre-ated the stranglehold of the full-service, $150-per-trade broker was an ability to access information. Current news, research, and, most im-portantly, pricing data from the world's financial markets were sim-ply not within the reach of average people. Until 1996, most people checked the prices of stocks and mutual funds in their portfolios in the morning newspaper. The information they were reading was the security's closing price of the previous day. It's not that the bankers didn't understand technology; on the contrary, the banking industry leads the way for the rest of the world, with regard to business systems. Think about the advantage of having a few bytes of information or getting an order into the market a few seconds before the next guy, when "the deal" involves trillions of dollars in volume. So, if the investment in technology is mind-blowing in the banking industry, why did it take the banks so long to get on the Net? Because their overpaid MBAs were scared, and many still are. The Internet has made banking technology available to everyone at once. So, ultimately (don't hold your breath), you might not need banks. This is often called "disintermediation." It means that the bankers might have to innovate to prove that they have some value to add if we want to pay them to deal with our money.

Brokers traditionally paid exorbitant fees for real-time or near-real-time data. In the nineteenth century and the early twentieth century, the data were delivered via ticker-tape machines with hard-wired connections to the exchanges. That delivery system continues right up to the present day. The hard-wired terminals from Bloomberg, Reuters, and Bridge cost thousands of dollars a year. The information stranglehold that started with Dow Jones in the 1870s was nuked by the Internet in about 24 months. Suddenly, everyone had access to real-time news, analysis, historical charts, graphs, sophisticated analytical tools, and more or less all the current market data they could swallow. All for the unbelievably low bargain price of absolutely nothing. NOTHING!

Talk about empowerment! The authors would like to go out on a limb and suggest that a major factor in the explosion of the stock markets from the mid-1990s to the beginning of the new century—an explosion referred to as "irrational exuberance" by Alan Greenspan—was in large part due to the availability of new information. Financial services are about risk management; that is what banking institutions get paid for. The best way to manage risk is to have more information, which is why all the world's banks employ platoons of PhDs to help them make sense of political, technological, and societal changes, and how those changes, in turn, move markets. Financial opportunity and upside come from having better information—or, more importantly— better analysis of the same facts than the next guy.

For the first time in history, the great consumer proletariat was awash in up-to-the-minute data and, to a lesser extent, analyses (of variable quality) that had previously been the exclusive domain of financial professionals. The entire world dove in to try to make sense of it and to ply their newfound knowledge on the stock and bond markets of the world. This introduced lots of new buyers and new sellers. The results were raging volumes and the creation of scarcity, which resulted in higher prices and higher overall markets. Big boom time, baby!

So where does that leave the pinstripe guys of the hallowed marble banking halls? Well, for starters, they're in a very different place. Banks are in the process of trying to electrify a great many of the relatively mechanical, repetitive tasks that fill their industry's workdays. What makes this process comparatively easy is that there are algorithms and formulas—sometimes quite complex, but still mathematically expressible—that guide many business decisions. Take mortgage lending, for example. A mortgage lender doesn't really decide whether to grant a loan. He or she identifies all of the elements of your personal financial profile that indicate risk, runs them through a series of complex equations, and, in the end, consults a software package that tells whether you are a yea or a nay. The vast majority of cases are clearly black and white, and computers deal with black and white really well.

The result has been an explosion of automated online lending services. Based on the profile drawn by a computer (and the credit reports that you authorize for retrieval), a website "decides" whether you are worthy of the bank's taking a risk on you.

Car loans, credit card applications, online bill payments, stock purchases, transfers of money between accounts, and on and on, are all quantifiable, mathematically expressible—and, in most cases, wholly electronic—tasks. Tellers who sleep on the job, take cigarette breaks, and demand time off for little Julie's ballet recitals are no longer needed or welcome.

What will become of financial services a few years down the road? For starters, they will be much smaller. The institutions that are still around in a few years will eliminate armies of tellers, institutional traders, and back-office operations guys. Tens of thousands of global financial services jobs will go the way of bowling pinsetters. Banks will become essentially giant software companies—more specifically, Application Service Providers (ASPs), that assemble customized packages of financial products and services over distributed web-based platforms. The majority of the financial services workforce will be involved in building and supporting an enormous web of systems that keep the virtual services humming 24 hours a day, seven days a week. Researchers and analysts will continue as the only major "human services"-focused groups in these massively downsized companies. A relatively few large institutional and high-net-worth retail customers will maintain their personal one-to-one banking relationships, but they will pay dearly for their human-touch experience.

The human labor involved in today's banking services may evolve to automated internet services. Bankers, who are usually human (despite appearances),[17] are not going to curl up and die. They will undoubtedly come up with better products and services. The real value of bankers is in their ability to solve financial problems, whether they involve retirement planning or financing a space-shuttle mission. As the problems get more complicated, the solutions to boring old problems can become more elegant. So, although the banking institutions we know and love to hate may change, the work of bankers will be in demand as long as there is money.

■ EXCHANGES AND MARKETS

Let's say we want to buy a baseball bat. It's a good thing to keep in your office, actually. A friend of ours at eBay, the biggest auction site on earth, keeps one by his desk to scare (and beat) people—mainly vendors, consultants, and such.[18] Consider purchasing one.

Instead of going to a store, or getting a price from a sales agent on the phone, or looking at a catalog of some seller of baseball bats, you can price it over the Internet. Is this exciting? No. Because who really cares that we can get an instant answer to our inquiry, using our mouse? So what that we can order the bat and have it shipped to our office without moving our feet. Granted, it may save us a few minutes, and some savings may be passed on to us because the transaction had a lower cost to the seller, but, proportionally, it's not too big a benefit.

Taken individually, shopping sites (the hip term is etailers) provide incremental savings. But what if we write a program that goes to the ecommerce sites of 20 baseball bat sellers, gets the best price for a bat, and orders it. That looks more like a home run. (Pardon the metaphor.) Now we have a real benefit. In the same amount of time that it took us to make one inquiry, we made 20. We have made a dramatic jump. We have created a virtual marketplace. This buys us more than incremental savings and efficiencies. The Internet gives us synchronicity and simultaneity, and these create new business capabilities.

B2B is a new craze for publishers. SAP[19] has announced that its new mission, called mySAP.com, will become the de facto standard platform for virtual marketplaces. SAP is well positioned to do this. Its business is to provide technology to manage transactions among vendors and customers, enforce business rules, ensure integrity, report on finances, and so on. SAP provides this technology for most of the large corporations of the world, and for many smaller ones. It is only logical for SAP to extend its technology so that all of these businesses (SAP's customers) can transact with one another in real time. The same system that manages your business will, one day, be able to seamlessly participate in various virtual marketplaces. From banking services to paper clips, the big software people believe we are going to do business through virtual marketplaces.

SAP is not the only player in this game. Oracle, SAP's major competitor, professes that "Oracle software powers the internet" and you can bet they are pursuing the virtual marketplace dream with vigor.

Oracle and SAP are in a very attractive position to make this happen. The question is: Can they go from providing stand-alone back-end business systems to orchestrating the future of networked commerce? There are also internet-centric companies, like Commerce-1, that come at it from the other side. These B2B companies started by creating marketplace platforms; now they are trying to tie into everyone's ERP system. Firms like Commerce-1 might seem less strategically positioned, but they are certainly benefiting from Wall Street's B2B hype, and an argument can be made that these start-ups are better equipped to build the new economy than the older, slower software giants.[20]

Looking ahead, everything starts to look like the stock market. This makes sense. Today's stock exchanges and trading networks are arguably the most impressive economic achievement in human history. They are a set of pure digital internetworks[21] connecting people and electronic entities. It is a foregone conclusion that all the separate stock exchanges will ultimately converge into a single unified network, and consolidation is evident in exchanges worldwide. Sounds like the Internet, doesn't it? We aren't economists, but, like most businesspeople, we appreciate a brilliant business model.

Exchanges don't have to be limited to stocks, and this is what the world is waking up to. Virtually, anything that has value can be traded openly through an exchange. To extend our baseball bat example, let's say you decide that you want a new tool to intimidate management consultants or create liquidity. The baseball bat has gotten boring. Is there any way to redeem your baseball bat, cash it in, and then buy a bullwhip? If the baseball bat was bought new for $30, its resale value is probably less than $10. Why did it go down so much? Why is it worth three times less? Did the bat's quality and usefulness diminish? No. The reason you can't get a fair price is because you don't have anyone to sell it to. There is no efficient way to find a buyer. Enter internet exchanges.

From a certain point of view, eBay, the auction site, is the largest garage sale on earth. But it's also the first example of a large-scale internet exchange. Because of the massive number of customers and merchants who use eBay, you can buy and sell items more efficiently through eBay than on your front lawn. A growing number of merchants now earn their livelihood through eBay alone. But the power of eBay to consumers is that we can get rid of stuff that we don't want anymore, and we can get a fair price. People refer to eBay as an auction site, but it is actually an exchange. It connects buyers and sellers, and the auction happens to be the method of matching bids and asks.

With time—and this is happening so fast that this statement will probably sound adorably quaint by the time this book goes to press—more and more items become more and more efficient to buy and sell. There may not be a baseball bat exchange, but you can bet there will be a sporting goods exchange, and the next step is that people will become sporting goods investors and try to corner the market in baseball bats. When enough people get together and want to buy and sell stuff, and when there is a network and a business protocol to support that desire, suddenly liquidity and volatility surface, and the people who participate the most tend to be the best informed to understand the products.

And while the eBay community and others are using the Internet to make consumer product markets efficient and liquid, the same thing is happening in the corporate space. Fruit and vegetable dealers around the world are getting ready to jack into networks to do real-time open bidding on shiploads of grapes from Chile. Energy companies are doing the same. At night, in eastern Siberia, unused power that is dissipating without being used while everyone is sleeping can be piped (conducted) across the continent to Paris. Bandwidth futures, diamonds, and embroidered blue jeans are all candidates. If there is a market for something, the dealers and the buyers and sellers are looking to the Internet to provide a platform for doing business. Think of the ancient Greek idea of the agora, but on a global scale. Even the stock exchanges are going through a process of democratization and openness; the days when bankers sat behind closed doors and restructured the world may be coming to an end. Individuals and institutions, now more than ever, can independently trade and settle transactions without the help (or interference) of large financial services companies.

Running an exchange is profitable. Typically, the exchange makes money on every transaction, whether the markets are up or down. Most of the software to manage these exchanges and markets is not particularly complex or expensive. The difficulty, as with any exchange, is getting enough buyers and sellers. Without masses of participants who are ready to transact, there is no liquidity, no exchange. But once the exchange or marketplace is established and running, it is very difficult to compete against it. When an exchange has enough liquidity, it attracts more buyers and sellers, and they add more liquidity, and so on. Arguably, in exchanges and markets, being first to reach critical mass is probably more important than in any other internet business model. eBay is a perfect example. It has locked up consumer resale. Other players who are well positioned may be able to specialize in specific consumer exchanges (e.g., our sporting goods exchange), but there probably won't be another eBay, just as there probably won't be another New York Stock Exchange.

■ ASPs

Let's explain this much-abused acronym.[22] ASP stands for Application Service Provider, but it's not quite that simple. In fact, it's a little confusing because Microsoft, the Roman Empire of software, also uses this acronym for one of its products. In the Microsoft product universe, ASP stands for Active Server Pages, a web technology for creating dynamic content and accessing services such as databases and other applications. This kind of verbal bullying should not come as a surprise from a company that uses "Word" as a trademark for its word processor. Because of Microsoft, the ASP industry has been tossing around the idea of renaming itself the ASM industry (Application Service Manager), but, in an effort to keep things clear, we will use ASP in the "non-Microsoft" sense.

ASPs are a relatively new but enthusiastically welcomed breed of business. They offer an increasingly popular way to outsource business applications. Typically, this is the way it works: Instead of purchasing a license for a software application, running it on your own hardware, and supporting it and your users, you contract with an ASP to manage the application for you, and you connect to the application via remote—usually over the Internet.

For example, no small company wants to deal with managing its own files servers, email services, scheduling software, running backups, and so on. Furthermore, most cannot afford to provide adequate service. Sites like www.visto.com are popping up all over the place and offering all of these services at a one-stop shop through a simple web interface. And they are doing it for free. It is a no-brainer when it's free, but even when there is a fee, it often makes more sense to go with an ASP.

Typically, ASPs are not free; you pay a subscription fee, usually monthly. All kinds of applications can be outsourced this way. The services available in the growing ASP marketplace run the gamut from back-end financial and accounting systems (such as SAP and Oracle Financials) to groupware (like Microsoft Exchange and Lotus notes), departmental file servers, and web traffic analysis tools. Several ASPs let you connect to them and run Windows 98 (and all the Windows applications you feel like running) remotely over the Internet. It's actually not running on your own system!

The difference between typical outsourcing and using an ASP may be a little fuzzy, but it boils down to the level of customization. If there is a big setup cost and a long time lag before you are up and running with your ASP, and if the solution you are getting only works for your company's special needs, then you are not getting an ASP. Your ASP-wanna-be vendor is possibly just using the term *ASP* as a buzzword, to make the service seem more attractive.

A real ASP offers something generic enough (and useful enough) to be provided to a broad customer base and get big economy of scale. If a huge customization effort and special knowledge are required for each customer, the economy of scale is reduced to the lowest common denominator among all the vendor's clients, and the bottom line shows higher costs.[23] Unlike traditional outsourcing arrangements,

ASPs should provide big net savings and superior service. As with a traditional outsourcing arrangement, the benefit to using an ASP is that you get to concentrate on your core business. The best tools are used without your having to manage them and keep them up and running, or to manage the staff needed to support that particular service.

To evaluate an ASP in terms of cost and benefit, you need to consider the total cost of ownership (TCO) of a software product. For example, a PC running Windows 98 with Microsoft Office might cost you $2,000. An ASP may offer you the same functionality, but you pay $1,000 up front, per user, and $300 per user per month. If you are just looking at $2,000 for doing it yourself, you are not looking at your TCO. Do it yourself, and *you* will need to support your users. *You* will have to set up and configure the software. When a workstation blows up, *you* will have to get it fixed. *You* will need to:

➤ Run antivirus software and keep it updated.
➤ Back up all of your users' data.
➤ Retain dedicated system administrators.

The TCO is probably more than the amount the ASP is charging, even before you include the headaches!

The key to the ASP business is economy of scale. ASPs focus on providing (relatively) narrowly defined services for the broadest possible customer base. In theory, the ASP's cost per user will always be less than yours. Furthermore, an ASP will be able to hire experts who would be unattainable and unaffordable to the ASP's customers. The only downside is that, so far, there are too few quality ASPs out there. It's a young area with a lot of talk and excitement, but few ASPs are delivering on the promise of higher quality and lower cost. This offers great opportunities to entrepreneurs with great products, but let the buyers beware. If you are going to go with an ASP, check your customer references and make sure you have a solid Service Level Agreement.[24]

■ ISPs

Internet Service Providers (ISPs) provide your business with the infrastructure to connect with and stay connected to the Internet. They offer basic services such as email, domain name registration, website hosting, and data storage. Basically, ISPs are the utility companies of the Internet. You simply can't do ecommerce without ISP services. It would be like trying to breathe underwater without scuba[25] gear or gills, unless you are Kevin Costner in the movie *Water World.*

ISPs are not limited to providing internet access to users at home and at work. ISPs connect the websites (and any other internet-based businesses), making them accessible to customers. If you run a website and your ISP goes down, you are out of business until it comes back up. You know those friendly "cannot connect to server" responses you sometimes get when you are surfing the Net? If you run a site and your ISP breaks down, that's all your users are going to see. Think of your ISP as your umbilical cord, but don't put it in the same category as your mother. That's not healthy.

ISPs deal mainly in bandwidth. Your connection to the Internet, or any kind of network connection, is like a road, except that all the cars go at or near the speed of light. The term *bandwidth* refers to the amount of data that can simultaneously travel across a connection. Using the road–car analogy, bandwidth is the number of lanes available to these great speed-of-light cars along a stretch of road. You will often hear people talk about bandwidth in terms of a pipe, as in: "I am so happy I got my cable modem. Now I have a fat pipe to download lots of wholesome content!"

Bandwidth is a two-way street. To be on the Internet, you must be able to send *and* receive data. Users tend to receive much more data than they send. Contrarily, websites generally send much more data than they receive. Like a two-way street, the traffic in one direction does not affect the traffic going in the other. This is convenient because an ISP can buy a pipe, sell the downstream bandwidth to its home users, and still have the upstream bandwidth available to sell to website operators.

Bandwidth is measured by how many bits per second can be transferred. It is sold in many sizes. Analog dial-up modems are the tortoises of bandwidth at 28.8 to 56 kilobits per second. T1 lines, at 1.544 megabits per second, are medium; DS3 (also called T3), at 45 megabits per second, is large; and OC3 and OC12 are really huge fiber-optic pipes used only by ISPs and telcos. A T1 line, which has about the same speed as 24 64-kps modems, will cost anywhere from $500 to $2,000 per month. In contrast, a 56-kps dial-up analog modem connection, under perfect line conditions, lets you transfer a maximum of about 56 kps from your computer to your ISP. The ISP, in turn, needs a much wider connection.

ISPs have to walk a narrow path between paying for unused capacity and not having enough capacity when there is a rush. It's risky and expensive to be in the game of predicting how a growing number of individual users and businesses will use available bandwidth. For example, if a consumer ISP doesn't have a wide enough connection to the Internet, its bandwidth will be consumed very quickly when more than one user dials up. It is as if 20 two-lane roads, with cars on all of them, suddenly merge into a four-lane highway. The result is a major jam. Or, if you like plumbing analogies, this is what happens to water pressure if every resident in an apartment building flushes a toilet at the same time. When your analog modem gets a busy signal[26] during the Internet "rush hour," which occurs after normal work hours, it's very obvious that the ISP doesn't have enough modems or phone lines. Even worse, but subtler and more deliciously irritating, is getting connected and then being unable to get anywhere. So, it doesn't necessarily matter if you've established a nice 52,000 bits-per-second connection, or have a T1 connection from your office. If your ISP doesn't have enough bandwidth to the Internet, your transfer rate across the Internet will be slower than smoke signals. Unfortunately, this happens a lot. A reliable ISP with good customer service—at any price and at any scale—is almost a myth. Think of your telephone company. The big telcos have pretty much taken over most of the ISP business anyway. There are very few exceptions.

➤ Broadband

Broadband,[27] the latest trend in bandwidth, refers to high-speed and low-cost ISP connections that are being deployed to consumers and small businesses. Broadband primarily consists of two technologies being deployed today that promise to bring industrial-strength network bandwidth into your home or office.

The first technology, Digital Subscriber Line (DSL), is physically based on the regular copper phone line coming into your house. The second is the Cable Modem, which is based on your coaxial-cable TV connection. Both are being widely deployed as we speak, and will offer internet connections that are 40 to 100 times faster than today's slow-dialup analog modems.

Both of these broadband technologies are rapidly supplanting older technologies, such as the traditionally slow analog and unreliable dial-up lines, and ISDN (Integrated Services Digital Network), which tops out at 128 kps.

➤ NSPs

If ISPs sell bandwidth, whom do they buy it from? Good question. There is also something called a Network Service Provider (NSP). Sometimes, ISPs and NSPs are used interchangeably, but, to boil it down, an NSP is just a massive ISP. NSPs are often called "backbone providers" because they comprise the "Internet Backbone"—originally, the U.S. military's experimental communications network for researchers. That network has since grown into a huge cloud[28] of commercial NSPs, such as UUNet, BBN, AT&T, and Sprint. Just to confuse things a little, all of the NSPs (wholesale) also have ISP (retail) divisions, but the NSPs focus on larger organizations and rarely provide service directly to consumers. Also, very large ISPs look and act much like NSPs, but there's a difference. NSPs are much bigger.

NSPs sell bandwidth to ISPs, but whom do they buy it from? An even better question! The answer is: From each other. Each NSP is a network unto itself; it connects thousands of organizations and ISPs. But one NSP cannot service more than a fraction of the whole internet. Some NSPs account for larger fractions than others, but all of them are needed to make this "internetwork" function worldwide. ("Internetwork" is the full term; "internet" is the short form.)

For all the users and systems on the Internet to be able to talk to each other, the NSPs have to connect and allow mutual access. This is called "peering." Mostly, the NSPs don't charge one another for peering because the traffic is pretty evenly distributed among all the "peers." There is one major exception: UUNet[29] is so large that, for now, it really has no peers. The lion's share of internet traffic never needs to leave UUNet's domain, and UUNet threatened in the past to start charging the other NSPs as if they were ISPs.

➤ NAPs

This is a good time to mention the Network Access Points (NAPs). You may hear people talk about "MAE East" and "MAE West," which are two of the biggest NAPs. NAPs are "public peering" locations that were originally set up by the U.S. Government in Virginia, California, New York, Illinois, and other places. They are superhigh-capacity clouds that big ISPs and NSPs can use for interconnecting their networks. Every major ISP and NSP can connect to any other through a NAP.

NAPs used to be a much bigger deal than they are now. People in the ISP business used to love to talk about being just one hop away from MAE West, or "the Backbone." Not anymore. The NAPs are very crowded, and the NSPs have consolidated enough and become large enough so that the traffic is more efficiently transferred across private connections (private peering) between NAPs. ISPs also have private peering relationships with each other, but it's not a practice that creates substantial efficiencies. Most of the ISP traffic eventually has to go through the big guys.

➤ Types of ISPs

There are a few kinds of ISPs. All ISPs are in the business of buying and selling connectivity, but bandwidth is increasingly just a commodity, and it is already being traded on the futures markets. There are no monopolies for ISP service, so ISPs have to work for a living. ISPs make money and attract customers by adding value in at least nine different ways.

1. The Freebies: Email and Personal Web Page Hosting. ISPs give these services away to all customers and try to make them as easy to use as possible. They want users to get very comfortable with them. What's important is that the services' addresses are always tied to the ISP (e.g., jon@his_isp.com or http://www.his_isp. com/users/jon/). If customers leave the ISP, they are moving to a new web "home." Their email address and home page have to change, and it's not as if they can just go to a local U.S. Postal Service office and leave a forwarding address. Email and home-page addresses, if used, are a reason to stay—or rather, a reason not to leave. It makes sense to give away services that encourage stickiness.

2. Basic Home Dial-Up. Most people connect this way, but this is a tough place to make money. It is very difficult for any companies to compete with AOL's economies of scale. Many smaller ISPs (and even big ones like RCN) tend to focus on newer, more expensive, and less mature technologies—Digital Subscriber Line (DSL), for example—because the newness levels the playing field in terms of price and quality of service. Still, to be in the consumer/small business ISP game, ISPs obviously have to offer dial-up or no one will use them for anything else.

3. Business and Secure Dial-Up.   This capacity of ISPs offers businesses the ability to connect to their corporate network while on the road, or from home, using a connection called a virtual private network (VPN). This connection, while it uses the ISPs' shared network or parts of the public internet, is secure and encrypted. It allows the users to attach to their firm's network as though they are directly connected from within the building, and to access their corporate servers and services.

4. Dedicated Hosting.   Many ISPs have facilities with servers that can be "rented" by users who want to outsource all or part of their server needs. Server space and services for the web can be obtained cheaply if users don't mind sharing their server with an untold number of other users, or, if they want, they can have any number of servers designated for their exclusive use. In any case, the servers are owned and are totally managed by the hosting facility. The shared servers are referred to as being "virtually hosted" since to you, it seems as though you have the server virtually to yourself.

5. Co-location.   You can put servers that you own in the ISP's hosting facility and take advantage of the ISP's bandwidth, redundant electric power, and other services that you may not have or may not want to invest in. In this arrangement, you are responsible for managing your own servers, and you have 24/7 access to the "cage" where your equipment is located. Companies like Exodus, Global Center, and AboveNet are big players in this space. Typically, they provide basic system administration services, such as network monitoring and tape backups. They often offer more sophisticated "professional services," such as database administration and performance tuning. Some will also offer to develop your whole ecommerce solution for you. Beware. Professional services usually come at a high premium and are not always of the highest quality. ISPs are in the bandwidth business, and although their goal is to provide less commodified services (with higher profit margins), what you get is not always of the best quality. Unfortunately, people don't scale the same way routers and cables do. Big ISPs have enough problems managing their crowded networks and data centers while still providing quality to their big customer bases. Professional services is not their strong suit.

6. *Edge of Network.* A number of specialized ISPs have complex systems that allow for faster transmission of web content to the end users. The theory here is: If your content is sent out from a place that is closer to the end user than your own web servers are, then your content will download faster. Akamai (http://www.akamai.com) has built a network of thousands of servers scattered all over the Internet. When a user requests an "Akamaized" piece of content from your web server, Akamai will rapidly move it to a place closest to the "edge of the network" before sending it to you. A number of different firms now offer this kind of high-speed distribution, including Mirror Image (http://www.mirror-image.com), Digital Island, Adero, and Epic Realm.

7. *Jim, the Local ISP.* We used to know a guy in South Dakota—"Jim"—who worked for Gateway. He told us he ran an ISP out of his basement with one Linux server connected to three modems (and three phone lines). Jim used one modem to dial up to a "real" ISP. The other two lines were left open for his paying users. Did he actually charge his friends to crowd virtually through his already slow internet connection? Yes, he did. He smiled and said, "As if they are going to know it's supposed to be any faster. Plus, I give them access to my personal file libraries and there is some really cool stuff in there."

The point is, with small shops, you don't always know what you are getting, but, for our money, a good local ISP is generally better than any national or regional outfit. Good local operators care and know about their communities; they are knowledgeable about local internet businesses; and, overall, they are better positioned to serve your needs. What these businesses lack in selection and savings, they often make up in quality and in responsive, helpful (even friendly) customer service. On the other hand, just because someone is local doesn't mean he or she has a good business.

Local ISPs usually try to cover as broad a base of users as possible. Most of their big margins come from business services.

8. America Online (AOL). AOL is a category unto itself. With the largest and most captive user base, AOL is the 8-million-pound gorilla. AOL's mission is to completely dominate the mind of internet consumers by making everything VERY EASY. If something can't be made easy, AOL just won't offer it. AOL takes firm control of the entire experience of being on the Internet. Many or perhaps most AOL users don't even realize that the Internet actually extends beyond the proprietary software that is famous for declaring, "Welcome. You've got mail!"

AOL isn't really an ISP. It is better described as a monolithic application. The software does absolutely nothing to help users get out onto the World Wide Web; in fact, it is designed from the moment of installation to discourage use of any service or site that is not entirely controlled by AOL. To be fair, AOL does provide internet access, even if it is sometimes strangely implemented.[30] If you want, you can just log in, minimize the AOL window, launch your favorite browser, and go where you want. But the WWW is still pretty confusing to some. Many users would just as soon stay inside the AOL desktop application, where they feel "safe." Everything there is easy and spoon-fed, step by step.

As the user becomes more and more familiar with the user experience and the capabilities provided by AOL, he or she becomes less and less likely to look elsewhere for comparable (or superior) service. With a devoted or captive user, AOL gets recurring revenue and "mind share"—a fancy way of saying that AOL gets more of the user's attention to advertised products and services. This wins more mind share, which puts the user deeper and deeper into AOL's pocket.

To understand AOL's mystifying breadth, consider that "AOL Keyword:" is often used in advertisements as an alternative to Universal Resource Locators (URLs) such as http://www.threeclicksaway.com/. This means that AOL thinks of itself as an alternative to the entire WWW. And it is!

AOL is not in line with the way most ISPs position themselves. Usually, an ISP tries to be the on-ramp and jumping-off point to the WWW—a source of access, communications tools, news, and guidance, encouraging users to explore the web.

AOL began in the 1980s as an online service, which is very distinct from an ISP. Today, online means "on the Internet." Back then (less than 10 years ago), online really meant offline. An online service was something members connected to, but it didn't connect to the Internet. Members worked within the proprietary network of the online service. Genie (defunct) and Compuserve (now part of AOL) were also popular online services. Online services had a "membership" model. Members (mainly geeks) got some of the same kinds of services that can now be found on the Internet, but the selection was limited. Typically, there were live news services, discussion groups, email, tools for home and business, shopping, interactive games, and file-download libraries. Members could dial up and hang out with other members, but they couldn't interact with members of other online services. Each online service was a proprietary closed system.

As the Internet became popular, the online services began to accept it, but slowly—in many cases, too slowly. The first form of internet access provided by the online services was email. To send an internet email message—as opposed to a "normal" message in the online service—the sender had to write the address in a special way—something like: internet:'jon@some-little-isp.com'—or the special online service software wouldn't work.

The online services had captive audiences, and they liked that arrangement. There were several sources of revenue. Users paid a subscription to the service on a per-minute or per-hour basis, and it was common to charge additional fees for special services such as stock quotes or access to content libraries. Online services would also charge vendors' fees to set up storefronts or target advertisements. What a great business! Users had no choice but to pay to get "online," and then they had to pay to do anything once they got there. But, for the few million people who wanted to interact/transact electronically, there were no other choices.

Enter the WWW and ISPs. At first, there wasn't much to do on the web. But, very quickly, there was a lot of excitement. People took the "If you build it, they will come" attitude and started putting up websites with compelling content and capabilities. The online services hoped to dismiss the web as a fad that would fade. That's exactly what Bill Gates said would happen, in his shortly-thereafter-recalled-and-revised book, *The Road Ahead.*

Across the country and around the world, there were a lot of people who wanted to build sites, and even more people who wanted to visit them. Thus, the ISP business began to grow very quickly. AOL and the others watched this growth. When it turned out not to be a fad, they moved as only several-hundred-pound gorillas can: slowly.

9. *Giant Consumer ISPs.* These companies, such as Mind-Spring (http://www.mindspring.com), focus on delivering dial-up internet access to consumers and providing "user-friendly" software for email, shopping, and the capability to publish personal web pages. Personalized news, chat, and other nifty services are other popular offerings.

The fact is, even if you are only a slightly savvy consumer, you can get almost all of these services for free, very easily.[31] The Giant Consumer ISPs try to bundle all the popular capabilities together and make sure the unit is "idiot proof." In a nutshell, here is the game plan for an ISP or ASP business:

➤ Once customers are captured, they are sources of recurring revenue.

➤ The user–provider relationship becomes increasingly sticky and profitable as more value-added services are attached.

➤ As the number of users increases, the same level of service is cheaper to provide.

Giant Consumer ISPs are involved in a cutthroat business, and there have been enormous consolidations over the past few years. For the winners, however, this is a gold mine!

There are enormous complexities and details involved, but ecommerce has become an integral part of the web and the Internet; it crosses every venue, from a dot-com start-up to a large corporate customer. This terrain needs to be well understood by anyone who hopes to compete and succeed in the ecommerce arena.

■ XXX ON THE WWW

When you looked at this book's contents and saw this section (pushed discreetly toward the back of this chapter), did you skip right to it, and then look around to see if anyone was watching?

This section is not here just to be controversial. Pornography was one of the important early drivers of the World Wide Web.

The authors neither condemn nor endorse the pervasive business of "adult" content on the web, but it can't be dismissed either. We choose to avoid a discussion of the actual business models of online pornography (maybe we'll save that for another book and use pseudonyms); we just want to point out some very important aspects of this shadowy but enormous sector of the new economy. There are some important lessons to be learned, and we would do readers a disservice if we ignored what has arguably become the most successful part of the Internet industry.

More than 50 percent of all internet traffic—the majority of the data transmitted over the Internet—is pornography-related. Until 1999, the majority of ecommerce revenue was from adult content sites. According to *Newsweek* in 1997,[32] "Nearly one third of all wired Americans accessed adult content in May." Also according to *Newsweek,* this time in 1999: "Adult sites were a $1 billion industry in 1998. . . . More than half the requests on search engines are 'adult-oriented' . . . 25 percent of teens in a recent survey . . . said they had visited X-rated sites."[33]

Don't be afraid, and don't think this is anything new or strange. The porn industry drove (virtually single-handedly) the adoption and growth of VCR technology, is currently driving the DVD business, and will drive multimedia distribution and technology for the foreseeable future. Let's face it: The web is a perfect medium for lascivious content. In the privacy of his or her own home (or office) a willing user can instantly find and download all manner of smut without divulging his or her identity or compromising security.[34] Pornography is also one of the only products for which internet users have always been willing and eager to pay. The first wildly popular sites to appear on the World Wide Web weren't really Yahoo!.com and Netscape.com. They were popular, but they didn't become "destination sites" until much later. They were just jumping-off points. Many (or most) people came to the web looking for sex. Many WWW veterans will remember the famous French site, *"Femmes, femmes, femmes, je vous aime!"*[35] One of the first sites to employ dynamic content, it showed a different naughty picture every time the page was reloaded.

The Internet porn industry has been the key driver for user interface and multimedia technology, and XXX software developers consistently blaze the technology trail for the "straight" ecommerce community. For example, the broad use and acceptance of SSL/HTTPS[36] and several other less well-known security technologies, such as First Virtual's VPIN, are directly attributable to porn sites. In fact, porn sites taught everyone else how to make users feel comfortable about doing any kind of business transaction over the web. In the early days of the web, most users felt that sending a credit card number over the Internet was unthinkable. Today, there is a general trust in the strength and safety of encryption technology. In this sense, the porn site operators were the pioneers of ecommerce. Without them, companies like VeriSign (the SSL giant) and CyberCash would not have had any business, and legitimate websites would be seeing far fewer credit card transactions. Ecommerce technologies have all been road-tested in the "adult" arena, in much the same way that the Russian and American armed forces have always tested their own technologies in foreign conflicts.

Video streaming and compression technologies have also been driven—almost exclusively—by dirty sites. If you think that movie trailers, dot-com news clips, and annual stockholder meeting "webcasts" account for even 10 percent of the Internet's video content, think again. It is all porn! The XXX industry has consistently pushed the envelope, innovating to create hosts of homegrown multimedia applications that don't require any special client software, even though almost all internet video applications do. Special client software has almost always been a big no-no with ecommerce. You don't want a user to have to do any extra work as the "price" for shopping on your site or using its functionality. If it takes too long to download the special software, the user will lose interest. Also, if an average user has to install software, he or she may have problems figuring out how to do it and become frustrated. In the cutthroat competition of the adult content industry, there is no room for these uncertainties.[37] In many cases, these single-minded, must-develop-faster-better-easier-to-use video technology engineers have created homegrown multimedia solutions that exceed the products provided by software giants like RealNetworks, Microsoft, Macromedia, and Apple.

XXX sites on the WWW have also pioneered the use of built-in browser technologies, such as JavaScript, VBScript, and Dynamic HTML (DHTML) to extend the browsers' capabilities. Some of these innovations can often be very annoying. Many users have had the experience of being "accidentally" directed to a porn site and finding the "back" button of their browsers rendered ineffective in trying to escape the onslaught of filth. You have to give the technologies credit. They are effective.

Whether you were aware of this "dirty little secret" of the Internet or not, the industry certainly is. American Express recently announced that it would stop having its card accepted at pornography sites because of excessive credit card fraud. Recently, in a conversation, George Conrades, chairman and CEO of Akamai, the "edge of the network" internet content distribution experts, acknowledged that a significant part of bandwidth was going to websites that were using the "Akamaized" network to distribute their adult content. His larger problem wasn't the nature of the content but who on his staff would agree to examine "those" sites when they were reporting technical problems. You can bet that there are technicians who might not want to be asked to look at a porn site as part of their regular job, so Akamai devised a policy that only those who have assented or "opted in" to working with those particular clients would be called upon to do so. What an interesting human resources problem!

In the end, you don't have to enjoy or respect these sites, but you should keep your eye on what they are doing with technology and ecommerce. If something new and innovative can be done successfully, they will be doing it. Innovations developed at these sites can often be applied very advantageously to legitimate businesses. If you can get past the nastiness of their content, you will find the sites are always on the cutting edge.

■ INTERNET-ENABLED MOBILE DEVICES AND WAP

Most of the sections of this chapter have discussed internet business models or types of ecommerce sites. Mobile devices and Wireless Application Protocol (WAP) are types of technology. They are an important new part of the Internet, and it is critical to see how they fit in and what they mean.

Let's start with an example of how to put great technology to seriously silly purpose. You're in a supermarket that is offering a special discount on some big packages of AA batteries. You know you always need these annoying little overpriced things, but it's not urgent. Can you buy them cheaper on the Internet? Is this a good deal? It would be a pity to pass up the chance to get cheap batteries, but it may not be such a bargain, after all. You want to know, right now, because it's certainly not worth the time and gas money to go home, log onto the Net, look up some prices, and compare them to this sale price. You dial up the prices on your WAP-enabled phone, and marvel at your $1-a-package savings at the supermarket.

When we began writing this book, WAP and the other technologies that let users connect to internet sites through their mobile phones, PDAs (personal digital assistant), and other handheld devices, were just a murmur in the industry. Now, they are a full-on craze. There is a mad rush to claim the new and expanding territories that are opened up by these capabilities.

Mobile internet is the beginning of ubiquitous access, constant communication, and electronic commerce solutions that are tailored not only to individual shopping preferences but also to the method of connectivity. In the WAP-enabled environment, you begin to see the emergence of companies that are divorced from any particular distribution mechanism. A retailer is a provider of products that have many faces all tied together under the same brand, with integrated systems. Customers choose their access method: physical retail store, mobile phone, website, commerce-enabled email, voice, fax, snail mail, and so on. Customers choose when, how, and where they want to do business. Companies extend themselves and allow their customers to reach out to them, using whatever means is available or preferable. WAP dramatically changes the game. Now, every physical environment is a computing environment.

The WAP environment is characterized by the connection technology—a telephone. A mobile phone is, by definition, mobile (read: small). Among the great challenges of developing for WAP are: the tiny size of telephone screens and the slow connection speeds. WAP development is tricky from a user's experience because delivering anything compelling in an area of just one or two square inches is fiendishly difficult. Heavy internet users have become accustomed to large screens, animation in full color, and increasingly high-quality sound and video. Although there are tests going on for "broadband" wireless (wireless connectivity robust enough to support mobile TV-like experiences), this innovation is not expected to reach consumers for a couple of years. At the moment, surfing the Internet via WAP is something akin to going online in 1994. Slow and texty. Yet, unlike the early days of the Internet, when sites were purely informational, WAP commerce is a huge push in the industry.

WAP sites are built using WML—a variation on HTML, the main technology for displaying information on the web. At present, in the United States and Europe, WAP phones cannot browse ordinary websites, and ordinary web browsers cannot browse sites intended for mobile phones.[38] Instead, like the early online days before the Internet, each cell phone company has its own WAP portal—a collection of a few sites that are specially modified for mobile phone browsing. In most cases, the companies whose sites appear in a WAP portal have paid a fee to be included within the mobile internet offering. Unlike browsing the Internet, at the present time, most users are limited to browsing the special services that have signed tenancy agreements with their mobile phone provider.

In the world of ecommerce, the mobile commerce (mcommerce) revolution has begun. An interesting feature of this latest development in electronic commerce is that it is not being driven by companies in the United States. The two leading mobile technology firms in the world, Ericsson and Nokia, are based in Sweden and Finland, respectively. The affluent, sophisticated, and technically savvy Scandinavian market has become the leader in the jump to mobile commerce. Finnish banks have been providing mobile phone-based banking and brokerage services since the end of 1998. These services were just beginning to emerge in the United States in the second quarter of 2000.

With WAP comes email—accessible and answerable while standing on a bus. Expect the ability to receive alerts about changes in your stock portfolio. Besides informing you, they will let you take advantage of the information and complete a transaction while sitting in a meeting. Strike one more point for the ever-encroaching modern problem of Attention Deficit Disorder. With WAP, you have limitless, relatively discreet distraction anytime, anywhere. Expect interesting applications to emerge in the beginning of 2001, when WAP-enabled phones are further enhanced with Global Positioning Systems (GPS). Mobile websites that know where you are in a museum, for example, will be able to send more information based on the exhibits at which you linger.

From an ecommerce perspective, the opportunities are fantastic but have a hint of Big Brother. Special offers from your credit card company, delivered on-the-fly to your phone, may be based on your balance and the jewelry store you happen to be standing in front of.

Already, websites are offering an integrated approach and technical solutions that extend functionality into the mobile environment. WAP sites will allow you to make changes to an internet bank account, and on and on. Watch this space carefully. Expect a slightly tempered but feverish race into mobile internet. It will smell a lot like the heady days of the web in 1995.

Chapter 3

Advertising on the Web

For many years prior to the introduction of the WWW, the Internet was a land of pioneers, geeks, academics, scientists, and lonely computer lovers who lived by a "flower power" code. It was a land devoid of commercial content. E-commerce was anathema to the culture of the early netizens, as they termed themselves. Around the middle of 1994, the first glimmers of commercialism began to appear on the WWW, and e-commerce began to creep into the network. With the dawning of the age of commercial sites, internet advertising arrived on the scene.

The first ads were clunky and amateurishly produced. As bandwidth improved and the experience of using the web sped up, more sophisticated companies, designers, and ad agencies struggling to join the new media world got involved. Ads themselves started to improve, and new industries developed: online media buying agencies, ad serving companies, media performance analysis, online ad production houses, dozens of software companies, and, from them, tools to produce, administer, monitor, and analyze ads for the Internet.

■ THE BANNER AD

The humble banner ad is the most ubiquitous form of online advertising. It usually appears as a thin strip of text and graphics at the top of a website. The user jumps to the advertiser's web site when clicked. The idea behind the ads is simple: You buy the right to put your message on someone else's site. If a visitor reads your ad and likes what it says, one click on it instantly transports the visitor to your website. Originally modeled as analogs to fractional ads in a newspaper, banners evolved quickly in technology and sophistication. Today's banner ads have motion, animation, scrollable menus, interactivity, and even sound and video. Although members of the "old school" internet community cite banners as symbols of all that is wrong with the web, banners were the beginning of a marketing revolution.

➤ What Is a Banner?

Banners are "units" (as web media people like to call them) that take the form of a skinny strip. They are usually rectangular and are placed at the top of a page, above the site's main navigation, but they can appear just about anywhere—at the bottom or in the middle of a page, and so on. Their physical shape came about because ads were intended to be obvious yet not overly disruptive. The vertical dimension of a web page is at the highest premium, so banners usually extend all the way across a page but their height is truncated.

"k-size" is another key issue that influences the look of banners— and, indeed, of every graphical element that appears in a web page. This is a measurement of the amount of information that is contained in a given element. The larger the k-size, the longer the download. The longer the download, the more frustrated the user; the more frustrated the user, the more likely he or she will hit the "stop" or "back" buttons on the web browser. Managing the k-size of banners (keeping them small) is a constant battle. How to deliver a compelling, clever, or interesting message in a strangely shaped area, while doing whatever is possible to minimize the amount of information that the user has to download, makes this a difficult advertising vehicle. People tend to be highly critical of banner ads because they are, in general, rather annoying to users of websites. The truth is: Producing anything compelling, given the constraints of the form factor, deserves some respect.

All sites that sell banner ads publish specifications as to the physical size of the ad, as well as the k-size. Unfortunately, elements that make banners interesting usually increase the size of the banner. These elements include: each "animation" or transition of a banner, the resolution of photography used, the number of colors, and the notorious "fat" elements: sound and video. Producing effective banner ads is a true study in compromise. It involves the convergence of increasingly sophisticated science and solid creative design and copy. These all work together to make a valuable marketing statement in a tiny space.

➤ Banner Ad Design

Often, people make a mistake with banner ads (and with web design in general). They assume that offline related design or advertising experience translates to the Internet. For the vast majority of ads, this is a recipe for disaster. Solid creative designers from the print media are likely to have a lot of skills and experience. These will help to make them good web creative designers *some day*, but the transition takes time and effort, and usually involves significant frustration for them and for anyone trying to get useful work from them during their adaptation period.

Specifically, print designers are quite accustomed to dealing with "mechanicals"—the size constraints dictated by print publications—but they have never had to worry about "k-size" weight. A standard four-color glossy magazine ad would take three to four hours to download over a typical home user's slow internet connection. Learning how to slim down graphics and photographs so that they become fast downloads, while keeping them attractive or even useful, takes a great deal of work, knowledge, and experience. If you are planning on spending money to advertise online, be sure to engage someone who has a proven track record in this area, even if it seems more complex or expensive up front. If you don't, you'll likely be wasting media money. Buying the media (the space) is the most expensive part of advertising, so maximize your investment with people who know their stuff.

■ OTHER TYPES OF ADS

Advertising is based on creating hype and buzz, so it stands to reason that advertisers love to create hype and buzz about—what else—ads! No sooner had banner ads become standard fare on the web than marketing communications people began clamoring for something online that went "beyond the banner."

The first "beyond the banner" ad unit was the banner wrap. Essentially, it is a banner ad at the top of a page but it extends down the left or right side, creating an upside-down L-shaped area. It allows the advertiser to create a message that is longer and more involved, merely because the space is larger. More importantly, it allows the advertiser to ensure that the ad stays visible even after the user scrolls down the page and the top portion of the page is no longer visible. An ongoing theme in online advertising, and website interface design in general, is the concept of being "above the fold." This concept, taken from print newspapers, refers to the part of a site that is visible without scrolling. (In newspapers, the top portion of a page that is visible without unfolding the bottom.) One of the great political issues surrounding a corporate website is which department, division, geography, and so on, controls the prime real estate above the fold.

Another type of ad, the interstitial ad, takes two basic forms: (1) the jump page and (2) the pop-up window. A jump page is often used in association with a banner ad. In a jump page, clicking on a banner ad or a text link brings the user to a separate page that lies outside the navigation of the site. Its purpose is usually to provide specific information about a product or service, often as part of an introduction or launch campaign. The pop-up appears as a second browser window, layered on top of the first window. It allows a promotional message to be delivered with impact, without removing all the navigation of the main site. Many advanced users find pop-ups a particularly loathsome form of advertising, but the ads still have their place if used sparingly. A well-known internet company, GeoCities (http://www.geocities.com), notoriously spawns interstitial ads whenever a member's website is accessed.

■ TRACKING

Tracking. Impact. Return on Investment. Effectiveness. Efficiency. For most of the history of advertising, these terms have been more about marketing rhetoric than marketing reality. The movement to direct-response advertising and direct marketing changed the equation substantially. It became easier for companies to measure the value of their marketing efforts. Yet, the possibilities afforded by online advertising and online selling are changing the dynamics in the most dramatic ways to date.

Let's examine a few plays from the Gateway book. Gateway, a Fortune 250 company, is one of the leading marketers of personal computer products in the world. It also happens to be one of the largest direct marketers of products in *any* category. Until the middle of 1996, the majority of Gateway's sales came from direct-response print ads, mostly in computer magazines. To track the effectiveness of these ads, each magazine, and sometimes each ad within the same magazine, was assigned a unique "800" (toll-free) phone numbers. Calculating the cost per call for each magazine was straightforward. The media spend per magazine per month was divided by the number of calls received on the associated 800 number. This was obviously very useful for deciding the spend per magazine, and for beating up publishers for better media rates when any cost-per-call figures began to climb.

The problem with this direct-response system was that it did nothing to ensure the quality of the calls. It was very powerful for cost-per-call and for maximizing the number of calls received for every marketing dollar spent. The heart of the problem was a small technical issue. Gateway, like many telesales companies, could track a call when it came into the building. Once the call went into the call queue to be accessed by the sales force, however, the company had no way of tracking which calls converted into sales, and which calls merely ate up a salesperson's time. This inability to track the sales conversion of individual calls caused Gateway's media buyers to make some bad decisions. Sometimes, the media people opted for magazines that drove lots of tire-kickers and few buyers, and canceled relationships with magazines that drove few overall calls but had a high percentage of actual buyers. Media buyers had to assume that a piece of media that created more calls was driving more business than a piece that was driving fewer calls. Usually, that was a good bet, but not always.

The problems in tracking media spend got worse as Gateway moved to television advertising. Blessed with a seven-character company name, peppering those ads with "Call 1-800-GATEWAY" at the end of every ad spot was a natural thing to do. The number was easy for customers to remember, but it seeded a huge media tracking problem for Gateway. The company had a large TV spend. Spots were running on cable, network, sports, sci-fi programming, prime time—you name it. Every spot had the same phone number: 1-800-GATEWAY. It was great for brand building, but lousy for media tracking.

Because all of the calls were hitting the same phone number, it was impossible, from a systems perspective, to track the effectiveness of time bought in one spot versus another. This caused huge consternation for Gateway because the skills to fine-tune the media spend were considered to be a core offering of the firm. The accountability of telephone-based direct marketing was a strategic advantage over other nondirect distribution players like Compaq or Apple.

Although it would be fairly easy to argue that most online advertising has less impact than the more familiar offline forms, internet advertising eliminates ALL of the tracking problems described above. Naturally, as in everything, the devil is in the details. But, with proper implementation, it is quite possible for a company on the Internet to know:

➤ Precisely how many people saw the page where a given ad was displayed.

➤ How many people clicked on an ad and, of all the people who saw the ad, what percentage they represent.

➤ The number of pages viewed or the amount of time each visitor spent on the advertised website.

➤ How many people saw the ad, clicked on the ad, and actually bought something when they arrived at the advertised site.

➤ Within a certain number of hours, the effectiveness of two different pieces of advertising in the same positioning.

➤ Whether a given piece of advertising is more attractive to customers or noncustomers.

➤ Whether an advertisement drives more "tire-kickers" vs. real buyers, relative to another ad.

➤ The effect of delivering different ads to active customers vs. occasional customers, or of delivering different ads to preexisting customers located in different geographic areas.

The World Wide Web is a digital, computerized environment; therefore, all advertising activity can be logged, tracked, and analyzed. The key point to remember is that an ad on the Internet is not dissociated from the actual sale, as is a print ad. If someone reading a magazine comes across an advertisement for a CD, how does the ad really influence the reader's behavior? The advertiser, if it is a direct marketer, hopes for the best case: The customer will put down the magazine, pick up the phone, dial an operator, wait on hold, and place an order for the CD. More likely case: The advertiser hopes that the next time the hypothetical magazine reader is in a record store, he or she remembers that the Rolling Stones have a new CD and will seek it out. Days or weeks could easily separate the event of reading the magazine and the event of being in a record store. On the Internet, a customer might be reading an article on a music-related site and see an ad for a new record by a favorite band. With one click of a mouse, the customer can be presented with an opportunity to buy the recording, listen to an excerpt, and read the critics' reviews. The ad itself is an active, direct, and immediate participant in the selling process. The connection between the advertisement and the sale is more closely linked than ever before.

All of the above is true, possible, and, in many cases, not terribly difficult to achieve. The problem is that, far too often, managers do not understand the tracking that they should be expecting or demanding from the technical groups that manage their website. It is also true that the technical architecture of a website—how it is built and programmed—can have a major impact on the ability to track certain types of data. If you are involved in a major web redesign project, or in building a new site from scratch, be sure to state your tracking needs up front. Although it is sometimes difficult for people without technical backgrounds to understand, the core architecture of a site has a tendency to become "digital marble"—frozen and immovable, once basic structures are established, and particularly after a site goes live. Work with the technical people who are designing and building your site. Define clearly the information that you expect to be able to garner, how often you expect to receive it, and in what form. The process will be less frustrating for your technologists and for you.

■ BARTER ADVERTISING

Traditionally, websites charge advertisers for placing ad media on their sites. This is a principal source of web business revenue. For a number of reasons, not the least of which is that many start-up websites are cash-poor, other currencies besides dollars have emerged. On the Internet, one of the most powerful currencies is traffic. "Loiterers" do not adversely impact online businesses, so having more visitors is considered preferable. Whether the business model is dependent on ad revenue or e-commerce, aggregating more traffic is always a principal website marketing goal.

The prevalence of barter advertising is an obvious manifestation of the "traffic as currency" trend. Barter can occur in many different forms:

➤ Where firms put each other's banners on their respective sites. Usually, they negotiate some level of exposure equity, based on the differences in traffic, demographics, and so on, between the two sites.

➤ Where an ISP gives free web hosting in return for having its banner placed on the website.

➤ Where any kind of service is granted in return for ad banner exposure.

There are endless variations on this theme. Barter of all sorts is a major force on the Internet. Don't be discouraged by what seems a paltry marketing budget. Take a long hard look at what your company can provide as payment for traffic. Remember, although the Internet looks progressively more like a suburban shopping mall, it still has a bit of the wild west. "I'll give you a gill of whiskey and two chickens for a banner, ma'am. . . ."

■ HOW WEB MEDIA ARE BOUGHT

In many ways, the financial structures around buying and selling web media have not evolved nearly as fast as the technologies in online ads. There are a number of reasons, not the least of which is that media companies would always rather provide less transparency than more. Web media are bought and sold on the surface, like print advertising, but there are a number of substantive ways in which they differ. It is important to really grasp these differences. They can have an enormous financial impact on an advertiser.

➤ CPM Basis

CPM, a term from the print world, means "cost per mil," or cost per thousand. It originally referred to the cost to reach 1,000 readers. In the web world, it means the cost for 1,000 impressions. An impression is essentially a pair of "eyeballs." One impression means that the ad was delivered (or downloaded) to one web browser, one time. To understand the CPM structure, it is important to understand a couple of fundamental mechanisms that allow online ads to work.

The advertising inventory of a print publication is constrained by physical space. Unless the publisher is willing to increase the length of a publication, the advertising inventory is whatever space is left over after editorial content is produced. In broadcast, the inventory is time rather than space. Whatever time is not allocated to content (TV shows) can be sold to advertisers. On the Internet, the split is not quite so straightforward. Ads are generally sold on a CPM basis, or cost per 1,000 impressions. The advertising inventory of a website is dependent not only on the space dedicated to ads on the page, but also on the number of people who actually visit the site. Let's examine how this works.

Yahoo! is the largest site on the Internet, based on the number of visitors to the site. As of the beginning of 2000, Yahoo! was experiencing traffic of around 400 million page views per day. To put that in perspective, the site was transmitting Webster's Dictionary about 125,000 times per day. We'll use Yahoo! as our example.

One of the Internet's prime advertising spots (the Superbowl Ad location on the web, in many respects) is the banner that appears at the top of the home page of yahoo.com. No one advertiser ever really "owns" that space for a given duration of time. No company occupies it the way a corporation might buy the back cover of *Forbes* for the month of July. Instead, companies buy a certain number of impressions at a predetermined CPM, to be delivered, over a given interval of time, for an ad in that position. For example, Toyota might buy 20 million impressions of its banner ad to be delivered as 10 million impressions on July 10, and 10 million impressions on July 11. In this structure, Yahoo! promises to deliver the ad when it fulfills 20 million requests to see the home page of Yahoo! over that period of time. In other words, Yahoo! places the Toyota banner in a rotation. If you were to go to Yahoo!'s home page 10 times on July 10, a day on which Toyota's ad was running, sometimes you would see the ad, and sometimes you might not. There might be 15 other companies' ads rotating in the same position at the same time. If we assume that there are 100 (we know it's more like 400) million possible impressions of the Yahoo! home page, approximately one out of 10 times you would see the Toyota ad, and nine times out of 10 you would see someone else's banner. Toyota bought 10 million impressions per day, so it owns approximately 10 percent of the traffic for that page. For Toyota to own that banner position and ensure that only its ad is seen on that page on July 10 and July 11, it would have to buy 200 million impressions (100 million per day)—Yahoo!'s total advertising inventory during that period. The difficulty is that the total number of impressions available on any given day, at any given site, is dependent on how many people decide to go there.

In magazine advertising, you pay for a CPM based on a historical audit by some outside source. Most commonly quoted, and most respected among such sources, is the American Bureau of Circulation (ABC). Once a year, ABC does a survey and says, for example, that the circulation of a magazine is 1 million. Naturally, the actual circulation of a magazine in any given month changes—maybe not by massive amounts, but if TIME or Newsweek puts an exclusive photo on its front cover and links it to an up-to-the-minute news story inside (recall the photo-and-print coverage of the crash that killed Princess Diana), you can bet that the issue will fly off the shelves and newsstands. If your ad is in that week's issue, you got yourself a huge media bonus for free. Conversely, if the complete memoirs of Herman Smith, Dishwasher Repairman, are announced on the cover during the week your ad is running, magazine sales might not be so brisk, and you might not be so happy. On the web, you actually get the circulation you pay for, for better or for worse.

It is critical to remember this dynamic when you are trying to ascertain what "share of mind" an ad will buy for you. Ad inventory ebbs and flows dynamically with traffic. A website where you plan to advertise should be able to reasonably predict the traffic on a given part of the site—say, 90 days out—but web traffic has enormous peaks and valleys. Thus, the exact presence a given ad purchase will provide can't be calculated until the second the impressions are actually delivered.

➤ Cost per Click

All e-commerce websites are, in effect, direct marketing engines, so the industry moves very quickly to try to manage its marketing expense with the same precision that the traditional direct-response advertisers achieved. The principal metrics for managing marketing expense in these businesses are *cost per lead* and *cost per sale.* Many early online advertisers discovered that their cost per lead—in this case, cost per click—was high. Sometimes extremely high. Advertisers began to look for a way to gain better leverage for their expense and to structure deals that provided more incentive for media companies to make their clients' campaigns successful. Thus, cost-per-click advertising deals were born. In these structures, a website establishes a per-click fee, rather than a cost-per-thousand-impressions structure. The advertisers pay for every actual click from a user. All impressions that do not generate clicks are free. This pricing scheme, which seems like a positive development, is actually at the center of a major online controversy: Is online advertising an effective vehicle for branding campaigns?

In a cost-per-click structure, the advertising vehicle gets no credit for an ad that a user sees but does not click onto. To date, most ads on the web are driven by calls to action: "Click for free trial!" "Click to save $100!" "Click to win 1,000 pounds of M&Ms!" The sole point of these ads is to drive the user to transact, or register.

Some of the biggest spenders in the offline advertising world, such as Procter & Gamble, Coca-Cola, and General Motors, have not been found online because their products haven't translated easily into the e-commerce setting, and there has been concern about how the effectiveness of their advertising could be tracked. Now, in the era of sometimes hypervalued internet companies, many of these traditional sponsors have come to the table in an effort to experience some of the "halo" effect of the Internet hysteria. Big-name internet properties have become choice advertising vehicles for companies whose reputation or product line is looking too staid and old-fashioned. Internet advertising conveys hipness, modernity, and a plan for the future. Whether this rush will bear fruit for companies whose products don't gibe well with the Internet's currency remains to be seen. (Are you going to be willing to pay $10 shipping and handling for your $6 jug of Tide detergent?) The corporate fashion statement for the end of the twentieth century was to have a "dot-com" after the company's name, and "dot-coms" in its media plan.

Section II
Organization

$$Chapter \ 4$$

Staffing

The explosion of the Internet has created massive demand for web people of all descriptions. Salaries are high. Turnover is higher. The best in the business are prima donnas who will ask for, and usually get, the moon. Staffing is an endless process, whether a web company is looking for employees and independent contractors, or is outsourcing pieces of work to development shops. This chapter will help you to know what to expect, to avoid common web staffing mistakes, and to get the most from your recruiting time and dollar.

■ CLASSIC CULTURE CLASHES

Recently, a colleague named Mark came to town from London to have a meeting/interview with a major New York e-commerce firm. This firm was interested in expanding into London, and Mark is an expert on the logistical part of the firm's business. A natural fit. They arranged to meet and have lunch at a little diner on Manhattan's East Side.

Mark was really annoyed. "I flew all the way out here from London at *my* expense.[1] I had an appointment with the president of this firm, and he blew it off. They want to reschedule it for another time. That is so discourteous and disrespectful. You'd think if he knew that I was coming all the way out here that he could have made the appointment. And besides, I walked around the office, and it was total chaos! What kind of place are they running?!? What kind of people am I dealing with?!?"

Mark, a former principal at a big UK firm, was used to working in the environment of a "proper" business, with established hierarchies and organization. We looked him in the eye (somewhat amused) and said, "Welcome to the pros." We grinned and said, "Hey, that's the culture of the e-commerce and new media world, and guess what? They are *all* that way! These guys don't know how to run a business the way you're used to—most of them have never run *anything* before!!!" After more talking, Mark calmed down. He eventually signed on with the firm.

On a superficial level, this experience exemplifies the gap between the freewheeling, bohemian new-media business and the mature establishment. More worrisome are the business interactions between the gray-haired or balding, business-suited, "We're experienced" culture and the blue-jeaned, young, trendy, body-pierced, "We're on the cutting edge" culture. The differences can prove problematic.

A few years ago, it was quite common for these two groups, or cultures, to clash, although in very subtle ways. Here's how it would go. The stodgy back-office IT (information technology) boys would walk into the room, hitch up their pants, dig in their heels, and be obstructionists to the web folks, claiming there was a problem with "security." They said that they wouldn't integrate their old mainframe systems, written in COBOL twenty years earlier, because it would breach the security of their data and systems. Bullshit! Whenever the word "security" came up, the issue was almost always a dead giveaway for cultural problems and fear. Security was a "safe" topic that could always be raised, even if there was no security problem. The real issue was that the IT dinosaurs were afraid that these new upstarts were going to come in and either take their jobs away or cause them to lose control over their air-conditioned raised-floor data environments. The reality is: Good technology and design have nothing to do with the web or security because if you do the job right, all of these issues are addressed. The web-vs.-IT clash is best addressed with patience and with management's ability to listen to, understand, and communicate effectively with both cultures. Ironically, this was much more of an issue a few years ago than it is today, mostly because the young trendy upstart web and e-commerce firms have realized that if they want to compete effectively in the market, they need *adult leadership,* which means bringing in experienced older people— "the gray hair," as a colleague describes it. An attorney we work with said recently that the management team of a dot-com, all in their early twenties, was initially working with a thirty-five-year-old lawyer from his firm, but the "dot-comers" told the firm that they wanted someone "older."

In many ways, the trendy crowd has it even worse than the "gray hair" because they don't have the same depth of experience to draw on when they need to solve problems. The survivors of this gold rush will be individuals who cast their personal preconceived notions aside, especially any cultural hang-ups, and look for the best ways to achieve business goals, even though some solutions will be old, tried-and-true, boring traditional ones.

Similarly, the people from the established traditional firms cannot possibly ignore what has been going on in the marketplace; dot-comers are turning conventional business models upside down and making themselves zillionaires in the process. A huge number of old-school businesspeople have crossed over in the past couple of years. A friend of ours, who went back to school and got his MBA in his thirties, told us that the entire MBA recruiting model has been re-vamped. Until recently, upcoming MBA grads vied to get interviews with PriceWaterhouseCoopers, Andersen Consulting, and other big consulting firms. Nirvana used to be landing a job with one of those big monsters. However, nobody at his school was interviewing with the big consulting firms, which went begging for candidates. Why? All the good MBAs hoped to go to, or to start, a dot-com because of the tremendous upside.

In big consulting firms, the only people who make the real money are the partners. Everyone else ends up being a grunt (albeit a well-paid grunt) who is invariably put to work in a distant city, working long but billable hours. We think that most of these people are seeing that if they are going to have to endure that lifestyle, they might as well work for a pre-IPO start-up. At least they'll have a chance to get in on the action and get some stock options, rather than going through years of the corporate hazing and backstabbing that are characteristic of the large, traditional, consulting firms.

Today's opportunities are historic. Smart flexible individuals will figure out how to adapt themselves to these unstructured environ-ments, and will probably find that they really like the resulting lifestyle. There will always be stodgy people out there, digging their heels in and saying why they can't do things. Too bad; they will miss out and will be bypassed, ignored, or replaced. Which lifestyle do you want?

As human beings, we have a tendency to fear things we don't understand, so the best way to understand the crazy web environment is to jump right in. No, we're not advocating that you go out and get a belly ring, but there are plenty of opportunities now to mix with these crowds and get a feel for their slant on business. Many leading universities offer programs on e-commerce management, so think about those avenues for gaining familiarity.

■ RECRUITING

People always make or break organizations—a given. On the Internet, however, the tremendous dearth of qualified people and the overwhelming swell from industry-in-search-of-staff have created a very difficult situation. Even with gyrations in the stock market, the real and actual need for people with web experience in all respects is going to be acute and problematic for years to come. Effective management of recruiting should be given careful attention, especially with the current lead times involved in hiring good staff. Never expect that you'll accomplish this overnight. If you happen to find someone quickly, consider yourself lucky. It is a fluke. Don't get lulled into a false sense of security. Because of the shortage, most firms are recruiting on a continual basis.

Recruiting is a very time-consuming process, so an early hire in any growing company should be a Director of Human Resources (HR) or Director of Recruiting. Both positions and departments should not be undervalued. That individual and his or her group will become the focus of attention when your firm gets in a crunch and needs people fast. This is a critical point to remember. In too many firms, HR is considered the bottom rung in terms of prestige. The department does not earn a direct profit for the firm; hence, its perceived value is very wrongly viewed as being low. A good HR person can be essential for building a web start-up or a web division in a larger organization. If you come from a company that is known for the vast quantity and variety of bureaucratic silliness that it is able to generate, it may be useful to examine your HR policies and procedures before embarking on a serious web project. There is nothing more frustrating and expensive than finding a great candidate and then losing him or her because you can't get the offer letter out fast enough. Make HR a strategic asset—not an impediment—to achieving your web goals.

If the firm needs people very quickly, consider hiring consultants or temps or outsourcing a project or a discipline. These options are discussed in later sections. The one fact that should be crystal-clear is: You can outsource some arms and legs, but you cannot outsource your brain.

Let's explain what we mean. Would you outsource:

➤ The core of what your business is?

➤ The definition of your strategic goals?

➤ The systems and people who control the systems that make your business run?

You need to understand that if you can see the future—or worse, if your competitors have already seen the future and have moved their business online—then chances are you will move your business online as well. The people who create your strategy and then operate it at a high level must be *your people.* This is not always possible in the short run because of the difficulty of finding good people, but don't lose sight of the goal. If the Internet is going to be anything more than an ancillary activity in your business, then hire your own web people. You don't need to staff for every web activity you can foresee, but, at a minimum, the generals who deploy the troops must be flying your flag. For almost every business, in almost every category, the Internet is an area of growth, a clear path for the future. You *must own* your own future.

A number of methods may be pursued for finding candidates. We will walk you through nine of them.

➤ 1. Word of Mouth and/or Referral

This is the most effective and the cheapest way of finding the best qualified candidates. Ask anyone and everyone who might know someone who has the skills you are seeking. The candidates who apply are then most likely to be good choices because they are known quantities.

People may periodically refer potential candidates to you, based on the kind of work you are doing, your reputation, or your business area. Be proactive; work your network. You may have done some networking to get yourself a job. It can be a powerful force for helping to find your employees.

➤ 2. Internal Referral

No one knows more about your staffing requirements than your own employees, and they also know with whom they want to work. Reward them lavishly when they bring in someone who eventually gets hired. You'll save a ton of money in recruiting fees, you'll get better people, and you'll focus everyone in the company on helping to build the business. Many firms wisely grant their staff $500 to $20,000 (or more) for each person who gets hired through their referral AND stays on for at least three months (the industry standard). Don't cheap out here. Cough up cash to your employees who do this. You will be repaid many times over. If you're forced to go the recruiter route or the advertising route, you will spend multiples of this in fees.

➤ 3. Contingency Fee Recruiters

In this category are firms that derive income solely from the fees they charge when they successfully place a candidate with a client. These *placement agencies* or *recruiting firms* are colloquially referred to as "headhunters," because of the hard-sell techniques they use for pushing warm bodies to their clients.

This avenue of candidate acquisition requires special care because many of the firms that supply potential candidates are not known for their scruples. Bad firms send resumes out to clients without the permission of the candidates, or they send out unqualified candidates. They can waste your time and your money, and they will hurt your organization by filling it with the wrong people. Watch out!

To be fair, there are many fine recruiting firms out there; unfortunately, they are in the minority. These firms take special care in

understanding the particular requirements or skills that you are looking for in candidates, and in learning about your firm's needs. The
best way to find good recruiters is through recommendations by satisfied colleagues.

Expect to pay *a lot* of money when you use any of these professionals. Typically, expect to pay a fee equivalent to 25 percent of the
annual salary that you plan to offer a prospective employee. Without
too much effort, these recruiters can usually be talked down to 20
percent by blaming the ceiling price on your boss or stating that it is
corporate policy. You have to question the quality and standards of
any firm that accepts a 15 percent (or lower) fee. If you squeeze a low
fee out of a firm, you risk its steering the good applicants to other
clients or just not giving you much attention.

When you hire someone through a recruiter, make sure you get
some sort of guarantee. Typically, the recruiter is entitled to the entire fee after the candidate has been on the job for three months.
Some firms charge one-third of the fee per month for three months;
others refund the entire fee if the candidate leaves prior to three
months. Another option is for the agency to find you another person,
free, if the original hiree leaves before the three-month period is up,
but there is no guarantee that the substitute will be satisfactory. Negotiate a guarantee when you negotiate the fee. Start with a fee that's
payable at the end of the three-month period, then negotiate down
from there.

A few years ago, only a few recruiters specialized in the new
media arena. Today, there are many more, but be careful! Many of the
traditional firms that profess to have lots of candidates have no clue
about the industry. Recently, a colleague was visited by the consulting
arm of Robert Half (one of the biggest national recruiting "chains").
The visitors professed to have a ton of "highly qualified" Java programmers. Our colleague asked them which middleware package was the
most popular among them, and, with great embarrassment, they ad-
mitted that they had no idea what he was talking about.

If you're recruiting for the Internet, or dealing with any area of
it, don't fall victim to the line: "You can't be a prophet in your own
country." Listen to yourself and listen to the people in your firm; just
because someone has had experience elsewhere, he or she is not
necessarily an expert. If you are part of a larger organization, poke
around internally before you go outside looking for help. There are

likely to be plenty of people in your firm who are destroying their health and their close relationships by spending weekends and evenings learning, programming, and building websites on their own time. They may be ecstatic to find that they can put some of these skills to work, and the added bonus is that they already know something about your business.

Some of the newer and trendier recruiting firms now call themselves "web talent agencies." This title evokes images of cartoons in which jugglers and animal acts are looking for show business management, and is nothing more than a new label on an old idea. However, you shouldn't particularly care how they describe themselves as long as they send you good people.

As in any client–vendor relationship, find agencies that get results for you, and reward them with further business. Trust your instincts. Just because you're hiring for the Internet doesn't mean that all the old rules of business don't apply. A person who submits a resume that looks scattered and undisciplined and has no continuity is probably a match to those traits. If you are looking for a senior-level web person, in whatever discipline, remember that managing budgets, managing projects, and managing people isn't radically different online or offline. Someone who has no experience in management but appears to have lots of web experience may be a fantastic single contributor but is probably the wrong choice for leading a web effort involving 30 people. Recruiters may try to steer you otherwise.

➤ 4. Retained Search

This is a variant on the contingency-fee agency arrangement, only the contingency has been eliminated. The agency expects to have an exclusive or near-exclusive agreement on the search. You pay a portion up front and, in most cases, you have to pay whether you hire someone or not. All of the major retained search firms—Russell Reynolds, Spencer Stuart, Korn Ferry, Egon Zehnder, and so on—have set up or are in the process of setting up new media/web practices. As is always the case with consulting agencies, good results depend on the quality of the people who are working with you. A fancy-name firm that is great for finding CFOs and COOs for packaged-goods companies doesn't necessarily have the knowledge or connections to find qualified web marketers.

This approach is the Rolls Royce of recruitment, and you need to enter into this type of relationship with real care. It is best to go with a firm that you really know well; otherwise, you may be giving an exclusive to a firm that will only end up wasting your time and cash. If you decide to go this route, you must do so with full knowledge. If you are in a large established firm, you should expect to pay the search firm between 25 and 40 percent of the total cash compensation (salary, incentive bonus, sign-on bonus, cash paid for lost stock options, and so on) that the new hire will receive during the first year of employment. If you are hiring a very senior-level person (these firms won't generally work on a search for an employee who will be paid less than $200,000), fees can easily amount to tens if not hundreds of thousands of dollars. As with any investment of this magnitude, you should be very aggressive in asking questions. Grill and regrill the people who are going to work on your search. Be sure that you are getting real experience and connections. Ask for references. Ask for details about the searches they have done online, and make sure they are not just recruiting generalists who have spent too many hours on AOL chat rooms and think being web recruiters would be sexy. This happens more than you would like to believe. A retained search recruiter is only as valuable as his or her Rolodex or Palm Pilot, as the case may be.

If you are working for a small firm or a true start-up, particularly a web start-up, and you have big plans but not big cash, retained recruiters will be happy to talk to you. There is a catch—a big catch. Having watched the dot-com IPO craze for several years now, the big recruiters would like a chance to taste some of the equity magic. So, if you cannot pay for your search in cash, they will be happy to take, or in some cases will even demand, equity. That's right, the recruiting agency may want to take, quite literally, a piece of your hide in exchange for helping you to find the people who might eventually make you a millionaire. We applaud their gumption, but what can you say? Proceed with extreme caution when you're asked to pay for a critical but, essentially, a "one-off" service with the lifeblood of your organization.

➤ 5. Pay Web Job Boards

These websites try to provide resources to applicants and companies. By and large, the applicants can post their resumes or background summaries on the site for free. The companies pay for the privilege of being able to search for candidates based on specific keywords, and to post their job requirements.

New job boards are popping up all the time; some of the better-known ones include monster.com, dice.com, and hotjobs.com. How are they ranked? That depends on whom you talk to and what experiences they have had. Rankings tend to be all over the map. Increasingly, job boards are based on very specific areas of specialty. It should be noted that monster.com, and all its associated international sites, is truly a monster in size. It represented, at press time, approximately 25 percent of all online recruiting on the Internet. Bad or good, it is unquestionably *big*.

All pay job boards try to get clients to sign up as members. The cost is many hundreds of dollars per month, although the boards will dutifully remind you that what you pay them is a fraction of what you'd pay as a single traditional headhunting fee. In return, they will give you full search access to their database of applications, and will allow you to post your open positions on their board.

The problem with these sites is that you will get as many unqualified applicants contacting you (and sucking up your time) as you would in a print ad, only now you have national or worldwide reach.[2] Even worse, recruiting firms lurking on these boards will send you unsolicited resumes and emails, even though most boards have rules against agencies.

If you don't hire that many people but think the boards might be useful, you can usually pay a limited fee for à la carte services, although the boards try to discourage this arrangement because they won't receive recurring revenue from you. With à la carte services, you pay a few hundred dollars on a one-shot basis, and you get limited numbers of postings and limited search capability (if any at all). However, this may be enough for your particular needs.

➤ 6. Free Web Job Boards

A number of organizations offer the chance to post job openings. There is also a tradition of posting jobs in newsgroups and in various internet community sites. In the New York City/Silicon Alley area, the top job board is run by the New York New Media Association (http://www.nynma.org), and the best thing about it is that you don't have to be a member to post your openings. NYNMA.org staff review the ads prior to their going up, which usually delays an ad from appearing on the site until the next day. The ads stay up on the site for only a couple of weeks, maximum, but these are small details compared to the quality of the applicants who are watching this board. The people found on this job board may be far superior to the applicants you can get through the expensive pay job boards, and you can't beat the price. These community job boards are effective for recruiting because they are naturally targeted toward a specific kind of professional. One caution here: Make sure you know the community you are talking to, and communicate appropriately. Otherwise, you run the risk of alienating the very people you want to attract.

A few recommendations about job boards. If you are looking for senior-level people—Director or VP level, or higher—you are unlikely to find them on job boards. The job boards function best for people in very early stages of their careers and/or for highly technical people. As time passes, the number of senior people available on job boards is increasing, and it is certainly the goal of monster.com and their online brethren to steal business from traditional retained and contingency recruiters, but they ain't there yet. If you are working for a large organization, have exhausted word-of-mouth and referral opportunities, and need to hire someone who is going to be managing more than 25 people, you will, for the most part, have no choice but to go the recruiter route.

➤ 7. Advertising in Periodicals

Paper ads and contingency-fee recruiters used to be the traditional sources for finding applicants, but the web has changed all of that. In the old days, there used to be several whole pages of ads for computer programmers, but the web has effectively wiped out these sources too. Dow Jones's venerable newspaper, so sexily named *National Business Employment Weekly,* closed its paper doors in early 2000 and embraced the web 100 percent. You can still place a classified ad in the help wanted section, or a display ad in the business section of many paper newspapers, but be prepared to spend a lot of time screening highly unqualified applicants, especially undocumented foreign nationals. That applies equally to the online counterparts of traditional newspapers. If you are going to spend the money, you'll probably do better by advertising on one or more of the pay web boards.

➤ 8. Advertising on Your Website

Is there a question here? Do it! This is free advertising. Anyone who shows an interest in your firm is invariably going to look at your website, and companies both big and small pay much closer attention to the applicants they receive this way because of the recruitment cost savings involved. If you notice, most firms these days have a link off of their home page where you can look at the current slate of open positions. Set it up so that it will automatically generate an email message to the appropriate person in your firm. Your HR person must keep this information current. If your web resources are modest, a number of external firms specialize exclusively in helping to maintain job pages in a private-label fashion. Not a bad idea if you are part of a large organization with a hundred or more job openings at any time. Just check the contract to make sure that confidentiality is properly maintained.

➤ 9. Keep Your Eyes Open

If you go to a trade show and hear someone give a lecture that sounds interesting, go up afterward and get his or her business card. Later, either ask via an email if he or she might want to "explore career opportunities," or have your HR person do it. If that person isn't interested, perhaps he or she knows someone who is. This is a dynamic industry, which is another way of saying it's "mercenary." If someone comes to sell you services or software and you fall in love, email, hunt down, and call that person. The reality is that the world is extremely hungry for talent right now, and its appetite is growing faster than qualified applicants are being produced. You need to be aggressive, creative, and fast-moving in this environment or you simply will not be able to hire. Go to interviews prepared to make a verbal offer. It may take some time to get your HR and/or legal departments comfortable with this tactic, but you need to have this tool at your disposal.

The best thing to do is to try all of these methods and see what works for you. Finding qualified people is arguably the most difficult part of building an e-commerce business. If you are heading up the effort to build a web company or a web group within a large firm, expect to spend 70 percent of your time on recruiting and retention.

■ CONSULTANTS

The tactical use of consultants in a corporation can be an effective tool for achieving your short-term business goals, but their strategic role in your firm must be examined.

One of the main issues to consider when hiring consultants is whether you want some of your firm's core competencies and intellectual capital centered in an individual (or individuals) who is not an employee of your firm. Your decision may depend on how strategic those skills are within your business. If you are engaging a programmer to do some straightforward work for a couple of weeks, then it might not be a big deal. If you plan on using some kind of specialized software for the foreseeable future, you will probably want to make sure that the person you are bringing in is invested in your company—in other words, an important and valuable full-time employee.

This larger issue comes down to a question of commitment. A consultant jumps around from client to client. The implication is that he or she doesn't have any particular commitment to you and your business needs. However, this is ironic because the staff turnover rate in a large percentage of new media firms can hit 70 percent or more.[3] A consultant is incented to your firm by the hourly rates you are paying and the contract you sign, which usually states some duration of months or weeks. An employee can quit at any time, so the question is: Who is more committed to your firm? When you hire a consultant to work on a project for you, you can sign a contract that obligates the consultant for the length of the project. Unfortunately, it is far more common for a key employee to quit a job (usually, in the middle of a project) because someone has offered a better or higher-paying job.

It is not uncommon for consultants to end up working for a client for long periods of time. Microsoft hires tons of contractors to work in Redmond, although the firm got into big trouble with the IRS because a lot of the contractors sued for benefits, contending that they were acting, for all practical purposes, like employees, and won their case.[4] At many large firms, consultants are given a status equal to full-time staff. Sometimes, full-time employees are even managed by consultants. We once met a consultant who had been on a project for Hughes Aircraft, in California, for *ten years!*

One issue needs to be considered. You run a risk when you use a consultant. Once the project is done, the consultant stops doing work for you and may not be available the next time you need advice. Consider structuring your projects so that they are contiguous and you can keep the same staff working together. If you don't have in-house capabilities to support, improve, and fix your technology, it may be necessary to retain your consultant well after the project is completed.

Here is the full list of reasons why you might want to consider using a consultant:

1. You need someone with specific expertise. Rather than trying to hire an expert in an arcane skill that you need for a specific project, bring in an expert to do the job.

2. You have a project that will run for only a finite period of time. Why go through all the trouble of hiring a bunch of people for a defined project of fixed length? Further, hiring a team of people and then firing them when the project ends is poor form and will give your firm a bad reputation. It's better to bring in consultants and pay for their skills only when you need them.

3. Resources are not available within your firm. You may have a department that does what you need to have done, but it may not have the bandwidth or capacity to get your job done any time soon, or the job may just be too big or too complex. By bringing in your own team from outside, you avoid a formal hiring process and any issues over why you are bringing in your own team, especially in departments that are very turf-conscious.

4. You want to hire someone quickly. The quickest way to get work started immediately is to bring in a contractor from the outside.

5. You want to avoid using your HR department. Especially in larger firms, the recruiting departments may be totally inept and useless, but your corporate hierarchy may dictate that you must go through them. Using consultants bypasses that problem.

➤ Consulting Rates

These are all over the map, and are based on experience, project duration, location, and, of course, whatever the market will bear. Expect to pay higher rates for managerial skills. Expect to pay more in big markets like New York, Boston, and San Francisco (Silicon Valley), than in Boise or Charleston. Rates for a short project will be dramatically higher than for a long-term one, so always negotiate a lower rate when you know the duration will be long-term. If special skills are required, expect to pay higher rates, but if the consultant has skills in a specialty area where there isn't a lot of business, you may try to negotiate a lower rate.

The active term here is *negotiate.* Consultants hate to be "on the beach" (not working) and therefore not getting paid. If they haven't been working for a few weeks, they will be anxious to be back on billing, and you can turn that to your advantage.

On the other hand, don't squeeze a consultant so hard that you aren't paying at least ballpark rates. You run the risk that the consultant may walk if a higher-paying contract comes along. Always make a proposal that's win–win (this should be a general business philosophy anyway). The people you contract with will be happy to work with you, and you'll be happy with the work they do.

➤ Sources for Consultants

Consultants can be found through sources similar to those used for obtaining full-time employees. Some recruiters place both full-time and consulting staff. Other agencies specialize in only placing consultants with firms.

Consultants can also be engaged directly and through consulting firms. In general, consultants will cost somewhat less when contracted directly; consulting firms mark up their rates anywhere from 30 to 100 percent. Some big firms actually dictate how much a consulting firm can mark up its consultants' rates to avoid a situation in which a consultant ends up leaving a project for a higher-paying project because the consulting firm is taking such a large percentage of the rate.

This brings up an interesting subject. Even though consultants are theoretically contracted to work on your project until it is completed, they are subject to the same career wants and opportunities as regular employees. If they become unhappy with your project, for whatever reason, they may leave. In general, you can't stop them from leaving (slavery was abolished a long time ago), and you don't want someone working on your projects who doesn't want to be there. If the consultant came through a consulting firm, you can demand that they send you a replacement, assuming they can find one.

Don't forget that, like your regular staff, consultants need to be managed. Make sure that they are assigned within the chain of command of your organization. You may be spending a lot of money per hour for a specialized Java programmer, but that doesn't mean that the programmer knows how to manage projects.

Finally, try to find consultants that are at least incorporated, to protect you from potential IRS rulings on their independent contractorship (as mentioned earlier in this section).

■ COMPENSATION AND EQUITY

If you have been watching Chairman Alan Greenspan at all, you may not agree with all of his misgivings—on the other hand, you may not understand his academic jargon, either. There is a massive labor deficit which is particularly pronounced in technology. The statistics are a bit fuzzy but it is clear that there are at least two hundred thousand jobs in IT that are unfillable each year.

To attract and keep talented contributors and leaders, you need to be pretty damn sexy! Having a successful and exciting business, charismatic leadership, a personally rewarding employee experience—these are all essential, but people are looking at their bottom line. Everyone wants to get paid a lot. And with a shortage of talent and a desperate demand, the inflation of compensation is hard to keep up with.

The Internet and the IT industry's salary surveys, which are published everywhere, are always stale and always low. Don't take them at face value. One of the deadliest mistakes you can make in management these days is to underestimate the demand for your talent. Does it make sense that the pimply-faced, inarticulate, utterly charmless HTML guy should be paid $80K and receive stock options every six months? Probably not. But you'd better believe that someone out there, right now, is ready to pay more and maybe throw in a personal masseuse. If you live in a small town and the only alternative to your web shop is a job on the local factory assembly line, you may think you are being very generous with your relatively fabulous compensation. Just wait. Your staff will be stolen and relocated, at fantastic expense, to a big-city company. Or your staff will leave you, set up shop by themselves, and attract clients from all over the world—without leaving town at all. Don't forget: The Internet transcends geography. It's an easy mistake to make. The scale of growth and the demand for even marginally experienced internet personnel is hardly possible to imagine, but there it is.

After you get over the staggering payroll required to keep your people satisfied, you have an even greater mental hurdle to surmount: employee equity. Some less financially sophisticated people are happy with fat weekly paychecks, but many employees expect to participate in the upside of the company they have graced with their abilities. Typically, founders of start-ups set aside no less than 10 percent of their equity to incentivize future employees with stock options. Well-established firms have, for many years, recognized that the best way to keep and drive senior management is with "golden handcuffs." For the movers and shakers, a salary is only symbolic; the stock is what matters. Recently, the demand for equity has mushroomed; now, everyone wants a piece. The result is that wealthy firms are losing all of their talent. Their panic is justified as they attempt to restructure their compensation structures. Microsoft (and Bill Gates) is famous for understanding that employees contribute more when they have more to gain through the success of their firm. Equity is not just for the suits anymore. Everyone wants equity, and it's good business to give it to them.

Some potentially sticky accounting and legal mechanics are involved in granting equity to employees (usually in the form of options). Lawyers, bankers, and accountants are the right people to consult, and it spares a lot of pain later if care is taken *early* to plan for employees' equity.

At a high level, you need to understand exactly how much equity will be allocated. For instance, with a start-up, if you don't have much cash in the beginning but you need to hire people who are in demand, expect to give more equity to staff. On the other hand, if you promise to give away too much, your company may become unattractive to potential investors. In an existing company, where this planning never happened, things can be more complicated. With public companies, the complications need to be thought out and then architected at a strategic level with the aid of professionals.

Legal and accounting issues aside, what is important from a staffing point of view is that option agreements are always structured to incentivize more work. Do not focus on rewarding past contributions. The question isn't "What have you done for me lately?" It's "What are you doing for me tomorrow?" When employees' options become fully vested, they are released from the golden handcuffs. If you want to keep them, slap some bigger ones on their wrists. In other words, if your employees don't have some more valuable options vesting in the future, they aren't going to hang around.

There are no rules, nor slide rules, for determining compensation. Be creative. Everyone has immediate needs and different aversions to risk. Risk-averse people obviously want more cash and a workplace that has a history of success and a bright future. Risk-inclined people want more equity and are willing to bet that they can make a difference in a less established enterprise.

The story of equity vs. cash has changed radically in 2000 relative to 1999 and previous years. In the fattest and headiest years of the dot-com boom, basically early 1996 through the Q1 2000 crash, very senior, seasoned players from the great blue chip companies of America were willing to throw executive perks and strong 6 figure compensation to the wind in exchange for millions of shares of pre-IPO stock in dot-com start-ups. Anything with a dotcom in the name held the promise of fabulous Vegas-jackpot-style riches in a NASDAQ instant. Now that stocks that were trading at $130 per share are trading at $4 a share, people are looking—looking hard—before they leap. Two hundred thousand shares worth a penny a piece isn't going to get anyone a beachfront spread in Malibu. The net result is the following: Strong, reasonable, profit producing, substantive business plans backed by real money and real management talent can still attract great people for comparatively low salaries and rich equity packages. More radical concepts laden with risk with lots of potential "upside" but no tangible "now side" are increasingly difficult sells. The market has changed dramatically: People are much more gun shy than they were. People want to get paid. People have discovered that packing 600 kids in an old garment factory without air conditioning while they sweat for the dot-com dream has lost its allure. The dot-com dream is far from dead, but it has matured a bit in the new millennium.

Chapter 5

Web Roles

This chapter will help you gain an understanding of what web people do for a living, and how some roles—which may have a familiar ring—change in an internet context.

■ INFORMATION ARCHITECTURE, USER INTERFACE, AND USABILITY

The unfortunate truth is that for many managers and executives the only part of a website that they can relate to is the user interface (UI). Basically, the UI is what you see on the screen when you view a website. The fact that the UI is the only "visible" part of a site leads to some rather dangerous behavior and to a strange focus of attention and time, particularly among senior managers. To many people, the Internet is wholly intimidating. The techies who make the systems work seem like strange medieval alchemists. It is only natural that people will gravitate to an area where they feel they can have a legitimate opinion. The look and feel of a site make it seem like a place where anyone can play and where specific expertise is not so critical. This is partly true, but only partly. Let us explain.

Websites are pieces of software and hardware. They are distributed systems. Most of the real programming or coding lives on machines that may be in Bangladesh, and not on your PC. But however it is put together, or wherever it resides, it is still just an application. Think about any piece of software that you have ever bought or used at your office. Usually, at some point, you end up referring to a manual or sheepishly asking someone, "How do you print?" The bottom line is that software takes time to learn. You only expect to be really able to use a piece of software after some period of time or training. Come on! How many of us use Microsoft Word or Microsoft Excel every single day? Think of the hundreds, if not thousands, of functions that appear in the online help list that you have never looked at.

The truth is, not a single website that has ever been created approaches the complexity of Excel—nor is there ever likely to be one any time soon. Also, there are no websites that come with user manuals. Think about the proposition of a website like Gateway.com. For years, Gateway had a very complex internal order-management and order-entry system that was used by its representatives in the call center to take orders from customers. It typically took Gateway three to five weeks to train its people in how to correctly enter an order, cancel or amend an order, check on the availability of parts, check on the time to delivery, and so on. Weeks! Now think about Gateway.com. Essentially, the goal of the site is to replicate this same internal functionality so that customers can take care of an order themselves. The issue, of course, is that they must be able to do so without weeks of training and without a manual. The system had to be designed so that when a first-time customer logs onto the site, it is intuitively obvious how to use every function—so obvious, in fact, that the newcomer won't have to ask a single question in the course of using the system. Avoiding expensive support and sales calls is, of course, one of the reasons to have a site in the first place.

To make a radical understatement, this is really hard to do. This is the goal behind designing and maintaining a user interface for e-commerce: To create a system that allows for the provision of information and the facilitation of complex transactions in a wholly intuitive environment. With the exception of video games, there is really no precedent in the history of software development that is this demanding. Let us break down the tasks for creating a user interface (UI).

We will assume, for the purposes of this discussion, that you have already completed a functional and technical specification. You know what functions the website is going to perform and what information it is expected to convey. The next step is the creation of the information architecture (IA). This is indeed a specialty—some people do this exclusively for a living. You don't necessarily have to contract someone to get your project built correctly, but if you can, do so. The role of information architects is to define what goes on each page. They build a flow chart that tells what information is displayed, what choices, what buttons, and what links appear on each page of the site. What they don't do is tell you how they should be presented, what the site looks like, what graphics should be included, or how to design the graphics.

Let's take a hypothetical example to make the concept clear. You are setting up a website to sell lemonade.[1] The products for sale are: lemonade and a host of wonderful branded hats, T-shirts, and lemon squeezers. On your home page, you might want to have a message welcoming visitors to Larry's Lemonade Shack—"Best in Cleveland" and then two buttons: (1) "Buy Lemonade," and (2) "Buy Larry's Stuff." If you click on "Buy Lemonade," you are presented with a form for filling out your address, credit card information, and so on. If you click on "Buy Larry's Stuff," you get a choice of images: a hat, a T-shirt, and a lemon squeezer. Clicking on any of those images will bring you to the same "check-out" form that clicking on "Buy Lemonade" brought you to.

That is information architecture. None of what we just discussed tells you what color the page is, what kind of font you should use, where the buttons are placed on the page, or whether you should have a horrible mascot that looks like a lemon with an enormous mustache and sunglasses. That part is design, the next step after information architecture. Even if your site is simple—and absolutely if your site is going to be complex—you should do detailed information architecture before you talk to a designer or spend a lot of time or energy thinking about how the site should "look." Both of these tasks go toward building the user interface and deciding the eventual navigability (i.e., how easy it is to navigate around the site, find what you are looking for, and so on) of the site. They are, however, discrete thought processes, and keeping them so will ensure a better result.

Design is the next task. Design is the creation of the look and feel that are used to present the information architecture graphically. This is where questions of brand, style, aesthetics, color, and art come into play. Tomes upon tomes have been written about this subject, but a few key lessons will help you make better sites.

In the immortal words of Ted Waitt, the founder and Chairman of Gateway, who uses them in response to just about anything: "Simple is good. Simple is better." In no effort is this more critical than in designing websites. Leave sophistication and complexity to wine snobs.

Keep your website as simple, obvious, and easy as you possibly can. Check out the highest trafficked and most popular websites: Amazon.com, eBay, Priceline, and the great-granddaddy of simple, Yahoo!. All of these sites are as simple as they can be, yet they still get the message across. Nothing fancy, nothing that you have to "figure out." Yahoo!, a now-profitable site with one of the richest market capitalizations in the dot-com world, has hardly changed at all, from a design perspective, since it was launched by a couple of Stanford graduate students. There is more on the page, and items have moved around to accommodate the increased functionality, but the design is the same: blue text on a white background. No pictures, no video, no sound, no animation.

This site is designed for speed, as nearly every website should be. It is critical to be aware of the expectations of the medium. There is a real expectation of immediacy on the web; web users want their pages *now!* It is an environment filled with distractions and populated by users who have ADD (attention deficit disorder), if you will. Any little hangup, any little delay, or any passing thought, and a customer can click away from your site in a second.

The Internet is, by definition, an unpredictable place made up of thousands of interconnected networks of radically varying quality. You need to ensure that the part of the Internet you control—your site—performs as well as possible. Without fail, you will be a victim of outages and network congestion at various points, and they will impact the quality of someone's experience on your site. In the vast majority of cases, users are not sophisticated enough to understand that the slowness that they experience is beyond your control. Keeping your site "light"—not loaded up with elements that take up a lot of disk space, and therefore take time to download—is critical. Never make the assumption that users will be willing to wait to be presented something "cool." Users want to get their information, transact, check their order status, do whatever their business is, and be done.

In working on user interface, it is critical to keep the concept of respect for your customers' time at the forefront of your mind. When customers visit your site, they are giving you a valuable gift—their time. You need to drive the UI so that it allows people to achieve their goals as quickly, painlessly, and obviously as possible. Users are impressed with flash and uniqueness only once. Utility and ease of use bring them back. Resist the urge to innovate with design.

The web is a difficult environment in which to work, not merely because of the issue of download time and the constraints placed on the size of pages. You need to keep in mind that the Internet is an internetwork—a collection of many networks. Those networks utilize heterogeneous technology. The users of the network connect to it with a whole variety of different computers that are running different operating systems with different browser software, with different languages and fonts installed, and so on. The bottom line is: There will never be a single version of your website. The configuration parameters of each individual PC that connects to your site have real impact on how that user will experience your work.

This is a frustrating experience for many people coming to the web for the first time. If you design a magazine ad, then, barring some sort of printing mistake, every person who sees your ad will see the exact same thing. The fonts and the colors will be the same, and the format and layout will be replicated exactly in every copy of the magazine in which your advertisement appears. On the web, this is never the case.

Ensuring an experience that is as uniform as possible demands a rigorous testing approach. Macintosh, Windows, and Unix browsers will interpret the HTML (hypertext markup language—the layout language for websites) somewhat differently. To ensure that a website is ready for deployment, the site must be tested in a number of versions of different browsers in different operating systems. How many you choose to test comes down to your level of risk tolerance, but at least the last two Netscape and Internet Explorer browsers should be tested in both the Apple and Windows environments.

There are a few areas to watch out for when you are overseeing design. Color blindness is one area people often forget. A large percentage of men are color-blind; red/green color blindness is the most common. If you design a page with red text on a green background, or vice versa, color-blind people will see no text—just a block of color. Another issue is text of one color on a background of the same color. If the shades are close, they are difficult for anyone to read, but remember that a person's monitor settings, or the sophistication of a video card, impacts how colors are displayed. What may appear as a dark blue text on a very light blue background, fairly readable on your machine, may be interpreted as the same color, or two nearly identical shades by a different video card. Remember Yahoo.com. Dark blue text on a white background. It is a safe bet that just about everyone on the web will find it easy to read, no matter what their equipment or software. To avoid color problems, most good web designers will use what is called the "safe color palette." This is a collection of 216 colors that are very basic and are nearly guaranteed to show up well on any computer.

Last, but certainly not least, is the issue of brand expression. This is an issue for any company doing business on the web, but in many respects it is the most difficult issue when companies with long-standing offline business are setting up e-commerce websites. If your company is well known for its striking retail store designs, how do you bring that onto the web? How do you replicate the experience of walking through a wood-paneled, English country manor-like Ralph Lauren Polo boutique? The answer is: You can't. Do not try to "bring a store to life" on the web.

The advice given above holds true regardless of the brand. This is a difficult change to swallow, and it has kept many luxury brands off of the Internet or delayed their entry. The key issue is accepting and working within the constraints of the technology, not ignoring them.

At the same time, numerous opportunities on the web are impossible or impractical in a physical store or in a paper catalog. If, for example, you are selling handmade, sophisticated Swiss watches, the Internet will allow you to provide endless amounts of documentation and explanations on the workings of the timepieces, the history of the company, the years of craftsmanship, and the rigorous apprenticeships of young watchmakers, ad infinitum. That is information that a retail clerk, selling many brands, will never take the time to learn. That information potentially would occupy hundreds of pages that would be too expensive to print on paper.

Your brand needs to find a voice and a look that connect to its history, but, at the same time, you must simply accept that you are playing in a different medium and the rules are different.

One area that is really a part of user interface design but often gets ignored is the copy—the words on a site. Copy falls into two basic categories: (1) navigational text and (2) marketing text. Navigational text is used to help guide a user through the web experience: submit, go, next, cancel, checkout, register. Well-thought-out information architecture and a simple and elegant graphical design can be quickly compromised with poor navigational text. The rule of thumb, as usual, is to adhere to conventions and keep it simple. It is worthwhile to spend time, or urge your development team to spend time, visiting the leading e-commerce websites to see how they tackle these issues. It is safe to assume that Amazon has tried hundreds of combinations and has settled on the navigational words that generate the least amount of confused and angry customer service contacts. There is no need to relearn the expensive lessons that Amazon has already learned for you!

Marketing copy is all of the information that is not site-activity-oriented. This text primarily describes products and services. Here, as in all aspects of user interface design, it is key to remember the need for speed. Customers will simply click away from long-winded product descriptions. At the same time, as in the luxury watch example above, you want to exploit the opportunities that the web gives you for providing customers with lots of detail. The issue is that it must be an OPPORTUNITY for detail, not a mandate. Sites work best when customers can choose to drill more deeply or to stick with information in summary form. The presentation varies with the product that you are trying to sell, but it is best to build navigation that allows customers to choose whether they want to go from product selection to check out—never more than *three clicks away*—or to while away the hours caressing every detail of your product's unique genius.

The key lesson here is that design is a specific discipline involving a complex mixture of art, human factors, marketing, and technical utility. Simple is always better, and simple-and-clean is almost always harder. Do not be afraid of navigation that appears standard or conventional or even boring. Conventions of navigation and user interface design have become conventions because they work. Spend your time and energy on innovation of service, or innovation in functionality, and keep your design as user-friendly as possible. Your customers will thank you by coming back again and again.

■ PROGRAMMING AND DEVELOPMENT

Development is technology delivery. Developers (or programmers) design, build, integrate, and extend software. Developers write code, test it, fix it, and, if they have time, document it and help support it. In a perfect world, developers are given a business problem, a set of requirements, and a framework (called *the architecture*) that is exhaustively documented and well thought out. This almost never happens, although a well-managed firm with thoughtful leaders can get close. If a nonprogrammer (i.e., a businessperson, usually) could express the desired functionality with rigor, and could clearly measure the business impact of introducing the technology to enable such functionality, there wouldn't be any programmers. There would simply be a notation for rigorously expressing business factors and calculating outcomes. We call this notation "code." Developers do much more than write code. They take on business problems, analyze them, and create solutions. The code is just what's left when they finish the project. It looks like magic, but code is actually very meticulous, and thoughtful work (unless it's bad code, in which case it is sloppy and thoughtless work, and the developers will usually claim they had vague requirements from the business!).

There are all kinds of developers. They come in all shapes, sizes, and skills. They speak many human and computer languages. Larry Wall, the man accredited with inventing PERL (practical extraction and query language), a rich scripting language designed to manipulate text and thus very popular with web developers who often use PERL to manipulate hypertext/HTML, said that the three "great virtues" of a programmer are laziness, impatience, and hubris. This is pretty true.

The laziness part is actually not as bad as it sounds. The reason laziness is a "virtue" is because software must be kept simple and easy, otherwise it runs away and becomes unmanageably complex and impossible to improve or manage. Laziness means that, rather than writing new code to solve the same problem over and over again in different places, you write it once, but in such a way that it can be used everywhere. This kind of laziness is good. It makes the software faster to develop and easier to maintain and understand. We would call this kind of thinking creative and wise, but a developer will most often smile and call it lazy.

The opposite of laziness, busyness, can be an enemy of success. There are many famous (and other shamefully hidden) stories of hundreds of millions of dollars spent developing new and integrating existing software products for years, with no result other than hefty tax write-offs. Large consulting companies like Anderson Consulting, PriceWaterhouseCoopers, and Ernst & Young have a failure rate much higher than they would be comfortable admitting in their IT and internet-specific development. Typically, these projects fail because the systems under development become so large and complex that no one can make them work, much less understand them. Maybe if the development practices at the big consulting firms were a little lazier, these projects would succeed. But that's a lot to ask of firms that make more money when they work more hours. Note: It is sometimes more attractive for consulting firms to have a lot of people billing with no result, than to have a few people billing with valuable results.

Developers are impossible to manage, and they usually cannot manage themselves. This is a paradox that is surmounted only by mysticism or, sometimes, very hard work and luck. Developers, especially the talented ones, are often prima donnas. Some developers are timid and awkward, some are stereotypical nerds, some are boisterous manic depressives. In San Diego, where many high-tech companies do their software development (Intuit/Quicken, Sun, Qualcomm, Gateway), developers run out of the office as soon as they see nice waves on the beach. There are actually surf-cams up and down the coastline that broadcast to surfer websites. Most of the time, developers aren't just in it for the money (though they like to get paid as much as possible). They like to have fun.

Good developers are hard to find. A good development *team* is rare. And it's hard to separate the wheat from the chaff just by meeting these people. Anyone can talk the talk, but can they walk the walk? Certifications, degrees, PhDs—they all mean nothing. So how do you know if you've got the right person or team? When products and product improvements and fixes are consistently delivered on time and on budget. Keep in mind that "Better late than never" is an important phrase in development. Software is almost always late. One of the first mistakes anyone makes when attempting to manage developers is to assume that software development is predictable. It's not an exact science, but if software is being delivered nearly on time you are in great shape. If a project consistently slips and the developers' estimates for completion are consistently way off, then you may have unqualified or mismanaged developers.

Perhaps the most important thing to understand is that no programmer knows about every kind of programming. There are database developers (DBAs), game developers, and folks who write the software that drives your cellular telephone. Some work in financial services, some work for the military (remember the War Games?), some write little applications for small businesses. Some work at home, alone, and pick up freelance jobs on the Internet. Some work in seas of cubicles. The kinds of applications, the technologies they use, and the physical and virtual environments they work in are as varied as the businesses they serve. Just because a developer has written missile-tracking systems doesn't mean he or she can make web pages or even understand how they work. Many developers are smart enough and confident enough to learn new skills and apply them, but many others are stuck in their ways.

Technology changes very quickly, but certainly no technology changes more quickly or as sweepingly as information technology (IT). A friend of ours, David Hock, a brilliant developer and architect, is fond of the aphorism, "If you ain't busy learning, you're busy dying." The best quality in a developer—going beyond Wall's "Three Virtues"—is a love of learning. But relevant experience is indispensable. Many developers have been left behind during the past decade. If you meet a developer who has never worked on a website before—and, certainly, not all websites are alike—think twice about letting that person sharpen his or her teeth on your dime.[2]

One last note on developers. Along with their great diversity of experience and skill sets, developers have a great disparity of productivity and talent. One great developer can literally do the work of 20 or more average ones. The key with managing developers and development is: Recognize achievement, reward, and retain.

■ ARCHITECTURE

In the physical world, architects are the brains behind buildings. They usually dream up the big picture of how the structure will be made, how it will be used, how it will look. They build models, do calculations, and deliver the blueprints to the contractors, who actually build the buildings. Typically, the architect is on hand until the project is done, but his or her biggest role is in the critical early stages. Eventually, after everything has been designed, researched, planned, costed, and decided, most good architects step back a little, observe and guide from the sidelines, and let the builders do their thing.

In the web world, the architects are IT architects. They are the gurus who dream up the blueprints for end-to-end e-commerce systems. If you have a business idea and—as with virtually all new web ideas—you can't buy an out-of-the-box system to support it, you will need to talk to an architect to understand what it will take to execute your idea. By the way, if you don't like the answer you get, you can always ask around. Good architects talk to each other constantly, to try to learn whether others are succeeding or are failing to solve different kinds of technology problems.

They also figure out how to integrate business systems that already exist. For example, when AOL buys (swallows whole) a little web shop that provides some neato tool like Mirabilis's ICQ—a chat program[3]—someone needs to figure out how to integrate it into the monolithic AOL world of "Welcome! You've got mail" so that the user interface can be branded with AOL advertising, and so that AOL users can be tracked (they capture every click!) while using it. This is where the AOL architects come in; they review the acquired technology and determine how to go about reworking it to fit into AOL's technology.

Unfortunately, architecture is often (usually) forgotten in the rush of initial e-commerce efforts. The zealous entrepreneurs—or newly appointed e-commerce executives—say: "We got no time for planning and meetings. We'll do that later! Let's get some programmers in here and start cracking." Usually, this sequence brings abject failure. There are no results; there is only frustration, and managers learn a lesson about "measuring twice and cutting once." Sometimes, serendipitously, some kids write some quick-and-dirty solution using PERL or ASP or ColdFusion, and it actually works. And sometimes, that's OK and nothing more is needed. But eventually (and sooner rather than later), a poorly planned architecture (or an unplanned architecture) will reach its limit and fail unrecoverably. This doesn't always kill a smart business. Smart businesspeople figure out a way to keep the ship from sinking. Then they hire skilled people to build them a completely new boat while they bail water out of the old one.

Sometimes, the difference between architects and developers—and even system administrators—can be subtle. Their roles and skills often overlap. In some shops, the roles are entirely blurred, and the developers and architects are indistinguishable. Think of architecture as a combination of big-picture thinking and deep technical understanding.

Architects have a talent for understanding and anticipating your business needs and selecting technologies that will serve you today and grow with you tomorrow. This saves you and your customers a lot of time and pain. Having an architecture and a plan for building it out doesn't mean spending lots of unnecessary capital up front. It means having an understanding of where your system will need to be as your business grows. Architects select the technologies you need, when you need them.

The problem with architects is that—as with developers—it is very difficult to find good ones, and there are many charlatans out there. Unless you are an engineer (and even then), it's pretty hard to evaluate them. Look for a proven track record and good references.

■ OPERATIONS

Operations (a.k.a. Ops) involves the maintenance and support of systems. Any systems, whether they are software components (e.g., COM objects, Enterprise Java Beans, PERL scripts), network devices (routers, hubs, switches, load balancers), servers and workstations (PCs, Macs, Suns, HP9000s), or business processes (like uploading fresh content), typically are part of the Operations organization. When a product is delivered by the development group, *Operations* is the name on the delivery tag.

Operations is concerned with things like: system implementation, day-to-day administration, performance monitoring and issue (the business world's euphemism for "problem") resolution, disaster recovery, security policy enforcement, and capacity planning.

Operations is all about uptime—the percentage of time a system is operational. The goal is 100 percent. When something goes wrong with a website, a good operations group knows about it first, springs to action, and communicates its status to the right people.

The general operations professional is the system administrator (a.k.a. sys admin or SA). Sometimes you may hear the term "system engineer," but we prefer SA. It's old-school lingo and it still makes the most sense, so use it and sound like a pro.

It may make sense to refer to specialized system administrators as "network admins" (do not abbreviate as NA). Network administrators are the router experts. They specialize in designing networks, configuring the routers' switches and firewalls, and dealing with network connectivity (especially internet connectivity). Network admins are especially important in the e-commerce world because systems rely on complex networks and the Internet more than ever before. A lot of (arguably, *most*) network admins in the WWW biz are hackers. They like bandwidth.

DBAs (database administrators) are concerned with implementing, configuring, tuning, and otherwise maintaining database systems. Databases are little worlds unto themselves, so DBAs make it their business to know the ins and outs of products like Oracle, MS-SQL Server, and Informix.

System administrators are a varied bunch. They support systems of all kinds. The easiest way to think about their role is to consider the three main "layers" of the web systems that they support: (1) the network, (2) the operating systems, and (3) the engines.

► The Network

A network consists of the cables, the switches and hubs, the routers, the Internet connectivity (T1s, T3s, and so on), dial-up connectivity for remote access, firewalls—you name it. This is "the plumbing," so to speak. Network admins, as we mentioned above, are the experts in this layer.

► Operating Systems (OS)

These are the platforms that applications run on, such as PC/Windows, Sun/Solaris, Linux, and others. There are many platforms, and no SA knows them all. When selecting a platform (part of the architecture process), it's important to make sure that you have staff to support it. If you are looking to hire SAs for a specific platform, make sure they have experience in your particular platform. Most of an SA's work revolves around the OS layer. For example, if you run out of hard-drive space, you have an OS-level issue, and your Ops people probably didn't do the required "capacity planning."

► The Engines

The engines are software applications such as web servers (Netscape Enterprise Edition, Microsoft IIS, Apache), application servers (Java Enterprise Platform, Microsoft Transaction Server, BroadVision, Bluestone Saphire, Dynamo, ColdFusion), database engines (Oracle, Sybase, Informix, MS-SQL Server), and search engines (MS-index server, Excalibur, Oracle). These are shrink-wrapped or homegrown products that web applications are built on. In the case of application servers, these engines are often referred to as development platforms, application environments, and middleware servers. They are not the same as operating systems, which provide lower-level services to applications such as disk access and network connectivity. Rather, they provide application-type functionality such as business transactions (e.g., "Add product to shopping cart" and "Store customer address"). Basically, engines sit between the developer's code and the operating system.

This last layer, the engines, is a very important layer. In e-commerce, this layer is often an area of great dispute between Operations and Development. In traditional IT organizations, this conflict is often compounded by the fact that Operations is the domain of the "old guard" IT, and e-commerce development is usually the domain of newfangled web people. Old IT Operations managers often draw the line at the OS layer. Many traditional Ops people think that the engines should be managed by the web people, and that their responsibility is only the traditional layers of the network and operating system. We think this is *very bad.* In the old days, it made sense to make this distinction because business applications were developed directly on top of the operating systems, instead of borrowing functionality from application servers. These big applications rarely changed and were maintained by specialists who knew every aspect of them. For example, if you bought IBM's vertical solution for your widget business, you also bought a support service that included access to these specialists for any issue that might arise, as well as day-to-day "care and feeding" of the system. The in-house Ops people never needed to know about anything beyond the operating system, and sometimes even that was outsourced to the business application vendor.

In today's world, this division of labor doesn't make sense. Application engines are sold off the shelf, but companies are generally expected to handle the custom development separately, on top of the engines. A modern Operations group needs to understand how to configure and tune these engines, and how the code that sits on top of them works. Today's systems just don't have neat and orderly layers that can be neatly divided for labor assignments. As businesses become more specialized, so does the technology. Operations organizations must rise to the challenge of these new *n*-tiered systems by engaging, learning, and taking responsibility for their successful operations.

Web people tend to be rather antiauthoritarian, but one unit absolutely must have order: Operations, which has the most important role in an e-commerce organization. Without effective operational support, the business simply will not run. If your business runs 24/7, then so must your Ops team. At all times, someone must be standing by who knows what to do, no matter what happens. While everyone was out partying on the eve of January 1, 2000, Ops people all over the world were standing by soberly, watching their consoles, looking for alerts in case of an issue. Chains of communication must be established, recovery processes must be practiced. All systems—every component, every configuration of every piece of software and hardware—must be documented and understood. Ops is kind of like the military.

Sometimes, Quality Assurance (QA) is rolled into Ops management. The thinking is: If these Ops people are going to have to support what they are delivered, they should be the ones to evaluate whether all the criteria (documentation, good performance, no bugs, and so on) for delivery have been met.

What are Operations people like? They are stressed! When was the last time you wrote an email to eBay saying, "Great Job. The site did not go down today, yesterday, or all year for that matter. Thanks. You Rock!!!" This NEVER happens. Operations folks never hear the praise. They just get the complaints. As a result, good SAs are a rare breed. Though the demand is always high, the job is not desirable to most sane, intelligent people. The right description of an SA is "confident and easygoing." "Unperturbable" is better. You need the kind of people who take pride in their work, don't need to hear how great they are, and—most importantly—stay totally cool under pressure. It's not easy to stay calm when a mission-critical system crashes and you know that the only person who can get it up and running again—and restore the halted revenue—is YOU. Experience is the only teacher in the world of Operations, so look for people who have experience in running heavy-traffic sites and no tolerance for downtime.

■ LEGAL

Law and the Internet do not mix terribly well. Lawyers, and the books that make them feel comfortable, function best in an environment of predictability and precedent. The online world provides neither. Yet, as everywhere in business, but particularly in America, the law is a major factor in many of the decisions we make. We will walk you through a number of the places where law enters into the world of building and managing e-commerce.

Disclaimer: We are not lawyers. We are businesspeople and technologists who have been around law and the Internet over the course of building commercial sites during the past five years. **Always seek professional legal assistance.**

➤ General Contracts

When contracting with web development vendors, a couple of structures work well. We'll first outline a basic contractual framework for working with larger organizations—the ones that you expect will assign you a number of projects over time. This structure is too cumbersome for working with individual independent contractors.

Master Agreement. The first document you need to get in place is a master agreement, or general consulting agreement. It outlines the general terms under which business will be conducted between your organization and the contractor. Key areas include payment terms, rate card, ownership of any intellectual property that is created (an enormous issue), conflict resolution, and so on. This agreement shouldn't cite any specific deliverables related to the project. It merely creates a framework for doing work.

Statement of Work (SOW). The statement of work is, as it sounds, a detailed description of a specific project. This is the document that should outline, in detail, the expectations for the project. The agreed-on and signed basic project brief, functional specification, technical specification, and project plan should be attached as appendixes to the agreement. This is the agreement that outlines the responsibilities of the vendor and the client for completing a certain project. This document contains the what, who, when, how much, and, to a lesser degree, how the work is going to be attacked.

Once you have a master agreement in place, you can attach individual projects under separate statements of work. A point that is often overlooked by clients and by inexperienced and perhaps overeager contractors alike, is that the client has just as much capacity and responsibility to make the project succeed or fail as the vendor that is doing the actual development. Ensuring proper response to work, managing scope creep, and having at least a somewhat formalized change management process are all critical to the success of your projects and are, by and large, the responsibility of the client. The basis for dealing with these issues should be addressed in your contracts.

➤ Licensing Agreement

Another form of contract is the licensing agreement. The long legalistic discourses you see on envelopes containing software, or when you download software off of the web, are usually licensing agreements. The purpose of these licenses is to protect the rights of the software owner. Big corporations have entire departments that deal only with software licensing. Microsoft will often conduct audits of large corporations it has relationships with, to ensure that they have been paid for all the copies of their software that exist at the firm. Start-ups need to be very careful about protecting their products through copyright, patent, trademark, and so on, especially if they are going to be marketing on the web. The right to a software license, the ability to build strong intellectual property packages out of software, can be the key to a technically anchored dot-com.

➤ Incorporation

Traditionally, people went to attorneys when they wanted to start a corporation, and they would end up paying several thousand dollars for the service. Today, this is totally unnecessary because all of the relevant information and forms are easily available to the public. If you want to start a company, the information and forms for doing so in your state should be available on the web.

If your firm is dealing with investors, angels, venture capital firms, IPOs, acquisitions, or mergers, you will need legal representation by someone who knows how to navigate that particular maze. Start-ups should look for attorneys who can help secure funding. Attorneys who are operating in the technical environment often have good contacts with the venture world. Work the network.

➤ Sourcing Legal Help

There are three main ways to source your legal help: (1) hire a law firm; (2) hire a sole practitioner; (3) add a lawyer to your employee roster.

1. Hiring a Firm.   Engaging a big law practice tends to be very expensive, especially when you use the firm's partners. Often, your work will get handed off to less experienced staff, but very high rates will still be charged. An attorney we know well says, "I can't tell you how many clients get billed at the partners' rates for work that was done by an $11/hour paralegal/secretary/slave." If your company is a big corporation, big law firms might be attractive to you because of the depth of resources they bring to the table, but don't forget to bring lots of checks when they offer you a chair. Another issue is: Unless you are a large firm yourself, a big law firm will simply not be overly concerned with your happiness. You will invariably represent a larger percentage of a small firm's business and are likely to get better support.

Start-ups often work hard and pay extra to be associated with a fancy legal name that can add a patina of credibility. In today's insane business environment, many "branded" law firms (and PR and advertising firms) are turning business away because there is just too much action. If you are truly in a small, start-up situation, think twice before going through the hassle and financial pain of running with the big legal dogs.

2. "My Cousin Vinny."   The second option is to hire sole practitioners. They tend to be much less expensive and, generally, they give you more personal attention and better responsiveness. The downside is that they have fewer resources to bring to the table. However, a good sole practitioner usually has a wide network of legal specialists and colleagues who can be brought in when conditions warrant. Like everything in life, there are trade-offs.

3. One to Call Your Very Own.   The third way to get legal assistance is to hire your own attorney. This is the most cost-effective way of managing legal resources *if* you have a lot of legal work. The question is: Can you justify the expense rather than using "pay as you go" services from outside attorneys? Try to forecast your legal needs, and run the numbers before you hire. Firing underutilized in-house attorneys is not generally good for your health. When you employ an in-house lawyer, your work becomes his or her priority, not just one more set of tasks from a bushel of clients.

➤ Law and the Web

The General Counsel at Gateway described it best: "The Internet is the legal Wild West." That was a few years ago, and the situation has since improved, but it is still true that legislation has not kept pace with the rapid development of business on the web. The one thing you do need to know is that lawyers are very nervous—and rightfully so—about working on the Internet. Law is a profession based on analyzing and understanding precedent. The web is an environment that, from a legal perspective, is largely without precedent. Legal opinions without precedent are unanchored and make it difficult for lawyers to understand the level of risk implied in a decision. It may require hard work to drive your attorneys to make decisions even when they are uncomfortable doing so, but you also must recognize that new ground creates a world of unknowable risk. Unknowable, unforecastable risk is anathema to the legal profession.

In spite of the immature state of law regarding the web, a number of principles are emerging that are critical to understand if you are going to manage e-commerce:

From the perspective of the law, web pages are essentially considered to be *advertisements,* which, in effect, are implied contracts. Company A asserts "X" about a product. Company A agrees to sell the product at the "X" price. Truth-in-advertising law in the United States and in most first-world countries means that advertisements are commitments. Websites are, therefore, commitments.

What that means is: All of the rules of false advertising that are in force on television and in print are equally valid on the web. The implication here is rather staggering: Your firm is accountable for **everything** on **every** page of your site. Every statement you make about the content of your product, the price of the product, the delivery schedule, and so on, is a commitment. Your customers can, will, and are legally empowered to hold you accountable for all such statements. Naturally, there is a level of reasonableness about errors, but a determination of whether you commit sins of omission, are guilty of carelessness, or attempt to defraud the public, is ultimately in the hands of a judge. The level of seriousness and potential danger should be appreciated.

This question becomes fairly prickly in relation to your management of your website. If you are running a small website with just a few pages that have basic e-commerce functionality, it will be easy to control what you say, and therefore what commitments you are making. This becomes far more complex in an organization like IBM, which has tens of thousands of employees, in more than a hundred countries. Corporate IBM is responsible for **all** of the content on its site. Any attempt to read all the pages of content on IBM.com is not possible. By the time you completed reading even 10 to 15 percent of it, the sections you read initially would have been updated, deleted, expanded, and so on.

The WWW is, at heart, a publishing medium. Websites tend toward complexity and size. That size usually comes in the form of depth of content and, for the most part, that is good for your business because it means more for your customers. You certainly don't want to create barriers to producing content on the web; at the same time, you need to have a control mechanism to ensure that a rogue employee, or a careless employee, doesn't commit the organization to something that might cost it millions of dollars.

Let's walk you through a real incident. At Gateway a few years ago, an engineer was uploading, to gateway.com, some new pricing data for the high-end server product line. He made an error. He listed the retail price of a top-of-the-line server as $150 instead of $15,000. The error was caught within a few hours, but, given the volume of sales on the website, quite a few customers had already placed orders. (The ridiculously low price probably prompted some less-than-scrupulous customers to see what they could get away with.) Most customers who had ordered the product at the $150 price accepted the fact that it was an error and were willing to pay the higher price when a sales rep contacted them and informed them of what had transpired. Several customers, however, understood the legal obligation of the company to stand behind its advertised price. They demanded that Gateway sell them the high-tech machines for $150. Gateway had no choice but to do so. This was a relatively expensive set of zeros.[4]

The job of legal departments is to protect the firm. They will often try to mandate that all pages on the company website must

receive legal review and approval before being posted. This is usually the reaction of the legal advisers in a company that has either
no web presence or only a minimal one. Unless your site is a few
dozen pages long and is not likely to change with any frequency, this
is simply not feasible. One of the main powers of the web is the ability to make changes quickly, to respond to the competition, and to
react to product availability—all in a matter of minutes or hours. The
logistical nightmare, not to mention the enormous cost represented
by having every word on the website reviewed by lawyers, is something to be absolutely avoided. Here are six strategies to keep your
business safe from lawsuits and still satisfy overbearing internal
legal watchdogs:

1. *Sensitive areas.* Work with the legal staff and examine the crit-
    ical areas of your site. Most often, these are disclaimers (price
    subject to change, availability subject to change), guarantees,
    warranties, and terms and conditions of sale and shipment.
    These areas will need to be written, owned, managed, and re-
    viewed—comma by comma—by the legal department. Offer a
    useful internal negotiating point: Allow them to dominate at
    least one part of the site!

2. *Control access.* There are numerous technical ways to
    achieve this control. However you do it, it is critical that the
    ability to post information on the company's website be con-
    trolled and monitored. Work with your technology depart-
    ment or technical consultants to create ways of monitoring
    who logged in, who made what change when, and so on. At
    the very minimum, create a system with a password/log-in
    scheme, and keep your group of "authorized content creators"
    small and accountable.

3. *Authorization.* Even though your website is probably a critical
    part of your business strategy, and even though the implica-
    tions of errors on the site can, as we discussed, be onerous,
    chances are that the people actually posting material, editing
    material, and deleting material from your company's website
    will be relatively junior. It is therefore essential that the peo-
    ple who *manage* the "content creators" understand the impli-
    cations and choose their staff carefully. Depending on the
    formality of your firm and the aggressiveness of your legal

staff, you may want to circulate a signature document that clearly outlines, to the content creators and the people they report to, that they are taking personal responsibility for the veracity and accuracy of the information they promote into the live web environment.

4. *Training.* Work with your legal department and your designated content creators. Train them in how to spot areas of trouble. Circulate a series of questions that the content creators should ask themselves, to help determine whether something they are about to post should receive legal review. A standard that works pretty well is the "new" rule. If a creator is putting on the website a document that involves a new type of arrangement, a new product, a new service that falls substantively outside of what has been posted before—it should go to the legal department beforehand. If you are changing prices on existing products, or changing basic information about product content, those postings do not need legal approval.

5. *QA procedures.* Be sure that someone checks all the work and content on the site before it goes live. Nobody should be allowed to proofread his or her own material before sending it to the public website. Organize the exchange in any way you want, but make sure that, at the end of the day, at least two sets of eyeballs (neither set needs to be imported from the legal department) have reviewed every scrap of content before it goes onto the website.

6. *Security policy.* These days, any website that is worth its salt and is engaged in management of any type of personal customer information (name, address, phone number, credit card, account number, and so on)—in other words, any e-commerce site—has an official security policy. That policy should be posted in prominent places on the website, particularly when sensitive information is involved. The policy should commit your firm to a set of secure practices for managing data and respecting customer privacy. Most importantly, you should be absolutely sure that what you say in your security policy is what you do! Check out the security policies of the big guys: Amazon.com, LLBean.com, and others, and check the sites in your industry to get a feel for the standards.

➤ Jurisdiction

The challenge here is to determine whose set of laws applies to a business contract, a sale, or a crime. What is a sale? What is a crime? Different legal jurisdictions—a county, a state, or a sovereign nation—have different laws. The Internet makes assigning jurisdiction very complex.

Let us provide you with a rather extreme and bizarre example. The Singapore Authority (a.k.a. the government of Singapore), decades ago imposed very strict laws for governing "immoral" content. Given the size of the country—262 square kilometers—it has been relatively easy for the government to keep a tight grip on naughty books, naughty photos, and naughty movies. Ironically, what the Singaporeans consider naughty and illegal in *their* country is shown daily on prime-time television in the United States.

Here's what happens when you throw the Internet into the mix. The Singapore Authority has decided, rather quixotically, that if a website transmits contraband information to a computer in Singapore, it is deemed to have broken Singaporean law. Suppose a Singaporean surfs to the French site of *Vogue* magazine. The Singapore Authority can deem that *Vogue* magazine *and* the licentious surfer are in violation of the law. Technically, although essentially unenforceable, the French web manager scofflaw could be arrested upon arrival in Singapore.

The question is complex. Where is a website? Is a website where the managers live and have their office? What about a company that uses a virtual or distributed office structure? Is a website where the physical web servers operate? Or, is a website where the website is visible, for example, anywhere someone who has a browser and an internet connection decides to access it? A host of philosophical and metaphysical questions are involved here, but when commerce began in earnest, this whole question was brought into tactical daylight by one of the most powerful forces in the universe: the tax authorities.

➤ Tax Nexus

Dealing with the issue of tax is an enormous, complex, and specialized task, but it is worthwhile to examine this particular area of law because it highlights the complexity of doing business on the Internet. The issue here is: Under which state's jurisdiction is sales tax charged? Is it charged by the state of the person purchasing the goods? Is it charged by the state that hosts the company that is selling the goods? Or, as in some more tax-aggressive states such as Michigan and Massachusetts, is tax charged in the state where web servers are hosted, regardless of where the company that owns them is located? The lesson from all of this is: Proceed with caution and consult attorneys, but also realize that they don't have all the answers to these online issues.

➤ Intellectual Property

It is amazing how people can get lost in the trees when it comes to the source of their livelihood. They get confused between cause and effect. For instance, they see that diamonds are scarce and therefore valuable, but that doesn't mean they can make diamonds scarce. It just so happens that they *are* (or at least are made to appear so by the huge DeBeers diamond cartel). But if perfect diamonds suddenly could be manufactured everywhere by machines, and everyone could make them by buying a cheap piece of equipment (this will probably happen in the not-too-distant future), you can bet that some people in high places—people who make LOTS of money because of the scarcity of diamonds—would do everything in their power to stop people from making their own diamonds. They might say that using these diamond machines was the same as stealing from them.

Silly people. We all know that the cost of goods is dictated by the factors of supply and demand. As soon as something is no longer scarce, it isn't expensive anymore. Technology has a sometimes nasty habit of quickly turning supply and demand upside down. People who make money from these no-longer-scarce items tend to get very touchy when this happens, and are willing to spend an incredible amount of effort to thwart technical change. So it is with "intellectual property."

For those unfamiliar with the concept, intellectual property (IP)[5] refers to ideas, literature, images, logos, mechanical inventions, software, trademarks, and music. Businesses that deal with patents, copyrights, royalties, and licensing are dealing in intellectual property.

The Internet lets people transfer anything to anyone as fast as their bandwidth will let them. This poses some problems with many kinds of intellectual property. For example, if you have a movie on DVD, or the new Microsoft Office CD, or the digital file of the "swoosh" logo from Nike's website, you have an electronic copy of something that technically belongs to someone else. If you have a PC and an internet connection, you have the capacity to pirate and internationally distribute—instantaneously—stolen intellectual property. This is the problem that strikes deep fear into the hearts of executives in the world's IP businesses: entertainment, software, art, and so on.

There are laws that protect intellectual property owners from (intellectual) theft. But when it comes to individuals, these laws are often very difficult, if not impossible, to enforce. Consider this: Does anyone take seriously the FBI warnings that appear at the beginning of home videotapes? How many pieces of real "shrink-wrapped software" have you copied from a friend? How much shareware software have you never paid for? Well, that's theft. But the owners of these properties have usually determined that it isn't worth it to try to enforce these laws when "personal use" is involved. If you try to open up a bricks-and-mortar movie theater and show films you haven't paid for, you will have some very angry lawyers sending you nasty-grams!

But who is going to stop you from downloading a music CD, a computer program, a picture from *Playboy* magazine, a special research report from Lexus-Nexus, or the latest *Star Wars* movie? The simple answer is: No one can. As soon as digital content hits the wire, it is as ubiquitous as the public wants it to be, and the only thing to stop it is bandwidth,[6] which is growing for consumers as fast as Jack's beanstalk.

Naturally, content owners, artists, software developers, journalists, publishers, record labels, and cable operators are very upset by this, and they are beginning to scream and moan. They will sue internet people who seem to be enabling this free-for-all. They will try to pass legislation. They will appeal to our sympathy for starving artists, hardworking engineers, and strung-out actors, and you can't blame them for trying. After all, they have a lot invested in the old distribution models that allowed them to capitalize on the actual scarcity of videotapes, CD-ROMs, paper, and so on. But try as they might, they won't be able to stop it. It's just too easy to use the net.

There are great benefits to no-cost distribution. One advantage is that, to a great degree, it democratizes the content and software industries. In the past, content distribution was so costly that most voices went unheard, most stories were unread, and most intellectual products were unshipped. Some might say this is a good thing. But the point is: The distributors used to hold the cards. The owners of the distribution channels had the power to decide what we—the public—would get. When distribution is free, the distributors lose all their power and the public gets to choose! It's kind of like what happened with Al Capone and booze. When prohibition ended, the rumrunners disappeared. Legalize drugs and Colombia falls off the map.

Another benefit of digital distribution is that it makes the products (or content) usable in entirely new ways. For example, if my music library is shackled by plastic CD-ROMs, then I have to physically alphabetize them, organize them, and load them into my player. Even the big 100-disk players require me to load 'em in and keep track of what is where! But if every part of my music library is digitized, I can automatically sort music by album, by name, by artist. I can sample selections, speed things up, change the pitch. In short, I am limited only by the software I have (and now I can download that for free) and the information that is associated with the content.

So, you ask, "How is anyone going to make money?" and "Why will anyone want to work on creating anything digitizable if they can't earn a living doing it?" What needs to be understood is that the value of "digitizable" intellectual property has moved away from the distribution side to a more conceptual place. With economics, things don't have value because of their intrinsic worth; they have value because of supply and demand. If there is an unlimited supply, then it ceases to have value. If air was scarce—and it may become so—there would be a breathing fee and everyone would pay up.

If copies of pop records become free, because there is no way to stop people from getting them for free, the value chain has to move. Perhaps concert tickets will cost thousands of dollars apiece because the singular experience of attending a live performance is ephemeral, undigitizable, and therefore scarce. Who knows? What is clear is that the old businesses based on intellectual property distribution are in the process of being severely disrupted.

There is an ever shifting change in supply and demand, and technology plays a huge role. Just as railroads and electricity changed things in the twentieth century, so has the Internet changed it in this one. Folks are going to have to start paying attention to technology, understanding how (and when) it affects distribution, and learning to provide products and services that have value. The good news is that this isn't happening overnight. There is no replacement for watching a live performance, or seeing a film on a big screen with lots of other people. Just because you have a free copy of PhotoShop or Microsoft Developer Studio, you are not necessarily going to be able to do anything worthwhile with it. You may get the software for free and pay high prices for tech support, for example. People are going to continue to pay for experiences, capabilities, and material goods. People are going to continue to trust brands and people. Aim at where the value is moving, not where it has been.

■ QUALITY ASSURANCE

Quality Assurance (QA) is generally viewed as the evil stepchild of the production process, yet it is absolutely critical if you want the highest quality in what you are intending to deliver. QA is the first thing to get overlooked when a firm is in a crunch to deliver, but QA is even more important when things get chaotic. Think of it as your last line of defense when you are in search of excellence.

The web production process starts with development, whether it is done by software developers, graphic artists, or HTML editors. These groups generally do their own testing (sometimes referred to as alpha testing) on their own equipment—usually, a combination of development workstations and development servers. When they are satisfied that what they have produced is complete and error-free to the best of their ability and knowledge, they physically move their materials to another special set of servers. This phase is usually referred to as Staging, Quality Assurance (QA), or User Acceptance Testing. Whatever you call it, it is the stage in which a different set of eyes and hands examines and tests this material in a realistic environment. Often, there are several isolated technical environments that allow different groups to test various aspects of a product simultaneously or in sequence. Finally, someone needs to release approved materials to the public. With the WWW, this usually means that someone in QA makes the call to promote it to the "live" (also called "production") environment.

QA testers perform a variety of activities. To begin with, they examine the newly developed material to see whether it meets users' criteria or specifications. This may or may not be a set of written descriptions; the better shops provide their findings in writing. If the material tested does not meet the requirements and specifications, it will be sent back to the developer for changes or additions. The testing and promotion process is then repeated.

The material is also examined for "bugs." The QA personnel may do this manually by going through all of the permutations and links on the site, or they may do it with the assistance of special testing software, which automates part of the process by worming through all of the material and generating a report that states actual or suspected problems.

QA testers' special area of examination in the WWW space is web browser compatibility. One of the important questions that is decided in the specifications for a website is: What version of the popular web browsers will be supported? This can have a major impact on the kind of design features that will be used. Typical questions include:

- ➤ Do you support frames or not?
- ➤ What aspects of Dynamic HTML (DHTML) will be used, if any?
- ➤ What version of the Netscape browser will be supported?
- ➤ What version of Microsoft Internet Explorer will you support?
- ➤ What version of AOL will you support?
- ➤ How does it work under different operating systems (i.e., Win 3.1, Win 95/98/NT/2000, Macintosh, Sun, and so on)?

Good QA teams will have a laboratory set up for testing these different versions. The lab will create full environments so that each version can be tested separately. A shop we know has computers set up to work with external hard-disk subsystems. There is a whole slew of different hard disks, and each one has a different combination of operating system, web browser, and browser versions. The technicians merely plug a different hard disk into their PC when they want to test using that version.

If the quality of the product or website you are producing is of importance to you, your QA department and its testing process will need strong support from senior management. The tendency in any firm is to want to skip QA to make up lost time.

Nine times out of ten, omitting the QA process will come back to haunt you. You will lose if you go down this slippery slope, so **don't skip testing!**

Your QA manager must be able to withstand this often-challenging job. This means:

➤ Being a good project manager, because every piece of the delivery puzzle must coordinate with and fit into the general delivery schedule.

➤ Being able to manage the availability of staff members to fit with this schedule.

➤ Hiring good staff members who enjoy this kind of work.

➤ Screening out ambitious but relatively low-skilled people who want to join the firm on the QA side and use that entry as a stepping stone to other jobs in the firm. This makes staffing difficult.

Find someone who is "into" QA and understands the process and its role in the overall project flow. Wise investing in this area will pay back your firm many times over.

■ PRODUCERS AND PROJECT MANAGERS

The first time you work with a web development firm, you will inevitably be introduced to someone identified as a "producer." You may be amused by the trendy "webby" attitude of this peppy person, and immediately think of that stereotyped Hollywood phrase: ". . . But I really want to direct!"

What is a producer, anyway? This is the web, not the motion picture industry. Most new media firms evolved from an ad agency model, so, unfortunately, the term "producer" survives that legacy. Originally, when websites were nothing more than online brochures, the producer had a combination role: account manager, project manager, project accountant (generating invoices), and just about anything that needed to get done. A producer was expected to roll up his or her sleeves and get involved with whatever was needed to ensure that the customer was happy and the project was delivered profitably. This was a sort of "jack of all trades, but a master of none" role.

The role of producer also became somewhat of a status role, at least in the late 1990s. It was cool to say, "I am a producer at Blowfish Digital." It sounded much more impressive than it actually was.

The role evolved beyond overseeing the development of bro-chureware, and required more developed skills that were equal to the task. Often, new media firms, not really understanding the dynamics of running a complex project successfully (few members of those firms actually had that kind of experience), would relegate those roles to administrative assistants or similarly unqualified and un-trained individuals.

The problem was finally stated: Web agencies didn't understand the fundamentals of how to manage a project. The term *producer* sounded glitzy, but its definition was unclear. The term *project manager* is fairly unequivocal: If you are a project manager, you *manage projects!* This may require all of the skills needed to be a producer, as well as the skills and tools that project managers use for delivering and achieving goals for projects of all sizes and complexity. These skills will be examined later.

A producer is a project manager. It is a term that is usually used to refer to project managers whose job is focused on the coordina-tion of the development of the front end (user interface) and the in-corporation of content. What that means in practical terms is that the producer acts as a liaison, a shepherd, and a task master between the designers, information architects, the basic web programmers, whomever is generating content, and the business owner driving the work. The job is stickier than you might imagine. Yes, it is true, that producers seldom get their hands dirty with deep engineering prob-lems but often the deep engineering problems are much less fought with politics and emotion than the look and feel of the site or where, how much, and in what form contents make it onto the page. This is a producer's bread and butter. Whether you are doing your web work 100 percent internally or working with external agencies, don't skimp on your producer. People tend to assign very junior resources to this role. That can be a successful strategy if that person is thick skinned, incredibly energetic, and as tenacious as a Gila monster, but a more experienced person will usually fare better. First and fore-most, however, remember that this is a project management role and your producer needs to be able to manage a schedule, lead teams, and drive toward on-time delivery.

Fortunately, some firms started to catch on. Organic Online (http://www.organic.com) was one of the first of the premium new media firms to actually integrate sound project management methodologies with the web development media. None of this was really new; large consulting firms and corporations had project management down to a science for years. The *application* of these methodologies to the development of large and complex websites involving the integration of back-end technologies—*that* was new. As a result, Organic became the firm to beat, although its success became its undoing. It grew so rapidly that the quality control of its staff suffered.

The role of a project manager is to provide and manage resources for project staff so that they can do their jobs to the best of their ability and achieve and deliver projects successfully.[7] Project managers have a very difficult job, but it can be boiled down to very basic elements: identify goals, devise a plan for reaching them, gather resources, follow the plan, and complete the job.

Section III of this book addresses many aspects of project management that are peculiar to the web.

Some firms believe in promoting managers from within the firm. Realize that only a minority of staff have the personality and organization of thought to actually run projects effectively. Expect your project managers to be able to build project descriptions, write specifications, perform a task analysis, work with users and clients to establish these goals, and track their projects through the use of a tool such as Microsoft Project. If a person does not have these skills or experience in these areas, then he or she is not a project manager. It is also important to remember that project manager is just that—a manager. They need to be able to manage people and process. Be sure your project manager has the leadership skills necessary to inspire, motivate, and discipline a team.

■ SENIOR MANAGEMENT

What does it take to run an internet organization? A CEO is always someone with a combination of skills, someone who is comfortable in a multidisciplinary environment. On the web, that is even more the case. A website makes strange bedfellows of technologists, marketers, and others in a way that almost any type of traditional business never would. As is the case with most technical revolutions, the web is additive. An internet executive needs all the skills of a traditional executive, in addition to specialized internet knowledge. It is just more to know. It is just harder.

The key point about finding a CEO, President, or Head of the Web Division is that this is a senior management job, with emphasis on "management." A web CEO still spends most of his or her time managing people and processes. The CEO's core skills need to be in this area. The major differences appear in two factors: vision and environment. Let's take environment first; it is a bit easier.

The e-commerce world is dynamic. Among its traits are: massive competitive pressures, recruiting and employee retention pressures, and a rapidly evolving set of tools and technologies. All of the skills that a CEO in the offline world needs are in evidence here, they just happen faster. Let's probe a concrete example: advertising testing.

If you are a graduate of the Procter & Gamble school of advertising, you know that it takes six months for an essentially finished TV commercial to get on the air. Why? During those six months, a dozen different versions of the spot are shown to customers. They are allowed to touch, feel, smell, and launder their dirty clothes in the astounding new product. Should the bottle of Tide say "New and Improved" in green? Red? "The bottle is red; can the 'New and Improved' be red too, but a different shade?" Radical. Better test. Show the ad, show the bottle, show a photo of the bottle to 1,000 people in 10 different markets, and tabulate, formulate, calculate, and forecast exactly what it all means. Why? It is an issue of risk mitigation. When this ad rolls, when this new jug of Tide hits supermarket shelves, Procter & Gamble already knows, with 96.5 percent security, exactly what the reaction is going to be.

If you try to play this game on the Internet, your competition will innovate right around you and put you out of business. It doesn't mean that the process is bad; everyone working on the WWW wishes they had more time, but the environment just does not allow it.

Web CEOs tend to fall into several different categories. The correct style for your organization depends on the surrounding people, systems, and structures. It goes without saying that the CEO of a web company, or the head of a web division, should be pretty web-savvy, but it is possible to be successful with a strong manager and strong marketer who isn't as web-experienced. Take this step with care, but remember that leadership, focus, marketing, and financial acumen can be enough to make a successful web CEO even if he or she has not had web management experience. What will prove disastrous is to give a web CEO spot to someone who not only does not have dot-com management experience but is also not a heavy and enthusiastic web user personally. Ask all senior management candidates—particularly those whom you are considering despite their skimpy e-commerce experience—lots of questions about their own internet usage. What are their favorite sites? Where do they buy gifts, book travel, get their news, research vacation destinations, research car purchases, and so on? It is an easy and extremely revealing line of questioning.

➤ Start-Up CEO

This is usually the founder of the company—the big visionary who is focused on the overall direction of the site and on hiring the right senior management team. Ideally, the CEO is also familiar with the capital markets/investment banking world and knows how to raise money. The web environment tends to take companies that would traditionally have been competitors and make them highly effective partners. The CEO usually takes the lead role on corporate alliances. A good start-up CEO knows how to quickly get people who can manage operational issues. The CEO can then wheel, deal, build the brand, get PR activities moving, and build the traffic and product-enhancing relationships necessary to make the company viable.

➤ Intrapreneurial CEO

This person could also be the head of a web division in a larger organization. This person is operationally focused, knows about the web, but also understands how to operate in a larger organization. He or she will be less concerned with grandiose vision, which may be dictated from above, and more concerned with figuring out how to get the job done, the teams built, and the budgets managed.

➤ Techie CEO

Many internet companies are based on a few key technical insights, so, in quite a few start-ups, the CEO is really a technologist. There are examples where this works well, but, in general, deep technologists don't fit the right archetype for strong chief executives. A true professional manager who can work with a CEO engineer/founder can make all the difference.

➤ COO

The chief operating officer, particularly in a start-up environment, is usually the person who is actually running the business. The skills of the CEO are a factor, of course, but every single part of the business, with the possible exception of business development and strategy, reports to the COO. If the concept is based on some technical insight that is really the product of the CEO, the technology unit may report directly to the top as well. The COO of a start-up company, particularly one that is well funded and is able to grow the staff and the complexity of the product quickly, needs several characteristics to be successful. He or she must understand all of the basic business areas, just as a traditional COO would. Additionally, there must be a tremendous ability to bring laser-sharp focus, prioritization, and drive to the organization. Web companies often suffer from massive scope creep. There are so many opportunities, so many ways that the product can develop, so many potential partnerships, so many potential competitive threats, that the organization begins to diverge and fragment; it is chasing too many things without integration. A strong COO has good project management instincts and is able to keep the place on track and make smart bets.

The COO, unlike the CEO, must absolutely have deep web knowledge. Particularly after a website is running, a huge amount of work is focused on optimization. A review of web metrics, made on a daily basis, is one of the key drivers that determines the allocation of people and money. The COO needs to understand the web well enough to be able to make good inferences from the metrics data that are reviewed. It is also critical for the COO to be fairly tolerant of sleep deprivation. (We're being realistic, not cute here.) Everybody works hard in the dynamic web environment, but during launches of new sites or sections, or when there are breakdowns, the COO is often at the office late into the night. These instances are much more common on the web than in traditional businesses. To be honest, we can't explain precisely why this is the case; it just *is*. Even in companies with hundreds of employees, late-night sessions are commonplace. Look for endurance, smarts, and dangerous levels of ambition in your COO.

➤ CTO—Chief Technology Officer

Finding a real CTO for a large company is probably the most difficult recruitment task. It is important to note that the Internet CTO is positioned very differently from a traditional IT CIO or MIS executive. In many businesses—in financial services, for example—the IT department is viewed as a group of sweaty workers who are responsible for bringing some brilliant businesspersons' (the business owners, the P&L owners) visions to life. Technologists in investment banking are responsible for maintaining trading systems, getting orders through quickly, and keeping budgets under control. Their input is not considered to be a strategic part of building or defining the business. Their role is execution and maintenance. End of story.

On the Internet, this is not the case. Technology sits at the senior executive table and serves a number of roles. Technologists maintain their traditional responsibility for building the systems that support the business, but they are also a key part of building the product strategy and, to some degree, the marketing strategy as well. The issue is: Innovation in product functionality, marketing, and sales in a web environment is heavily reliant on the possibilities and constraints of technology. The technology group is often the originator, not merely the implementer, of great customer functionality and marketing ideas because it has revelations about new ways to use systems. Some traditional business areas are ill-equipped to generate these types of ideas because they do not understand the capabilities of the technology well enough to do so.

Still, a CTO has an enormously high bar to get over. He or she must have technical expertise, managerial strength, a curious and energetic personality to keep up with the rapidly evolving technology, and enough business understanding to spot opportunities and to translate business requirements, hopes, and dreams into practical technical implementations.

One of the particularly difficult issues with finding truly web-capable CTOs is the Catch-22 that is inherent in the newness of the web. Because the web has existed only since the early 1990s, anybody who is truly senior enough to be an executive—and, for example, to be the CTO in charge of building a site for Ford Motor Company to sell cars over the Internet—will not understand the Internet well enough to do so. Anyone who understands the Internet technology well enough to do the job is probably too young and inexperienced in project management, people management, and business in general, to take on such a senior job. There are those few (very few) who have all of these capabilities, but you can't count on snaring one for your firm. Due to the strange situation created by the sudden and explosive growth of the web, there tend to be two different types of CTOs. We call them the Punk and the Gray Hair.

The Punk.   Pretty much how it sounds; usually, someone who is technically sound, really "gets" the web, but is not terribly well prepared to manage big budgets or increasing numbers of staff. Often, serious cronyism creeps into a Punk organization. This is a small cadre of people who know a lot, work incredibly hard, but become rather defensive about their turf and do not delegate well. There are, in fact, some advantages in a small start-up situation because of the intensity and focus that a Punk CTO will provide. However, in a larger, more established dot-com, or a web project within a larger organization, particularly a traditional organization where the Punk must integrate systems and people with legacy systems, there can be a massive "immune response" from both sides. It does not lead to success.

The Gray Hair.   A Gray Hair CTO is most likely to be found in a start-up after a venture capital firm has given some preliminary funding and wants "professional management" running IT. A Gray Hair may also appear in a larger, established organization that wouldn't think of putting a Punk in charge of delivering its highly strategic and well-funded new internet group. The success or failure of a Gray Hair usually comes down to a quantity of arrogance and/or self-confidence. A confident, technically strong Gray Hair will get help in the new areas of internet technology that are highly specialized and scarcely understood. An insecure Gray Hair will miss the boat on the technology side of the internet, get mired in process, and have standards of testing and quality assurance that are so burdensome that the business stagnates.

A good leader for your technology organization is extremely critical and extremely hard to find. If you find someone who is strong and fits the bill, move fast, move smart, and pay what you have to. Mistakes or successes in this hire will make whatever extra amount you pay, or whatever money you save, irrelevant.

➤ CMO

Chief Marketing Officer is another role that has some interesting complexities. Running marketing for a web company means understanding not only all of the systems, arts, and sciences of marketing through traditional mechanisms, but a whole raft of new ones that are unique to the web. Many websites spend the majority of their marketing funds on traditional vehicles, but the key is understanding how they impact site traffic, site sales, registration, or whatever metric defines success for your business. There are a large number of differences in the way advertising, creative production, media buying, and planning function in the web environment. To be a truly strong head of marketing for an internet company, your candidate must "get it."

Unfortunately, as with CTOs, you are likely to run into two flavors of internet marketing heads. Punks understand the dynamics of the web, but they may not be good people managers or financial managers. They may not understand the classical disciplines of brand definition and brand building, and the processes for print ad creation or media buying. Gray Hairs tend to approach the web as though it's a novel form of magazine. Neither profile is optimal.

In contrast to technology, a group of traditional marketers tends to perform better on the web even if they are relative web neophytes. The Internet, as we have mentioned several times, is essentially a platform for direct marketing. Marketers who come from direct marketing/direct sales organizations tend to have the right instincts. They are accustomed to constantly tweaking their media expenditures, creative and positioning, based on real sales data. The web, if a system is architected properly, allows for a level of monitoring and control that goes far beyond what a paper catalogue can do. The general framework, however, is roughly the same. If you are in a position where you must hire a marketer for your website, even one with insufficient internet experience, look for a direct marketer.

➤ Head of HR

The human resources manager is another key executive at the top tier of the web organization. Here, look for flexibility and innovation. Internet organizations are tough places to live in. There tend to be fairly large numbers of young and not-very-experienced people.

Competitive pressures are tough; therefore, the pace and hours of work can be very intense. Strategies and priorities tend to shift more often and more radically than in traditional companies. Lastly, and certainly not least, is the tremendous, insatiable appetite of the business world for solid web talent from *any* discipline. Finding, hiring, and retaining employees is probably harder in the online world than in any other industry.

Because of the tremendous demand, there is a fairly substantial amount of prima-donna behavior among web employees, especially those in the technology areas. They can be quirky and demanding about the terms of their compensation, hours of work, office environment, dress code, decibel level of electronic music they demand to be productive—you get the idea.

These difficulties and quirks are simply a fact of web development life. Your HR staff needs to be willing to work with them and around them, without attempting to battle them. It is, of course, helpful if your HR staff actually understands what some of the web skills are and can help you spot them in resumes and in candidates' interviews. This has not been our general experience. Unfortunately, the HR field does not seem to have caught up and done enough homework to become helpful in the recruiting process, beyond the administration of recruiting logistics.

Chapter **6**

Starting a Start-Up

The dot-com IPO dream—images of 21-year-old geeks with old sneakers and Italian sports cars—has become the global "American" dream. This chapter will give you a basic understanding of the key characteristics of successful start-ups: how to find your niche, structure it, and fund it.

■ WHY START-UPS SUCCEED AND WHY THEY FAIL

It isn't hard to catch on. Every entrepreneur thinks that his or her ideas are going to be the greatest thing since sliced bread, and one special idea is the be-all and end-all on the road to success. NOT SO!!! The idea is actually the easy part. The hard part is structuring the company, getting money to fund it, building a team and a workable plan, executing, and achieving actual business goals! It is easy to sit back in a chair and come up with ideas. Making them into reality is a completely different animal, demands a completely different set of skills, and requires actual effort. This is the difference between wanna-be dreamers and the achievers who get the Porsche.

■ CHECKLIST FOR WEB SUCCESS

Here are some criteria to tell you whether that dot-com idea you've been kicking around has what it takes for a run at cybersuccess. If you can't comply with these criteria, you might not want to give up your day job.

➤ 1. Website Idea Showstoppers (quit here)

➤ You want to sell music or books on the web, or to any other already crowded market.

➤ You have no background in that business, nor do you know any experts. How do you expect to compete against the experts?

➤ Your idea came to you in the shower. You discussed it with your pals at bowling. They like it.

➤ Not a very profitable market? Not enough to sustain a full-fledged business? Stay away from marginal markets.

➤ Your idea doesn't harness the geographical reach of the web, such as a website for your gas station. What business goal does your website achieve for you?

➤ You just "want to be on the web."

➤ Your idea will require millions upon millions of dollars and take years to achieve profitability.

If any of these apply to your idea or situation, stop and do not continue. Think about what you do well and where your expertise is; then come up with another idea. None of those given above is likely to fly.

➤ 2. Website Idea Possibilities (at least one of the following)

➤ Your site is for your firm, which is an existing business with substantial market share. Having a name, resources, market share, and customers is an unbeatable combination, assuming you can successfully leverage it on the web.

➤ You are partnered with an existing business with considerable market share. In many ways, just as good. Leverage someone else's achievements.

➤ This market has no clear leader or major players. An untapped opportunity, but not for long. Double-check your competitive analysis and make sure you haven't missed someone who is already pouring resources into this market.

➤ You are creating a whole new market or product that leverages the geographical reach of the web. Risky, but the opportunity is to establish you as the first to market.

➤ You've developed some kind of web, internet, or e-commerce technology or product that requires a lot of work to develop or sets out other barriers to keep the competition at bay.

➤ You have some significant asset, such as an existing subscriber or customer base, or something of value other than just an idea.

These are all possibilities. They are legitimate bases for a start-up. Now all you need is money to get started.

■ BUSINESS PLANNING AND FUNDING

As the old saying goes, "It takes money to make money." To build a company, you have to have enough money available to reach your business goals and manage the company properly. This means having enough cash to develop your product (or website, or whatever), and to properly bring it to market.

How should you figure out how much money you need? The usual way is to build a plan and/or do a task analysis and assign costs to each item. Add up all of the costs, and that's how much money you need to execute the plan. This exercise should be part of the basic budgeting you do when planning your firm or writing your business plan. Do you have enough money to reach your goals? If not, you'll probably fail. Undercapitalization is usually listed as the single biggest reason why businesses fail.

A lot of complex issues go into the planning and funding of a dot-com start-up. This section is not meant to be exhaustive. The idea here is to give you a flavor of the planning complexities that go into starting a company in today's complicated and constantly changing web arena.

➤ Business Plans

One of the keys to starting a company is the compilation and documentation of your ideas. How do you expect to successfully take a company from a "good idea" to a thriving and growing business? Sometimes, the germ of this plan magically appears on a coffee-stained napkin as a result of an inspired conversation with a colleague or co-conspirator. At other times, plans arise much more formally. The web is full of brilliant dot-com ideas, and the vast, overwhelming majority of them show fatal cracks in the foundation after only a few minutes' planning rigor is applied. Even if you have millions to burn, look before you leap.

However you end up doing it, planning your business is an important first step; otherwise, you will end up wasting a lot of time on activities that have little or no relevance to your central goals. What are your goals? What do you want to do? Who are your target customers? How will you reach them? How much will it cost to reach them? Who is the competition? What resources will it take to get this show on the road? These are only some of the questions that need to be answered.

The usual document for recording all of this information is a business plan. There are two general kinds of plans.

The first is a true planning document. This kind of document is often produced internally by a company and is usually more action-oriented than a true project plan. Chances are that this document will contain your proprietary business models, methodologies, your detailed financials; and a detailed project plan/Gantt chart. This will be the actual blueprint for getting your business started.

The second is the "Business Plan," with a capital "B" and a capital "P." This is essentially the marketing document you will use for raising money, finding partners, or persuading internal people within your organization to fund and support your idea. When you want to raise money from external sources, this is a pure sales-pitch document. You will explain why the market is ripe for the taking, why it won't cost so much to take it, why your idea is so devastatingly unique it deserves Mr. Venture Capital's millions. This is always very different from the first kind of business plan. If your capital "B"/capital "P" business plan is successful, you will be forced to write a rigorous actual planning document—the first kind. Just be sure the assumptions that proved you were profitable 90 days from launch don't mysteriously morph after you get funding.

Entire books, and even software packages, are dedicated to helping you put together these types of business plans, so we will cover only the web-specific issues in this section.

➤ Return on Investment (ROI)

This is obviously a basic business concept, but sometimes it gets a little strange in the land of hypervalued internet IPOs (first-quarter-2000 NASDAQ crashes notwithstanding). This really comes down to how you are going to evaluate the success of an internet venture. If the goal is to generate profits, then this is pretty cut-and-dried. It is a straightforward ROI analysis: You put in one dollar, take out a dollar and a dime, and declare a 10 percent return.

The issue is: Many companies enter into internet ventures for a variety of reasons. Perhaps it is not to increase sales but to decrease costs through automation. Perhaps it is a critical marketing play to make the company seem more modern, or to get closer to customers through a more direct relationship. Perhaps, and this is often the case, the company assumes that the web venture will be a loss maker for a long period of time, but the existence of the website will help the stock of the parent company to appreciate in value. All of these are potentially valid reasons to begin a web initiative, but you need to think carefully about how you show the payoff. Upside can come in many forms, but, at the end of the day, there has to be some upside somewhere.

➤ Funding

One of the easiest and most common reasons for the failure of young businesses—whether they are pure start-ups or ventures within a larger company—is undercapitalization. They don't have enough money to properly build a business. Newborn businesses can be cash-hungry creatures.

The market for funding is very volatile; it depends a great deal on the investment community's current taste for funding dot-com start-ups. This funding, of course, is directly affected by the state of the stock market, and particularly by the types of firms that are dogs and darlings at any given moment. The Internet funding world's and the stock markets' views on internet companies are tremendously fickle.

In mid-1998, communities and portals were all the rage. These are big sites with lots of traffic monetized through advertising and sponsorship. By early 1999, the market had turned, and everyone pronounced that straight advertising models were never going to generate profits. The Internet was all about massive consumer retailing sites, the so-called "etailers." By the middle of 1999, everyone had decided that consumer etailers required too much expensive consumer marketing to keep the engines fueled, and they too would never make the grade. No, the real model was Business to Business (B2B): wholesaling sites that sold to the money-burning etailers, and on and on. The moral of the story is: If your brilliant category has been deemed a loser, keep plugging away; the environment could be very different in a few months. The bad news is: Your brilliant twist that makes an out-of-favor category a winner could be unfairly pushed aside forever. The world isn't fair.

These issues affect the market as a whole; they may not apply to you individually. A lot more depends on the strength of the management team you have assembled, the proposed market, and the assets you bring to the table. Despite all of the noise about a lack of concern among dot-com start-ups regarding profitability, success in putting a group together with a short path to profitability will always be an attractive proposition.

You are concerned only with getting your specific venture funded—not the entire marketplace. Here are eleven ways to fund your particular start-up.

1. If you are looking to electrify an existing business with some kind of market share, you can obtain your seed funding from the company itself, assuming that you can make a good case for why it should be on the web. This will, of course, require you to put together a business plan that includes good financials and a good marketing plan. The big advantage here is that you are (potentially) starting a dot-com with financial resources, a brand name, market share, and a built-in customer base.

2. A variant on the first method is to partner, or put together a portfolio of partners that have existing businesses and market share. These firms may want to get on the web, but may not have the internal expertise or resources for actually building a site. If you have the know-how, you may be able to persuade them to partner with you, fund you, and let you keep a piece of the business.

3. Are you a millionaire, or at least a thousandaire? If so, maybe you can self-fund your company. There is a lot of debate about doing this yourself. On one hand, if you have the money, you can do whatever you want and not have to answer to anyone. Another possible benefit is: If you decide to ask for money later in the process, you may not have to give away as much equity. Presumably, further down the road, the business will be more valuable by virtue of what you have already created. On the other hand, there is a school of thought that says you should always use OPM[1] when putting a venture together. Do you want to risk *your own* hard-earned money, or would you rather risk someone else's? Remember, OPM always means losing a share of equity.

4. With a bootstrap (as in "Lift yourself up by your bootstraps"), you quickly and cheaply get to market and your growth is based on your profits. This can sometimes work, but if you are trying to compete on the web, you may either miss your market or be outmuscled by firms with enough capital to outspend and outmaneuver you and not worry about pricing models that sustain profits. You may end up cash-starved, dying on the vine. To most entrepreneurial newcomers, this seems like a logical path, especially if they are strapped for cash, but it rarely works well in a fast-moving market. Study the other models for funding presented here, before choosing this path. Always keep in mind that the aim is to achieve your goals. Your job is to pick the most efficient path for achieving them.

5. Friends and family are very common sources for raising money. Hit up your rich uncle and your pal the stockbroker to invest in your firm. Some entrepreneurs are comfortable hitting these circles for money; others aren't because of the social ramifications of borrowing from people you know, even though their contributions would still qualify as OPM. These will certainly be the easiest groups of people to convince, but if (or when) your start-up crashes and burns, you will have to look these people in the eye for a long time. On the other hand, they can share in your success if good things happen.

6. Borrow the money from your bank. If you are sure of your success, maybe you can get your bank to write you a loan. This can often be the cheapest form of money. More likely, however, your bank will be happy to loan you the money as long as you are willing to put something up as collateral to guarantee the loan. What happens if your start-up fails and you have to pay the money back with your house? Hmmm; OPM starts to sound a LOT more attractive.

7. Incubators. These variants of venture capital money are very trendy now. They are also being called *accelerators*. They usually take a hefty piece of equity in return for providing you with basic services you need in order to get your company going—for example, introductions to potential partners, suppliers, and customers. The best incubators have true experts, in various fields of internet endeavor, who can help you refine your technical architecture, your market research, and your customer acquisition plans. The range and quality of these services are all over the map, so be sure that what they provide is worth the equity in your new dot-com baby that they will demand. Incubators seem to be very hungry for deals these days, so you should be able to comparison-shop. You should also speak to start-ups that are currently being incubated. Get some inside scoop on how the relationship is working.

One other thought about incubators: Any well-organized start-up should have enough expertise and management talent to obtain the services that incubators offer WITHOUT having to give away so much equity. Stated another way: You should be giving away the equity to your business partners and the senior management team that will be with you to grow the business for the long term. Incubators function something like outside consultancies. The difference is that because they are also investors, they have "skin in the game." They rise if you rise. They fall if you fall. If you aren't looking at an incubator as a funding source, then you should be asking yourself what is missing from your management team that is driving you to an incubator. Incubators claim that they can get economies of scale that are not available to individual start-ups because they are able to pool services across all of the start-ups under their umbrella. The reality is that so many services relating to e-commerce development are in such high demand that the level of discount anyone can expect, at any volume, is minimal. This is a complex relationship to enter into. Proceed with caution, consideration, and reliable information.

8. Angels. These investors differ from friends and family in that you don't necessarily have a personal relationship with them, but they get involved in early-round financing. Again, you will have to have a good business premise, business plan, and presentation. Remember, angel investors are still investors. They will want to get paid at the end of the day. Everyone needs his or her exit to real cash.

9. Venture capital (VC) firms. VCs (no, not Viet Cong), together with the investment banks, are largely responsible for providing the baseline capital that started the dot-com explosion. The business of these firms is to find entrepreneurs, give them cash in exchange for equity, and, usually, take a board seat or two to oversee their investment. Their attitudes and styles vary across an endless continuum. Some are speculative gamblers who want to put in money and get it out (more than they put in, of course) quickly. No muss. No fuss. They are almost sophisticated loan sharks. Then there are VCs like the famed Silicon Valley Group, Benchmark Capital, or Flatiron Partners in New York. They are famous for the support, advice, and connections they provide, in addition to access to their deep pockets. Typically, VCs get in on relatively early rounds of funding, when equity is cheaper. They will, however, also invest in later rounds, up to and including IPOs.

The key to remember here is that, unlike your rich Uncle Bob, VCs are professional investors. Many are professional dot-com start-up investors. Assume they know their stuff or are advised by people who do. They are increasingly selective regarding where they put their money; just any dot-com plan is no longer a sure thing. They are bombarded with *tons* of business plans on a daily basis. Getting their attention can be difficult if you send your plan in the front door. Your best bet for any substantive attention is to get in through some personal connection. If you are lucky enough to actually get a contact, prepare for your start-up to be stripped naked and examined down to the smallest detail. These guys do this for a living and their offices are populated by experts whose job is to determine the value of your business, its viability, and the ability of your team to pull it off successfully. Your business plan had better be nailed down tight.

10. Investment banks. These are often massive multinational corporations that are involved in any and all aspects of the financial services business: banking, merger and acquisition advising, stock and bond trading, security underwriting, VC activities. If your goal is an IPO, you will eventually end up working with an investment bank. But, increasingly, investment banks operate in the early rounds of funding for start-ups. Some investment banks have also set up true incubators, like J.P. Morgan's Lab Morgan (undoubtedly named to sound like Bill Gross's firm, IdeaLab, a legendary VC/incubator). Needless to say, the separation among all these groups gets a bit grey. The value of having an investment bank in an early round is that it provides cachet and credibility and makes your deal "smell" more like a real potential IPO, which might make it easier to bring in other investors. Be prepared for the same scrutiny you would expect from a VC if you approach an investment bank for early funding.

11. IPO. An initial public offering is a sale, to the public, of a portion of your company, represented in the form of shares of stock tradable on publicly regulated exchanges. Although this is without a doubt a funding mechanism, it is, for many entrepreneurs, the ultimate end-game. Forget about using an IPO as a way of funding your company in the start-up rounds. IPOs—the past few years of dot-com madness notwithstanding—are usually reserved for firms with several years of solid operating history, a clearly viable business, and a strong management team. Firms tend to do an IPO for one of two reasons (and sometimes both): (1) as a way of raising capital by selling equity in the firm, and (2) as a way for the owners to cash out, by converting their private equity positions into public stock salable on the open market for cash. (The next section, "Looking for Liquidity Events," gives more information on this topic.)

This should give you a feel for a few of the different ways of raising money for your start-up. The bottom line is that *you will need cash* if you want to get into the game. Happy hunting! But hunt with care.

■ LOOKING FOR LIQUIDITY EVENTS

Say what? Yes, perhaps it is a vestige of the kinder, gentler, not-for-profit days of the early internet, or of the generally more liberal, socially minded leanings of the new fabulously wealthy internet entrepreneurs, but "liquidity event" is an increasingly common term for finding a way to cash out. Finding a way to get to real money that they can spend in a store is the end-game for all entrepreneurs.

➤ IPO

The initial public offering of stock, almost always on NASDAQ, is a major component, if not the culminating event, of the dot-com dream. A number of high-flying, high-profile IPOs have indeed created millionaires—and even billionaires—overnight. Needless to say, this is not the norm.

All too often, young companies drive to the IPO for short-sighted reasons. An IPO is a financing vehicle, a way for a company to sell a piece of itself to the public in exchange for cash. This means that the founders of the company are giving up some fraction of ownership, sometimes a quite significant fraction, to get money to grow a business. The motivator for an IPO should be the need to get a large and rapid injection of cash. Undertaking an IPO is a lengthy, expensive (it takes money to make money) and excruciatingly boring and time-consuming task. It puts the key people of the organization—the people who have all the vision and strategy—in rooms with lawyers, investment bankers, government officials, and accountants for thousands of hours. Undertaking an IPO means that the people who are central to the organization are spending their time working like crazy—but not on the business. This period of massive distraction for the entire management team lasts anywhere from 90 days to six months. This is a huge amount of time in the rapidly changing online world.

With the recent wild swings in the NASDAQ, and the increasing rigor in evaluating plans for dot-com businesses, it is not wise to view an IPO as an easy exit strategy. It is a complex, dramatic, and difficult way to get money. It is the highest-profile way, perhaps, but not the only way and not right for every business.

Perhaps it seems a waste to even mention it, but there are viable, profitable companies to be built on the Internet. It has become a common mantra for businesspeople outside of the Internet that all dot-coms "never make any money," and therefore, the only way to extract value from a dot-com is with a hypervalued IPO. That is simply not true. It is true that many of the highest-profile names on the web—the huge consumer brands—are losing money. There is a correlation between the companies that are losing money and the Internet companies that you know. It is not a coincidence. By and large, the massively promoted dot-com firms share the same vision: We are, they say, in the early pioneer days of business online. We are much like the people who, in the mid-1850s, went "hell bent for leather" to California to stake their claims and get as much land and its associated gold as they could. This is clearly Jeff Bezos's (founder and chief executive of amazon.com) approach to the web.

In this case, the "land grab" is the arena of brand. Share of mind, share of the market, and share of wallet of the customers you succeed in wooing—this is the name of the game. The dot-com companies that are spending massive amounts on advertising do so because they take a LONG-term view of the web landscape. They are willing to lose many battles—particularly battles with equity analysts who are angry about continuing rivulets of red ink—in exchange for a strong position at the table and a dominant market share when the dust settles. Amazon could have been a profitable company some time ago, but it kept its marketing expenditures extremely high to continue its stratospheric customer growth. Until the stock price truly tanks, and Amazon begins to lose its currency (its market capitalization), expect them to continue to exchange profitability for a marketing blitzkrieg, sky-rocketing revenues, and exploding new customer growth.

The vast majority of internet companies or traditional companies that are not on the Internet do not operate like this. For them, the liquidity event, although not often heralded on the front page of *The Wall Street Journal,* comes as a profitable addition to their sales and distribution system. Lots of mom-and-pop shops and companies you wouldn't necessarily think of as being major dot-com players are making big money on the web, so there is no need for a big cash-out moment. Icelandair, the national airline for a nation of 280,000 people in the middle of the north Atlantic, sold 5 percent of its tickets online in 1999. This is not going to buy them a new fleet of aircraft overnight (not that they need one), but it probably has a huge impact on their bottom line. If the thought of working to build a sustainable, profitable, honest-to-goodness business online is not so attractive, there are other ways to extract value from your bit of dot-com paradise. Rather than sell shares of your company to the public in an IPO, you can sell out directly to another company. If the company is already public, you will then get tradable shares of stock for yourself and your staff. This is sometimes a good way to get cash and gain access to publicly traded stock, without having to go through the IPO process yourself.

One of the results of the dot-com IPO craze is that it has created expectations of massive upside, usually in the form of stock appreciation, from employees. Prospective employees will want to explore with you the "upside" potential for the business and, most importantly, for them personally. This has led some companies to drive toward an IPO because they needed, or felt they needed, the ability to offer stock options as a currency to attract and retain employees. For the founders/owners of a company, extracting liquid cash value from a venture is not necessarily so simple, but there are lots of mechanisms for employees. Force your HR people to work with you to find ways to create upside, incentivized compensation for your employees that does not have to be tied to a complex corporate financing structure.

■ THE NOUVEAU RICHE: HOW TO SPEND THE MONEY ONCE YOU'VE GOT IT

The second part of capitalization deals with how you spend your money. There is a saying that goes something like this: "When investors see the leather couch in the CEO's office, they run the other way." Money needs to be spent wisely and responsibly. The key here is *lean and mean*. If you are a start-up trying to build a business, your hard-earned capital should be devoted to achieving business goals, not spent on creature comforts or toys for the executives.

Avoid expensive offices and furniture. Do you need to be located on Wall Street or at some other expensive address? Where are your clients? If they are spread across the web, they don't particularly care where you are. Whom are you trying to impress?

Many of these things can come later, when you are successful. But don't feel that these trappings of success *mean* success. Don't create a justification for spending money on stuff that makes you *look* successful. Seeing a firm in the "lean and mean" stage tells smart people that, at least in theory, you are focusing your spending on the important things. Also, one sign of a good manager is that he or she spends the company's money as though it was coming out of his or her own pocket.

A dead giveaway of a firm that doesn't know how to manage its capital is how it deals with staffing. Look around the firm. Are there lots of staff, assistants, and secretaries? Or are the managers writing their own documents and setting their own schedules? Given the amazingly cheap office automation technology in use today, from Palm Pilots to desktop copiers, there should be no excuse for spending money on unnecessary staff. All of these things factor into what is usually referred to as the company's *burn rate*—the rate at which it is spending money. Here's the important point that management must understand at this stage: Just because you obtained money or funding doesn't mean that you will succeed. We've seen some managers of dot-coms seriously believe this. This couldn't be further from the truth. Obtaining funding is only a hurdle, not a guarantee of success. In fact, the only guarantee is that once you've taken on funding, you will have more eyes watching over your shoulder to make sure that you are spending the investors' funds wisely. If your investors or VC firm decides that you aren't up to the task, in many cases they can have you replaced by someone they feel is competent. In business, everyone is expendable—even the founders.

Have you passed the test and can you honestly say that your dot-com fulfills all of these requirements? Good. That was the easy part: idea and asset, money, and a great, talented team. You're on the road to success. Now you actually have to get out there and achieve your business goals, which is the hard part, and keep your company focused and on track.

Chapter 7

Growing Your E-commerce Organization

Everyone marvels at the way tiny start-up companies have become household names in only a couple of years. Old-economy companies are rapidly growing new-economy appendages. This chapter explains how to manage the commingling of the old with the new and anticipate the inevitable frictions before they damage your efforts. It also explains how to manage growth and build organizational structures that keep control but allow for things to move at internet speed. Lastly, it examines some of the concepts that allow distributed organizations to stay connected even when they are physically apart.

■ P&L RESPONSIBILITY AND CHANNEL CONFLICT

The web may be a sophisticated worldwide communications network, the next generation of commerce, and a host of other futuristic-sounding things, but, at the end of the day, e-commerce is direct selling and direct marketing. One of the fundamental principles of e-commerce is the concept of disintermediation: reducing to zero the number of intermediaries between you and your customers. The web creates a direct link for marketing, selling, and supporting.

That sounds beautiful. And efficient. Sounds like a great structure on which to conduct business. But it also can be the beginning of an internal nightmare known as *channel conflict*. Essentially this nightmare comes in two equally ugly forms:

1. Distribution method conflict—direct sales to customers vs. sales to wholesalers or sales to retailers.
2. Conflicts between different direct sales organizations—say, telephone or showroom vs. web.

It is absolutely critical to ask the hard questions and resolve channel conflicts before you launch your web effort. Here is an example from Gateway. Before the website, the only method of buying a Gateway computer was from Gateway's 800 number (there are now several hundred nonstocking showrooms, or "Country Stores," around the world as well). When the site was launched, there were no dedicated "web sales support" people. Just the general 800 sales line. To this day, first-time buyers of expensive products over the Internet often call nervously to make sure their order hasn't been lost. Those of us managing the website began to realize that any customer making a nervous call was more likely to cancel an order than someone who had just ordered online. Why?

After great frustration, we realized why. The phone sales reps, some of whom are fabulously successful, are commission salespeople. The website was stealing their business—plain and simple. A huge motivator for building the web presence in the first place was to remove the human cost element for sales and support—a particularly huge cost when tech support is involved. This is what was happening. When a nervous customer called to check on an order, the traditional telephone sales rep warned: "Gee, online order. Not sure I would trust my credit card over the Internet. I've heard that web orders get prioritized last. I've heard that web orders often get missed" and so on. The issue was clear: channel conflict. The telephone sales reps had every incentive to protect themselves and to do whatever they could to keep their customers from ordering from the website. The website was a great move for the company: less cost, long-term better margins, and the ability to lower prices and be more competitive in the market. But the organization wasn't well set up to promote the change.

At the time, Gateway was not able to solve the problem completely for a variety of organizational, political, and technical reasons. It did achieve, however, a reasonable half-solution. Gateway changed the phone number of the website to connect to a team of dedicated "web sales" reps. Rather than being compensated on an individual commission basis for every computer sold, they were paid a commission (split among the team) of one half the normal percentage of all computers sold online. The thinking was: Over time, as the percentage of Gateway's online business increased, the commission would gradually be lowered to keep the web sales representatives' compensation reasonable. As soon as this structure was put in place, the level of repurchase for web customers increased and the percentage of order cancellation plummeted—clearly, a good result. The issue that Gateway did not solve was how to incentivize the general sales reps to cannibalize their own business and tell their customers, "Don't call me ever again. Use the website. It's great!"

Expending energy, focus, and, most importantly, cash, to manage these channel conflicts introduces grave risk for traditional players operating in an online category populated with pure dot-coms. Take Amazon.com vs. Barnes & Noble. One of the major reasons that Barnes & Noble got off to a slow start was channel conflict. Everyone at Amazon was 100 percent focused on growing the web business, and all resources were targeted toward its success. Barnes & Noble had hundreds of stores in which managers were compensated for increasing in-store sales. Their own company was making it more difficult to achieve their sales goals. Barnes & Noble—like Charles Schwab, the brokerage firm—had spun off its web business as a separate company. The idea here was to give each type of business the space it needed to deliver what it was expected to do—build a bricks-and-mortar business, or build a web business. A somewhat Darwinian approach was used to see how each fared. Neither company talked about them openly, but there were internal naysayers. Traditionalists were predicting the eventual end of the web "fad." Part of the goal, at both companies, was to give the web guys space to build their business without having to justify their existence over and over. In the case of Schwab, Schwab.com now is, essentially, the business.

We are not saying that the web should be the only channel, or that, as the head of the web effort for your firm, your job is to seek out and destroy your more traditionally distributing colleagues.

Not at all. The web provides a channel, a platform, and one more way to communicate with your customers. Say a company has retail or telephone-based channels. If it plays its cards correctly, it can gain a much stronger position over time by providing customers with the ability to choose how, when, and where they want to do business.

In spite of the issues outlined above, Gateway has done a good job of letting customers choose how they want to buy and support their PCs. About 25 percent of the PC-buying world will not buy direct. These customers want a retail experience. Gateway built the Country Stores to let people touch and feel the product (something the web is unlikely to be able to provide any time soon) and to talk face-to-face with someone before spending several thousand dollars. Most customers get comfortable with buying software or add-on gear via the web. For those who need a calming voice when the hard drive crashes at 2:00 A.M. on the day a big presentation is scheduled, telephone technical support is available, supplemented by web documentation. Unless you are planning to build a pure dot-com for financial efficiency reasons, or your big idea, like an eBay offering, can only function in a virtual environment, don't forget to address the problems and to look for the opportunities that a multichannel strategy can afford. Brands that touch customers in lots of media, in lots of environments, gain power.

■ REPORTING STRUCTURES

There are many ways to manage a web organization, but some principles seem to hold true for most. Successful web shops—and this applies to technology organizations in general—are relatively flat. The collaboration among different disciplines and the cross-functional nature of web teams tend to undermine hierarchical organizations, and vice versa.

The senior officers of a Fortune 500 company actually need to spend time with their web designers and technical architects, as they would with their ad agencies or product suppliers, but the stiff hierarchies of most large companies prevent this level of interaction. It is not OK to delegate the development and execution of an internet strategy to an executive who doesn't understand the web.

The knowledge gap is too great. If you are the CEO and you have web visions, work directly with the Internet professionals. Don't delegate the realization of your vision to another executive who, like you, is a talented amateur at best. It won't work. Your vision will be lost. Michael Dell is famous in the web world for having recognized this immediately. The story goes that, in 1995, he moved his desk right into the middle of his company's fledgling web group and, for several months, he worked directly with those punky kids and their managers until he felt comfortable that they understood where he wanted to go, and he understood what was needed in terms of work, organization, money, and so on. Anyone can see that the web is non-hierarchical in its nature, and that's something to keep in mind. The line that has to be walked is between administrative convenience and stifling hierarchy.

Obviously, organizations need clear reporting structures with clear accountability. We don't believe that the lines on an organization chart should have anything to do with how people interact with one another in a company, whether horizontally, across different departments, or vertically, up and down the food chain.

Most WWW organizations function well with the layout shown in Figure 7.1. This is only an example and it's not complete, but it's pretty typical. The reporting structure indicates that a lot of cross-management is needed. For example, to get their job done, project managers who report to the administrative organization will need to manage creative staff and technology staff. Depending on management's preferences, there could be technical project managers and producers who work in the technology and creative groups, respectively.

There are no hard and fast rules. Don't be afraid to reorganize. Most growing e-commerce organizations reorganize themselves every six months on average. They do this for two reasons:

1. As a business's goals and focus change (these changes are inevitable; if you're not making them, you are probably doing something wrong), an organization needs to change accordingly.

2. As an organization grows, different kinds of management skills are needed. An org chart shouldn't be a theoretical stack of boxes. Each person has strengths and weaknesses, and some people are more dynamic than others. Reorganize your staff accordingly.

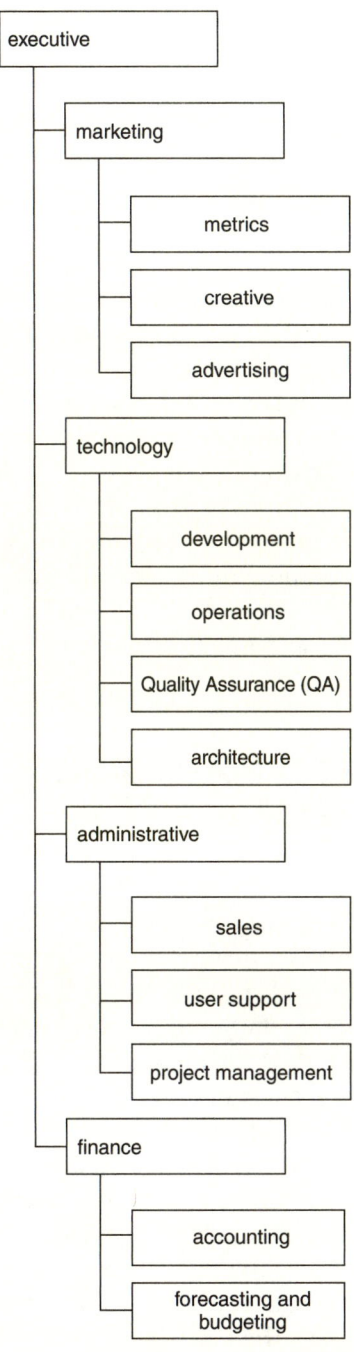

Figure 7.1 Generic web organization chart.

Some or even most of your organization may be virtual. People who report to you for the purposes of your company's internet programs may administratively report to someone else in an entirely different part of the company or even another part of the world. For example, people who have "off-line" professional skills may be essential to your project. You may have a "dotted-line" relationship with them (their connection is expressed in an org chart with dotted lines instead of with the "hard" lines that indicate direct reporting relationships). An organization that is filled with both hard and dotted lines is called a matrix organization because of all the implied cross-reporting. Matrix organizations are useful and generally necessary for doing e-commerce in large organizations.

If you are a very small organization or a very new company, be cool. Don't get hung up on titles or reporting relationships. They are a waste of time, totally unproductive, and just plain LAME. If four of you are starting up a company and you are arguing about who reports to whom, you should quit before you start. Hierarchy is needed to manage organizational complexity. If you have no complexity, you don't need a hierarchy to manage it. Grow up!

■ GROWING AND MANAGING YOUR BUSINESS

Guiding a company from inception to middle growth can be both exhilarating and terribly frustrating. Just as a baby goes through an incredible metamorphosis during its first year of life, a company changes dramatically, and those changes bring a host of challenges. How you deal with these challenges, while keeping your business on course and achieving your business goals, will make the difference between struggling and succeeding.

First and foremost, build a strong business plan and stick to it. Everyone who comes in through the door will have an opinion on what you should do, and you will be constantly tempted to change course. Stay focused on what you are trying to achieve, or you will bounce all over the map doing things that divert you and your firm from achieving tangible goals and cause you to waste a lot of time. Banish the "time vampires" and stay the course!

This is in contrast to the need to be flexible and responsive to what is happening in the world and the marketplace. Conduct periodic reviews of your business plans—and modify them if necessary—but be systematic about it. Have your finance person do the numbers, and try letting reality guide you. If you originally projected revenue growth from one area, but the numbers show that most growth is coming from somewhere else, decide whether it is time to go with what is working or whether your longer-term goals are still sound.

Keep reviewing your answers to some very basic questions: Who are your customers? What are you trying to achieve? What do you do? Try an easy test called the "elevator positioning exercise." If you were on an elevator and someone asked you what your firm does, could you describe what it does, in a clear and concise manner, *before* that person has to get off at the ground floor? If not, you've got a serious problem. If *you* can't describe it, how do you expect anyone else to?

We're not saying that what you do isn't or can't be complicated. But if what you do is so obtuse that it can't be easily and clearly explained, you're going to have a hard time getting everyone in the firm pulling in the same direction; or worse, you'll have difficulty getting investors excited about investing in your firm. You can start out simple and have more detailed answers available if needed. When you randomly meet someone who asks what you do, say that you work with the web and the Internet. If you're asked for more detail, you can tell them more. What really does *your* company do? You've got 30 seconds!

As your firm grows, you will reach a point where you are getting so busy that you cannot personally accomplish all of the things that you used to do when you started the business. You always need to be thinking of how you will be able to scale up to larger challenges as your company grows. Many senior managers plateau because they cannot mentally let go of some things that they were accustomed to doing themselves. Unfortunately, this can limit the growth of a company arbitrarily. The managers themselves become a bottleneck.

The question you always need to ask yourself is: "What am I doing that I need to keep control of, and what can I hand off?" Really good managers keep control of very few things, but those are the key elements that keep the firm on course toward maintaining its business objectives. Do you really need to manage that project, or can you hand the whole thing off operationally to someone else? Maybe all you really need to do is keep an eye on it by reviewing its progress periodically.

As an integral part of handing off responsibility, you must trust and empower the people who are working for you. Make sure they have an honest stake or empowerment in what they are doing. Don't micromanage them or go over their heads by issuing orders to their staff. You'll demoralize them, and that's a very quick way to drive them to hotjobs.com. A colleague of ours started a new job that had enormous responsibility, and he was really nervous about whether he was up to the task. His boss sensed his uneasiness and prophetically told him that the company wouldn't have hired him if it didn't think he could do the job, and it was standing behind him to make sure he could achieve the things it wanted him to do.

Don't feel that you have to be the expert on everything. That's why you hire specialists and experts. We've all had at least one boss who told us that there were two criteria for hiring people: they had to be smarter than the boss and know things that the boss didn't. This isn't bullshit. This is how you build an awesomely talented and amazingly loyal team.

Being focused on what you are doing is another key factor for achieving your goals. When you are in charge—the master of your own destiny—and nobody is telling you what to do or how to do it, there is a great temptation to waste a lot of time on things that aren't important to achieving your business goals. Do you really need to arrange your travel plans yourself? That's why there are travel agents. Do you really need to spend 30 minutes on the phone, arguing with customer service over a stupid three-dollar overcharge? Instead, ask yourself, "Is what I'm doing getting us closer to our goals?"

Keeping your firm on course in the midst of a changing environment can be very difficult. The key is: Always be flexible and adaptable, like the proverbial reed bending in the wind. If you are too rigid, you'll snap. Again, ask: "What are the important things here?" Keep careful tabs on the factors that are critical for success, and leave everything else open to negotiation and modification. The job of leading an endeavor can be extremely difficult. The leader has to have the vision to be able to see the fine line—the course that will bring the firm success.

Be alert to recognizing when you have outgrown your current systems. Overhead and cost, both in time and money, are involved in evaluating, selecting, and implementing a new infrastructure. Some problems will make themselves known, whether you want to deal with them or not. You're running out of office space, but the people you are hiring are specifically generating revenue for you, and the last thing you want to do is let a lack of space dampen your profitability. Make the call and execute the change. Change is good, or as Mr. Spock once said in his sagely way, "Change is the essential moving force in the universe."

It is also important to understand the role that evolution plays in the growth of a business. We've all seen firms where, instead of a proper LAN (local area network), there's a rat's nest of wires and ancient equipment, and the whole infrastructure is on the verge of collapse. You might say, "What a mess! What were they thinking?" But the whole scene is perfectly natural in the office of a company that has grown organically. Such a mess is the result of years in which systems replaced systems as requirements grew, but the old stuff never was completely removed.

Like a snake that naturally sheds its skin as it grows, an expanding firm changes its infrastructure. Expect this to happen in a firm that is growing rapidly. People often ascribe a high level of sophistication to the thought behind how things are done, when the plan or the answer is actually very simple. People usually create a solution that is just good enough to meet their current needs; then others add layers or build on top of it, if the foundation is sturdy enough. What works in a 10-person single-room office may not work later on when the company is distributed over five offices and now has 100 employees. There rarely are any sinister or idiotic motives, as the unenlightened might suggest. In the normal state of affairs, people build for today, and then do patchwork on top of what is there. Don't be thrown off course because your old ways can no longer accommodate what you need today. Recognizing when they have outgrown their usefulness is the key. Pull the trigger, fix them, or replace them. Then move along.

The ultimate growth challenge comes to a young firm when it gets to a point where the demands made on senior management exceed the abilities or experience of the people who originally put the firm together. A colleague of ours calls that "founder's disease." Rarely does a single individual have the skills needed to start a firm from nothing, make it grow, achieve success, and manage it as a multibillion-dollar firm. Among the notable exceptions are Bill Gates and Steve Jobs.

Usually, management needs to turn over and effect a transition when the firm enters its middle growth period. Two questions arise: (1) What should we do with the founders? and (2) How can we get them out of key roles? Some firms never solve these problems because the founders refuse to step aside. In other cases, a venture capital firm or a board of directors will wield sufficient power to force a management change. Sometimes, the founders themselves will be smart enough to realize that it is time to step aside. This isn't a humiliating problem. They are usually stinking rich, and some will drown their sorrows on their yacht or on a golf course. Others will take their money and start new firms. But don't forget that once you've been a *player,* it *is* hard to walk away and stand on the sidelines.

The inevitable casualty of growth and success is the loss of the start-up culture. This is sad; it leaves the original players yearning for "the old days": Everyone knew everyone on a first-name basis; employee badge numbers were single digits; the group bonded through working long into the night; and, for company picnics and group vacations, the firm picked up the bill. Today, creeping corporatism replaces the small-company culture. Is that a bad thing? Success isn't bad, and, invariably, economies of scale dictate that certain services be centralized. The ad hoc way of doing things in a new or small company is no longer adequate.

But this doesn't mean that all good things will be lost as you grow. Strive to make your firm continue to be an attractive place to work. Keep having the company picnics, parties, and sports outings. The cost of those activities is little compared to the cost of employee retention—and you still get to write off the expense. One firm we know bought a very trendy bar across the street from its office, to provide its staff with a place to hang out and entertain clients. Another mandated a basketball court in the blueprints for its massive new facility.

Don't be undone by your success. Remember, you only have one life to spend, and money will never buy time back. If you have the ability to increase your quality of life, along with those of your charges, do it! In the long run, those are the things that will be remembered, not the trivial amount of money they cost.

Finally, don't get wrapped up in your own self-importance. Instead of trying to show how successful and important you are to your company, do just the opposite. Show how involved and accessible you are. Set a shining example for those you wish to lead. Remember that you can only *earn* respect, not demand it, and by doing so, you and your firm will be able to achieve amazing things, no matter what the size of your shop.

■ THE VIRTUAL OFFICE

Offices are expensive and unpleasant: rent, furniture, heat and air-conditioning, insurance—not to mention office politics, noise, people with bad breath, body odor, and dandruff. Who needs them?! Enter the virtual office. With telephones, email, and remote access to file servers and business applications, it is possible to use internet technology to do internet business. For people who haven't been part of a virtual organization, it may seem harder or stranger than it is. It's really easy. Sometimes, you do need to be face-to-face, but you would be surprised how much force of habit can affect our perceptions. "Out of sight, out of mind." Leave that baggage behind. Don't even get on the plane. Stay at home and jack in.

Some people like to work at home because they are agoraphobic, have small children or for some other reason do not want to come to a "normal" office. Some people have valuable skills but live far away and don't want to move. You can't afford to relocate them, or they won't relocate at any price. These are good opportunities for a virtual office. At some companies (and their numbers are growing), there is no physical office. The officers of the company, and the employees, all work out of their own private offices or their homes.

A variant on the virtual office is the distributed office. Large global companies are used to managing communication and cooperation (or the lack thereof) among offices around the world. More and more smaller firms are doing the same, usually more efficiently. The goal of the smaller distributed office is to leverage talent wherever it is. If there is a team of 10 people in Chile who have skills in web design, development, and project management, and you want to bring them into your company in Prague, why ruin a good thing by trying to move them across the world?[1]

In most cases, it isn't even an option to lure talent away from where they already have a happy life. Talented individuals and groups know how valuable they are, and even huge companies with deep pockets are learning that it is a seller's market. Good web people can pick and choose whom they work for, what they work on, and where they work.

Managing a virtual office requires more discipline than a conventional office, but it is often worth the effort, and, to reiterate the very important point we just made, you don't always have a choice. You can't always have your team where you can see them. We worked with a terrific boutique web shop called Interactive Bureau (later acquired by Circle), and they made great use of their "virtualness." They had five small offices (30 to 50 people), located in New York City, Washington, DC, San Francisco, and Monterrey, Mexico. They were able to distribute complex work to different offices across time zones. They could get work done fast, and they got astounding synergies from the different specialties and cultures of each minishop.

The main tools for running an effective virtual office are the telephone, networked computers, and some central place to store shared files, such as project plans, reports, policies, and so on. A growing number of ASPs are specifically designed to enable virtual offices. The ASPs offer secure file servers, office applications, group scheduling, collaborative tools such as virtual white-boarding, application sharing (look-over-my-shoulder-type functionality), and more. They also offer a surprisingly high quality of service, and www.visto.com is a good example. It provides email, file sharing, and calendar. It's pretty good, and it's free! If you shop around, you will find some convenient services, and the best part is: You won't need to invest capital or hire IT people to keep everything up and running. See the ASPs section in Chapter 2 for more on this subject.

Videoconferencing is neat, but most of the home products are pretty weak. The software and hardware, and the connectivity required to make videoconferencing anything more than a cute gimmick, are out of most people's price range, and the truth is, you don't really need it. The phone is fine. If you absolutely need "face time," you should plan a physical meeting. Anyway, videoconferencing is totally overrated under any circumstances, especially with regard to the home office. The whole point of working at home is that you don't have to get dressed, comb your hair, or shave.

Chapter 8

Outside Resources

One of the major challenges facing managers who are responsible for implementing web strategies is: Where can they find competent resources? This applies to existing corporations and to start-ups. It even applies to new media firms, because, often, they don't have the resources or specialized skills to meet the needs of their clients.

All three groups must identify, engage, and manage the resources they need, so a logical strategy is to outsource the work, either by engaging individual consultants (see Chapter 4) or by going to outside firms.

The tight job market makes external resources an inevitable part of building e-commerce businesses. A complex industry has developed to serve the needs of e-commerce. It can often be difficult to navigate, and there are expensive consequences for wrong turns.

The issue, then, is: How does this work? What kind of outside firms are out there? What can they do for me? This chapter will help you get the lay of the web's outsourcing landscape, and will give you a better shot at driving successful and cost-effective development.

To understand how the e-commerce consulting industry works, it is first important to understand how it evolved.

■ THE EVOLUTION OF E-COMMERCE

When the web first emerged in the early 1990s, content was produced by webmasters, graphic artists, and a collection of others.

162

➤ Webmasters

The Internet was initially hosted almost entirely by Unix servers. These systems were controlled and operated by Unix system administrators; therefore they became a predominant technical group in charge of the web. Programmers weren't necessarily involved at this point, because little programming was involved with the web. Most web content consisted of static HTML pages, colloquially known as "brochureware." The webmasters were Unix "sys admins." They produced a lot of the basic content.

➤ Graphic Artists

This group also produced content. Graphic artists are not paid very well since theirs is a "creative" activity. Many people are attracted to these fields because of their artistic passions, and they create an endemic oversupply. Until the web came along, they mostly created content for print media. In general, graphic artists have not been able to demand the hourly wages that computer programmers receive, mainly because there is always an ample supply of people who enjoy the creative work associated with graphic design. In general, the only graphic artists who have done well financially have been those who have set up their own shop and hired other designers to work for them.

Computer programmers, up to this point, were still producing most of the graphics and layout for commercial computer software. However, once the opportunities on the web became apparent, graphic artists eagerly jumped to the interactive world because of the chance to earn greater income.

➤ Others

This group, a hodgepodge of people producing content, consisted of neophytes, programmers, and other people interested in working on the fringe.

As mentioned earlier, most websites were what we now refer to as brochureware; they were solely informational and provided pictures and text, with little interactivity. In those days, very little transactional work was going on; the tools—and more importantly, the business requirements—didn't dictate it, and no market forces were driving it yet.

Most early corporate adopters were primarily interested in getting their brands online. The so-called "web presence" was put in the purview of corporate marketing departments, which were responsible for the public presentation of the firm's brand. They either set up their own in-house groups for web development, or they farmed out the task to outside advertising agencies.

Unfortunately, at the time, there were no outside agencies! This created an interesting void, and pioneering graphic artists and savvy young entrepreneurs stepped up to the plate and decided to meet this emerging market demand. (Nature abhors a void.) They set up shop as *web design firms,* also known as *interactive agencies* or *new media firms.*

The business model that graphic designers were familiar with (and brought with them) was the one they used with ad agencies: fixed-price projects. They produced an agreed-on amount of work for a fixed price. With these projects, a design firm would estimate the size of a project, decide how much it would cost to produce and how much the firm wanted to make in profit, and then price it accordingly. An accurate estimate of the scope of these projects would translate to a good profit margin. Many firms flourished using this model.

Most of the people starting these new media firms had little or no business experience, or no knowledge of how to run projects. Because demand was there, it created a situation where neophytes could come in and start a business, and large companies were willing to pay a lot of money for their design skills. The downside was that these were young turks who had little practical experience. Mainly, they looked at how other people were conducting business, rather than bringing in seasoned managers—a sort of "blind leading the blind" situation. This pattern would cause a lot of problems later, when the industry inevitably changed.

In the early days of the web, fixed-price projects were relatively easy to estimate because of their simplicity. The client would issue a request for proposal (RFP) to a number of firms. The RFP would describe the size and scope of the job, and any other project details. The agency would count up the number of pages on the website it was being asked to design, multiply it by a price per page (including cost and profit), and that would produce the bid price. Although the bids were competitive, jobs would not necessarily go to the lowest bidder; rather (and this is still true today), clients would select a bid, based on a combination of price, quality of previous work, and other factors.

The period through the end of 1996 was a boom time for these fledgling web companies. New media firms sprang up like weeds. Many grew very rapidly and garnered projects with very large firms. The projects made instant millionaires of the founding partners, and the market seemed likely to go up and expand forever.

But in this very rapidly evolving industry (with time measured in web years), the model began to change. By the beginning of 1997, companies were waking up to the scaling power of the Internet, and projects began to have technology injected into them at an increasing rate. Firms began to look at the web as a very low-cost information delivery vehicle. They realized that they could integrate their back-end processing and information sources onto the web, and take advantage of its geographical reach in a way that no other medium could afford them. True transaction-oriented e-commerce sites began to appear, and the demand for technology-heavy sites began to grow.

Meanwhile, the big consulting firms, such as IBM Global Services, Keene, Computer Sciences Corporation (CSC), and Anderson Consulting, were still sleeping within the cozy, warm beds of Y2K and system integration—the mainstay of their lucrative, large, old-economy Corporate America projects. They still hadn't woken up to the huge market emerging in e-commerce, but it was pretty clear that when they smelled this kind of "food," they would be hungry. The reason was very clear. At this point, the projects were relatively small—less than $1,000,000—and they didn't come up on their radar.

As soon as project budgets broke the million-dollar mark, the hungry bears smelled food, and boy! were they hungry! They woke up like a bear after a winter of hibernation—famished and looking to feed on this tasty financial source. Too bad for their clients that they were such helpless behemoths and rarely delivered what they promised or charged for.

Most new-media firms had no clue about how to manage technology. They were only design-oriented, and many ended up committing self-immolation. They tried to apply their old fixed-price methodologies to pricing projects that now included significant amounts of software development and back-end integration. They often applied the "number of pages times the price per page" estimating model to these technology-heavy websites, and got killed in the process. They usually ended up severely underbidding the projects because they had no idea how much work was involved, or they mismanaged them due to a lack of technology leadership, or all of the above. Their more savvy competitors then snatched many of these teetering firms up at bargain basement prices.

That was what had happened to Avalanche, a premium web design firm. Avalanche was one of the early new-media firms to arrive in New York's Silicon Alley, and it had enjoyed rapid growth and a fair amount of success in the mid-1990s. Near the end of 1997, it was ending a destructive year in which it had taken on every web project involving technology that came its way, despite its lack of adult technology leadership. The principals were at the crisis stage. They were financing their company by cash-advancing their credit cards and not paying their creditors. They sold their firm off to Razorfish for a fee that mostly covered the debt that they had incurred, and they had little to show for their trouble. By the time the two firms were integrated in mid-1998, very few Avalanche clients or staff remained.

The smart firms realized what was happening and went in one of two directions. Some firms, after their awakening, brought in two groups of people to address the changing market: (1) industrial-strength project managers who had the skills needed to manage these complex projects, and (2) technologists with the skills needed to integrate the websites with serious databases and back-end processing.

Other firms put their heads in the sand and tried to imagine that the web world was still flat. They stayed totally on the design side of the equation and never went beyond the web server. To us, this was the cowards' way out. Change should be embraced, not shied away from. An example was Razorfish, which shrank in fear from technology, preferring high-profile, graphically pleasing sites that were technically and functionally shallow. Razorfish finally wised up and merged with a technology firm, iCube, at the end of 1999.

At about this time, programming shops began to appear that specialized in web middleware programming and technology integration. They either competed against the web firms, or were contracted by the web firms to do the technology portions of their projects.

Certain web agencies, such as agency.com, also began to market themselves as bona fide web ad agencies. They offered services such as branding, marketing, positioning, media buying, and strategy. They positioned themselves to offer web strategy in addition to web design. Some also incorporated technology into the mix.

Another breed of company began to appear. We call it the "full integration" firm. This type of firm saw that there was an opportunity between the huge hungry bears and the management-and-technology-light new-media companies. They sought to fill the gap between the technology-lean web agencies and the overbearingly large and expensive system integrators like Anderson Consulting and PWC. The full-integration companies provided an alternative source of expertise for projects such as the building of large, scalable web applications able to handle millions of hits, and sophisticated methods of integration with corporate-legacy back-end systems. Clearly not familiar ground for graphic designers! Examples of these firms include Scient (http://www.scient.com) and Viant (http://www.viant.com).[1] In the midst of all of this change and explosive growth, the huge consulting firms finally woke up.

The traditional large corporate clients of the hungry bears were moving to web, internet, and e-commerce in a big way, and by the middle of 1998 the awakening big players started touting e-commerce as though they had invented it. Where they lacked expertise, they bought it, hired it, or subbed it out to the more sophisticated programming shops. Mostly what they did (and continue to do) was pack their projects with inexperienced and underqualified staff and have them learn on the job at outrageous rates. Overpromise and underdeliver! E-commerce had arrived.

Today, a variety of firms offer web solutions through a mixture of different business models. Still alive and kicking (and IPOing) are the web shop agencies, as well as the boutique firms, the hungry bears, the Internet integrators, and all manners in between.

Here's a more in-depth look at each category.

■ WEB SHOPS

These are "interactive agencies" or "new-media firms" that provide the spectrum of web strategy and design, but are usually pretty light on the technology side. They tend to be good at branding and graphic design, but they rarely go beyond the web server, although our pal, Henry Bar-Levav, President of Oven Digital, tells us that his philosophy is that he is only "one hire away" from whatever skill he needs!

The dead giveaway is the "middleware" tools they use. If their web development software is limited to a product like Cold Fusion or

Macromedia Dreamweaver, they probably don't have much of a technology staff. Also, get a real answer as to how many *full-time employees* on their staff are actual programmers. Most will realistically only have a small number.

If they have a programming staff of ten or more full-time employees (FTEs) who know Java and middleware products like ATG Dynamo or BEA Weblogic, they may legitimately have some fairly good technology resources. Or, they may just be throwing buzzwords around. The question is: Do they have a track record and client references that fit with what you are trying to do?

■ BOUTIQUES

These firms specialize in design *or* programming *or* strategy, but rarely in any combination (or in all) of the above. Chances are, when you talk to them, they will claim to do everything *and* the kitchen sink when it comes to the web. But again, the dead giveaway is the configuration and skills of their staff. Probe, and get realistic answers.

We refer to these as building block firms. They are rarely the prime contractor, unless the client is small. Usually, they are either subcontracted or are one of a number of vendors that get glommed together because each one offers only a partial solution to what is needed for building a robust e-commerce site.

The only thing you have to watch out for is whether they really have the resources available to do your project. Because they tend to be small, it is easy for them to get fully booked up, and they are all endemically short of staff. You may end up having to wait for several months before their resources are freed up to work on your project.

By the way, the design boutiques put a premium on being trendy. If you are over 30, you'll feel like you're visiting your high school when you visit their offices.

■ THE HUNGRY BEARS

These are the behemoth traditional consulting firms. They suddenly realized, when the Y2K work was over, that e-commerce is very big, so they are now gung-ho experts in a field that they essentially ignored for years. Unfortunately, they are no better at it now than they were before. They're just taking the work away from other firms that are eminently more qualified than they are.

These firms have some good people working for them. But, in our opinion, the complex overstaffed models that they use don't lend themselves to the fast-paced, results-oriented, let's-get-it-out-the-door mentality of the dot-com.

We place these firms in two categories. In the first are the large, regionalized consulting practices—firms like IBM Global Services, Andersen Consulting, PriceWaterhouseCoopers, EDS, Keene, and CSC, among others.

In the second category are the consulting arms of major software vendors. The trend among these players is to have their consulting arms help propagate the use of their products in the marketplace. Oracle has a substantial consulting practice, as does Microsoft. Both categories have some very talented people working for them.

By the way, both kinds of hungry bears are having trouble keeping their fur on. The big firms are actually under a lot of pressure because staff is leaving them in droves to join start-ups. Don't forget that these firms have *regionalized* practices, which means that they draw on a talent pool that may range from Boston to Atlanta (the scope of an East Coast practice). All of these people have to travel and stay in hotels every week—at *your* expense. They are away from home every day of the workweek, so don't be surprised if most of the people you meet at these firms are either single or divorced.

■ FULL INTEGRATION

These are really interesting firms. As mentioned earlier, they are larger firms with a fair amount of technical sophistication and resources, in addition to design capabilities. They lurk in the open space between the boutiques and the hungry bears.

■ INCUBATORS

This is another interesting approach to getting the resources for building a start-up. An incubator takes start-up firms and provides them with the infrastructure needed to get their business started.

This usually includes office space with phone systems, computers, and development servers. Other incubators may also mandate the use of certain services such as production web hosting, software development services, web design, accounting, and so on.

In return for providing these services to the start-up, the incubator demands an extremely large amount of equity. Even some hungry bears—never too far from a picnic—have started chains of incubators (Andersen, for example).

Obviously, the incubators are betting on the success of the start-up so that the equity they receive ends up being of value. They may also take an active role in the management of the start-up, to protect their investment. Getting involved with an incubator is like signing up for "Big Brother." There are some clear advantages, but you end up giving away a lot of your firm in return. In deciding whether to get in bed with an incubator, you need to look at the resources you have on hand and your abilities and skills in obtaining the good things that the incubator provides. Then analyze the cost/benefit of using an incubator vs. getting these services on your own.

■ CHEAP SITE GENERATORS

OK, now we're obviously getting into the darker side of outside resources, but we might as well talk about these options for the sake of completeness. We're going out on a limb here, but we think there are three reasons why you (or anyone) would use any of the options listed from here to the end of this chapter:

1. Your business doesn't really depend on the web, and you just want to have a "web presence" or brochureware.

2. You don't really care about the quality of your site or the image used to portray your business.

3. You're really hamstrung for cash, and/or can't figure out how to get the money needed to build something of real quality that represents you well on the web.

Don't forget that the minute you put your business up on the web, you will be marketing to the world. Is this how you want to portray yourself?

Let's look now at the cheap site generators.

Quite a number of firms have popped up that offer low-cost-to-entry ways to put you on the web. They provide you with canned tools for laying out your website—a sort of "one size fits all" approach to website design. Here's the rub: One law of technology says that the easier the technology is to use, the more control you give up over how it works. This is an inverse relationship between simplicity and control. Does this meet your needs? Chances are, once you sign up with these guys, you'll have to toss out the whole thing if you ever decide to expand, which means starting from scratch at considerable expense.

If you have some skills at web development, you can merely contract any of a large number of web hosting firms that can host your domain name, give you email accounts, web server disk space, and bandwidth to the Internet for your site. These range from premium services that cost thousands of dollars a month for dedicated servers, to cheap hosting at around $20 a month for space on a server that is shared by dozens of other firms.

If you go the cheap route, don't expect to get much customer service or responsiveness. In fact, don't expect your site to load quickly or even be up all of the time. As in other industries, you get only what you pay for. What kind of service can you really expect for 20 bucks a month?

■ OFF THE BEATEN TRACK

Some perfectly good boutiques exist out of the mainstream areas of the web world, like Silicon Alley and Silicon Valley. Some of them probably put out some really good work, too. But, buyer beware! Realize that the reason why the Alley and the Valley attract the best and the brightest is because they *pay* orders of magnitude more money than firms located in the middle of nowhere.

Because of this disparity, many of these "cheap" firms do not produce anywhere near the quality of their more expensive brethren. Make sure you look at who their clients are, their portfolio, and so on. Do your due diligence. Check references. If they tell you that they expect you to put a link to their home page at the bottom of *your* home page, you should seriously question whether you want to work with them. We hate to tell you this, but most of them do pretty amateurish work, and again, you get what you pay for. When visitors browse to your website, they don't care how much it cost you; all they care about is whether it meets their needs. Will your site be competitive if you use one of these guys?

■ FREE

You can get free web hosting on the Internet, but it comes with a price. You'll be forced to include an advertisement of some kind or another—either embedded in EACH page or frame, or as an interstitial ad. If you are going to go this route, you might want to see if your ISP throws in free hosting as part of your membership fee (AOL does). You usually can't use your own domain name. You'll probably have to use theirs (such as http://members.aol.com/YourScreen-NameHere), and your amount of disk space and traffic will be limited. Some ISPs (mainly, local ISPs) will offer free domain name hosting (i.e., www.your-own-name.com). These are fine for family or hobby accounts, but no one will take them seriously for business use, and you can't have dynamic pages or services such as shopping carts or server-based Java programming.

Section III
Project Management

What is project management?

Think of the process of managing a project as being like a military unit in the field, trying to navigate toward an objective or location—say, a hill within the enemy's range. Your lieutenants have a tendency to veer off on the wrong course with their charges; your job is to keep them on track. You have to manage your supply lines to make sure you have what you need to make it through any number of project checkpoints. You have to regularly report your progress to your senior officers, and perhaps ask them to contact the Air Force and call in an air strike if the opposition gets too concentrated (if it were only that easy). Most of all, you must take that hill. At the end of the day, nothing else matters. You are evaluated on whether you reached your objectives or not.

Ironically, while you try to manage by consensus and empower those working around you, sometimes it feels like you need a *gun* to get everyone pulling in the same direction!

Managing projects in the web arena in particular presents interesting challenges because it is so inherently interdisciplinary and intercultural. When you manage software development, you deal mainly with programmers. With the web, you also need to deal with the "interesting" personalities of the creative designers, marketing folk, strategists, system administrators, hosting companies, and a rag-tag cast of many others—all in addition to programmers. Success in "herding all of these cats" lies in bringing a structure and methodology to what you are doing.

173

"Process" has become a trendy buzzword among the new-media firms, as if it is some amazing new discovery on their part. "Process" is an integral part of *all* project management, no matter what industry you're in or what you are managing. This section outlines a process that can be used for identifying, quantifying, shepherding, and delivering whatever you are trying to achieve in cyberland.

Chapter 9

Project Organization

No matter what kind of company you are or what you do, the first step in any endeavor is to figure out what it is you want to do—whether it is coming up with an idea for a web start-up, or a project for an existing company.

Whether you are considering a strategic corporate initiative or just an update project, as a project manager, you may or may not have a say in whether the idea is worthy. It may be a directive coming from your boss, or senior management, or your customers. No matter what the source, your duty is to determine whether the project can be delivered within the given parameters. When is it wanted? What resources do you have (or need) to deliver it? How much will it cost?

The ability to deliver is always built on three factors: (1) project scope, (2) resources, and (3) time. The larger the deliverable, the more resources or time it takes to complete. Sometimes, throwing more money at a project can speed it up by allowing you to procure more resources, but there is a point of diminishing returns, and our favorite expression to illustrate this is: "You can't put nine women in a room for a month and produce a baby!"

The alternative is to reduce your deliverables, or make them commensurate with the resources and time you have on hand. Time is a difficult resource to spend; we are in a society that wants things now, not later, and this is especially so on the web, where zillions of entrepreneurs are racing to build their companies so that they can nail down market share. Ironically, when a project runs into trouble, it is usually extra time that ends up being spent—you need more time to get your project done. Usually, this is the last thing that a web business wants to hear.

Knowing the interaction of these critical factors, you need to decide what you are realistically able to do. The best process is to have a preliminary conversation with your client or partners to gauge the scope of what you are being asked to produce. Some preliminary investigation or research may be in order. You may be able to come up with a rough plan or budget estimate, or if you have a lot of experience in what you are being asked to do, you may be able to do that on the spot.

The issue here is one of "orders of magnitude." For more complex or larger projects, more planning is needed. This estimate may be different from the one that is normally produced in the form of a project plan and a set of specifications, or, ultimately, it may be the same one. It depends on how accurate a figure is necessary, based on the business's needs. If someone is asking for a "knee-jerk reaction" price or estimate for a project, it will be orders of magnitude less accurate than the figures you might come up with if you are doing a project for a fixed price.

Once you have an idea of the scope of the project, the estimate can be shared with the user or client. That may result in the project's scope being modified, or its timeframe for delivery being extended. If you are a consultant, you may really be lucky and have them tell you thunderously, "Spare NO expense!"

■ BUDGET ESTIMATION

An amusing Catch-22 occurs when you are asked to come up with a budget for a project. Most clients (or management) want to know how much a project will cost prior to giving their approval or making a commitment. However, the most accurate way to estimate a project is by going through a detailed specification process, which usually, in and of itself, requires budget or funding to perform. How do you estimate resources, when it takes resources to do the estimate?

One solution, of course, is to grossly overestimate the amount of money that the project will cost. You should then be covered with sufficient funds, after you figure out what the project really costs. This is a "CYA"[1] style of estimating, and it has a danger. In a company, if your budget is too high, you run the risk that your firm will cancel or shelve the project—or, even worse, give the project to someone else. This may also occur if you are working for a client. The client may feel compelled to find a cheaper vendor. If you are bidding on a project, you may lose the project to someone who underbids you.

A better method is to have experienced people perform a limited analysis and come up with a budget for the project, using their best guesses. It should be more accurate than a huge overestimate, although seasoned estimators always factor a certain amount of "padding" into their estimates.

The most accurate approach is to put together a price for performing a detailed specification, and include a project plan. Once you hit the end of this process (described later in this section), you can deliver a relatively accurate estimate. Unfortunately, this doesn't meet the immediate need of calculating an overall budget for a project.

Sometimes you can use a hybrid approach, especially for business plans, when investors want a breakdown of the total amount of funding needed by the start-up. Rather than just say, "The budget for this is $2.2 million," you break it down into the constituent projects and assign an estimated cost to each one. Again, a seasoned and experienced individual must put together these figures, and they will not be as accurate as the numbers you have when you prepare a plan and specifications. But this presentation may be enough to get you started or at least take you past the budget process.

It's important to gauge the level of accuracy needed. Sometimes, it is enough to give a number and an order of magnitude, such as: "It may be plus or minus 50 percent," or whatever you deem the accuracy to be. In this way, you can at least give whoever wants the numbers an idea of what ballpark the cost is in. You may be asked to go back and come up with a more accurate estimate, or the money people may turn around and change the deliverable.

Estimating is an art as well as a science. Experience plays a big part, but your innate ability to visualize the breadth of a project and the scope of its constituent parts is based in large part on how you project your intuition and intellect, and this is difficult to teach. It may seem unfair, but good estimators can sometimes do the whole thing in their head, without running the numbers,[2] and have the results come out just as accurately. However, in the absence of someone whose intuition you can rely on, the next best thing is to sit down and actually go through the exercise of running the numbers.

There are highly metrical and systematic ways of performing estimates, but they all end up having the same basic method: breaking the project down into small pieces, estimating the individual pieces, and then rolling them back up again. These steps help you create a defensible estimate. One of the great features of a tool like Microsoft Project isn't just its ability to let you track a project, but its reliability when you must defend an estimate. One time, a colleague was in a meeting with a surly senior Wall Street manager who was famous for ripping apart the numbers put forth for a project, as well as the head of the person who was presenting them. When the yelling started, and he began questioning the numbers (the scene usually opened when he shook his head and said, "It's wayyyyy too much money!"), our colleague, who had built the plan, stood up, unfurled his detailed Gantt[3] chart to its glorious detailed length down the table, and said, "OK, you tell me. What pieces do you want me to eliminate? What is unrealistic here?" He pointed to one of the dozens of project steps on the plan. The surly manager looked at it, looked at him, and backed off.

■ THE IMPORTANCE OF PLANNING

When people get excited about starting a project, their overwhelming tendency is to dive in and start building, without any kind of plan or methodology in place. Programmers especially love to do this. They want to start writing code immediately. A friend used to call this: "Ready, Fire, Aim!" If you're just trying to put an idea together or maybe a proof of a concept, this may be OK, but don't expect to build anything of any significant size or magnitude without having some kind of project plan or specification. Running projects in a Ready, Fire, Aim mode is OK when you are the only person on the project, but the method rapidly starts to break down when it involves the cooperation and coordination of multiple people and resources.

A friend related this story: When General George S. Patton was marching across Europe in World War II, he came to a river that his army needed to cross, but there was no bridge. He called an engineer and asked, "How long will it take to build a new bridge?" The engineer replied, "Four months of planning and two months of construction." Patton called over a second engineer and asked him how long it would take. He said, "Two months of planning and four months of construction." He then called over a third engineer and asked him how long it would take to build a bridge. The third man replied, "We'll start building it tomorrow and I'll let you know." Patton went with the third guy.

Great story, except that everyone knows what a bridge is. We can all picture a bridge in our minds. But what about a website? Can you picture the entire information architecture? How about all of the back-end integration? This is where the idea of jumping into production without planning falls down. Even a child can draw a picture of a bridge, but a website? You first need to agree on what it will do, what will be in it, and how it will be built.

The friend who told the Patton story was from a real estate background. He had no clue or perception of what went into building an e-commerce system, nor was he willing to learn. He just wanted to start putting pictures up on the site and somehow magically have the thing get integrated—hopefully, prior to launch. A disastrous and failed project in the making.

Spend the extra time. Plan your projects carefully and thoughtfully. Any experienced project manager can tell you that the time you spend up front will be paid back handsomely because any change you have to make when you are in the midst of building a project will be enormously expensive. Your up-front planning will make or break your project.

■ GETTING APPROVAL

This step mainly applies to projects inside of corporations, but can also be adapted to small firms and start-ups. As mentioned earlier, getting a project approved can be a deceptively time-consuming process. In reality, very little of the time spent in getting a project approved has anything to do with any actual analysis or with having the merits of your proposal weighed by whoever is doing the approving. Instead, it is usually spent with your project sitting in someone's in-box, or waiting for a meeting to convene so that some committee can decide whether to approve it.

One thing you have to be clear on, prior to seeking approval, is where support for your project is coming from. In general, it must include support from those you work for, the people you work with, and the people who will use the site. If you are missing concordance in any of these three areas, you're in for trouble. No matter what the case, you have to ask yourself, "Whom does this project serve?" If you can't answer that question, or if the person or group that it serves hasn't bought into what you are doing, address that issue prior to seeking formal approval.

The approval process varies, depending on the kind of firm you are. Here is a description of the approval process in two different settings: a corporation and a start-up or dot-com.

➤ In a Corporation

When working in a corporation you must first identify the internal business groups that will sponsor your project. They most likely originated the idea, based on some internal need. This is particularly important because, in many companies, the projects are underwritten in the corporate budget by the business groups that requested the project.

Some people make the mistake of thinking that because their project is a great idea, everyone should immediately use it and adopt it. That's a big trap. Most people don't like having things imposed on them, especially if the way they have been conducting their business will be affected. Your project will die on the vine if you try to mandate that business units must sign on—unless, of course, you are the president of the firm. But even pulling rank can only go so far, and this kind of will is rarely imposed[4] effectively without engendering bad feelings. It is tough to try to force people to change the way they work unless they agree to the change themselves. Go around to a representative group of users and get their "buy in," so that they don't become obstructionists.

The first step in any project plan should include an initial "project organization" phase: You put together a proposal, estimate the funding and the time frame required, and present it to your management approval chain. Usually, several levels of approvals are required, which may bring in some of the usual annoying office politics that are inherent in big companies. Allow plenty of time—measured in weeks, not days—for these approvals to come through.

Why does this approval take so long? There are several reasons. To begin with, senior managers do get busy, and it may take a while to get their attention, make your presentation, and have them sign some form of approval.

The other main reason is that things can tend to pile up on executives' desks. Your project proposal may be in a full, but untouched in-box. This seems really *lame,* but it happens all the time. Also, a committee meeting may be required, and that may take weeks.

One countermeasure is to "walk" something around—make appointments, or just wait outside someone's office, catch him or her when you can, and ask for the necessary signature on your documents.

When you must get approvals, make sure that the business sponsors sign off first, then the lower-level managers, then the higher-level managers. This is important and will save you time. The higher-level bosses usually won't sign until they've seen that their own people have signed. Make sure you start out with either a cover page or a summary that shows exactly who is doing the project, the expected duration, cost, user base/customer, and any other key information. Don't expect all of the signers, especially the senior managers, to actually pore through your project document. If your document has an "at a glance" page, an executive summary, and the other signatures, you have a better chance of getting a quick decision.

➤ In a Start-Up or Dot-Com

If your firm is self-funded (or just your own firm, whether you have cash or not), you may be the decision maker. In fact, you may be the only person in the company.

If your start-up is funded through another entity, you may need to get its approval before you can spend the necessary money. The entities that you may need to get approval from may include: your VC firm, your bank (if you have a line of credit), your board of directors, or even your father-in-law (if you made the mistake of borrowing from him).

A small company, by its definition, doesn't have much bureaucracy, so going through layers of management shouldn't be a major problem or hold you up. The larger problem here is the ability of what little management you have to be able to act quickly and decisively. If your project makes sense and you've done your homework, including running the numbers, then go for it. Your insurance is your size; it will allow you to make adjustments much more easily if your work is in progress and things are turning out differently than you anticipated.

Chapter 10

Specification

Perhaps the greatest single cause of failure in e-commerce development is lack of rigor during the business definition phase, when you are "spec-ing out" the project. This chapter will give you some background on the kind of tools you need to drill down into requirements, make sense of time and cost estimates, and build plans with sufficient detail to guide and manage development.

■ JAD SESSIONS

Much has been written about joint application development (JAD) sessions. The simple point of a JAD session is to get the user and the developers in one room at the same time, so that all of the details for a website or project can be hashed out and put into a document that everyone agrees on. This document will become part of the overall project document. In a consulting relationship, this document can become legally binding.

The concept is relatively simple, but organizing a JAD session is not always easy. The first hurdle is getting buy-in and communicating the critical importance of getting all of the necessary information about the project prior to starting actual production. As mentioned in the previous chapter, some people don't understand why project specs are necessary and why the designers can't just start drawing pretty pictures.

Fortunately, this seems to be the exception and not the rule. Most techies and business folks are eager to set aside time for making sure that what will be produced is exactly what they have in mind—especially when the pricetag is large and the business is depending on a successful delivery.

Setting up the sessions is the second hurdle. Make sure to *overestimate* the amount of time you need to set aside, and measure it in days. It is easy to "give back" any time that you don't use, but it can be next to impossible to obtain extra time when you need it, especially given everyone's busy schedules.

When you all sit down together, most clients are surprised at the amount of time it takes to drill down to the level of detail needed for producing their site and having it operate the way they want. This session also provides an environment for bonding the team together—breaking the barriers that sometimes exist from the outset between different parties from different disciplines and backgrounds. Having a close working relationship can obviously foster the most effective setting for production, and help to minimize mistrust later on, when the inevitable "challenges" occur.

➤ Rules of the Game

To effectively run a JAD session, we advise setting some ground parameters and appointing people to fill some key roles. Consider the two following steps.

1. *Appoint a leader.* The role of the leader in the JAD context is multifaceted. The leader can set a positive tone for meetings, enact any necessary ground rules, familiarize the group with facilities, define any other particular roles that are needed, and review the tools or methodologies that are to be used. The leader can also proctor the discussions in a neutral way, and draw in all of the participants. He or she should set limits to prevent one person from dominating the discussion and to keep the session on track and on the subject. A good leader will produce a periodic summary of the session's progress and of all of the agreed-on points. This is an important role. Make sure that everyone agrees on the appointment of a leader and that this leader is empowered to properly do the job. Having an established leader will help to facilitate a smooth, efficient, and productive JAD session. Often the leader is referred to as a "facilitator" and has special training.

2. *Appoint a scribe.* You will need someone to take notes, to keep file copies of any charts and tables that the group produces on your white board or flip charts, and to record important points brought up in the discussion. Appointing someone as "the writer," up front, will ensure that the results produced will be recorded properly. The alternative is to hand off the role among the session's attendees, but this can sometimes be haphazard and, in the worst case, can result in the loss of some of your vital information.

It is also important to create a positive atmosphere based on courtesy and mutual respect among the group members. Follow the old saying, "There is no such thing as a stupid question," and make sure that all ideas and input from everyone are welcomed. Try to have only one person speaking at a time, and avoid the temptation to let group members interrupt whoever is speaking. Above all, maintain an open and positive atmosphere. The goal here is to foster progress and accomplishment, so try to make the achievement of that goal as easy as possible for all involved.

➤ Session Activities

Here is a list of the activities you may want to attend to during your JAD session. This isn't meant to be an exhaustive list, nor are all of the items listed here meant to be mandatory. Decide what is appropriate for your particular project, and mix/match them appropriately:

➤ Perform introductions of the JAD session members. Have each person state his or her name, company, job title and functional job description, particular interest in the project, and any important points that should be brought up during the course of the session or put on the session agenda.

➤ Review any existing website or related materials. Show what has worked, what hasn't worked, and what material should be considered for retention.

➤ View competitive sites. Review what looks good and attractive as well as any features that may be usable in the site you are planning.

➤ Review the original project materials, if any.

➤ Review any existing documentation, especially if the project is to migrate a legacy system onto the web.

➤ Go over any hard-and-fast deadlines that are associated with the development of the project. Perhaps you will want the launch of the site to coincide with some other major event that is immovable. These restrictions need to be revealed up front, so that the project milestones can be adjusted accordingly.

➤ Discuss the resources that will be available to the project. The obvious one will be the budget. Explore the availability of production groups, PR agencies, or any number of different resources that can be brought to bear on the project.

After you perform this kind of review, you can commence the definition of the site itself. A good place to start is by clearly stating the site's business objectives. This will set the expectations of the group from the very beginning.

One favorite approach to defining the functionality of a site is to describe everything that you could possibly want, as though it was being developed in a perfect world. This wish list will bring out a detailed picture of the complete range of your business's wants and desires. Begin to drill down on what is feasible, and get an idea of some early approaches. After you do that, you can drill down on the following areas:

➤ Refining of the objectives of the site.
➤ Laying out business rules and logic.
➤ Defining the content of the site.
➤ Identifying the functionality or back-end processing that will be involved.
➤ Sketching out a rough layout and information architecture.
➤ Identifying what third-party resources the site will be integrating.

At the end of the final JAD session (and probably at the end of each day, as well), review what has been accomplished and agreed on. Couple this with a restatement of any follow-on action items that will need to be attended to by group members.

■ ESTIMATING WEB PROJECTS

The art of estimating projects is not new or earth-shattering. Many books have been written on this subject. The process tends to break down, however, when you try to apply traditional estimating techniques to the widely cross-disciplinary medium of the web.

The absolutely best method for estimating a web project is to have some amazingly brilliant person on your staff listen patiently to a description of what the site will do, think about that description for a minute, and then deliver an extremely accurate number based largely on intuition. This requires that you have a "Moses" of estimating on your payroll—someone who can turn his prophesies into profits.

For the rest of us mere mortals, the usual technique in any estimating exercise is to try to put a limit on the boundaries of available intuition by breaking a project down into its constituent parts. First, perform a task analysis; then, brilliantly estimate each easily digestible piece of the project puzzle on an individual basis. These pieces can readily be entered into a project management tool such as Microsoft Project, a program that can roll up the numbers into an overall project cost, once you assign resources (people) to each task.

Many people in the web industry have no clue about what kind of process is required to come up with reasonably accurate numbers for a project estimate. We have seen enormously complex projects put out to bid on a request for proposal (RFP) basis. Teams are expected to come up with an estimate when there has been little documentation and certainly no JAD sessions, and the only results were in misunderstandings and unrealistic project expectations.

When you must come up with a project estimate and the information needed is incomplete, you have three choices.

The first choice is the "Road Warrior" technique: "All you have to do is walk away," said Lord Humongous in that cult classic. Don't even *think* of trying to come up with a number. You'll get killed. Sometimes you have to withdraw in order to fight another day.

Your second choice is to throw in the towel and come up with some kind of number. You plan to attach a bold disclaimer that will get you off the hook when the inevitable explosion occurs. You expect that you will have to go back to the till to get enough money to finish the project because so many unanticipated facets of the project weren't known at the time the estimate was given. A group of programmers in lovely Hawaii were building a system for a local television station, and the project had a specification built previously by individuals of questionable abilities. Fixed dollar costs were assigned to each module, and, of course, the people who did the estimates were long gone. Needless to say, the estimates were wildly off. The amount of money for each piece ended up yielding minimum wages for the programmers who were writing the code. Don't think that the TV station had such a great deal either; there is no winner in a win–lose situation. The programmers on the project quit, and no one in the Hawaiian Islands who had the skills to finish the job would do it for the money that was being allowed. Everyone who does consulting has at least one project like this in their deep dark past, but usually *only one,* because if you get burned this way, you rarely let it happen again.

Your third choice is to perform some kind of discovery phase and get enough information to perform estimates with some level of credible accuracy. Unfortunately, ours is rarely a perfect world, and the usual way to provide insurance against disaster is to build a fairly large amount of cushion into the estimates, in case unforeseen or unrevealed project details surface. One colleague has a very simple formula. He does his best estimate, using whatever information is available; then he doubles it and adds 50 percent. This, of course, translates to triple the original amount, but his description has a poetic sound. In all seriousness, this raw form of estimating is actually quite common.

If you have been blessed with an ability to lead JAD sessions and have compiled a fairly good amount of descriptive information, use it to put together what we refer to as an *estimating team.*

An estimating team consists of leaders from the major disciplines involved in the project. Each team may or may not include team leaders from the following disciplines: project management, account/relationship management, graphic design, web development (the HTML guys), programming, system administration, QA, and copywriting, plus producers, information architects, and production artists.

The purpose of an estimating team is to elicit individual estimates, for any work to be done on the project, from each discipline that is required, and for these estimates to be assembled in an interactive team environment. Having the group review the estimates, negotiate changes, and come up with a schedule that everyone can agree on while the estimating team is together in one room can save an enormous amount of time. By bringing multiple perspectives to bear on the overall estimate, issues are perceived realistically, and dimensions that might otherwise be unrecognized can be revealed.

After the team is assembled, create a multicolumn form like the one shown below. Build a high-level outline of the project in the leftmost column, and break it down to a level of detail that can be comfortably estimated by the members of the group. On the topmost row, list the various disciplines that are represented in the room. Your form should look something like Figure 10.1.

In one view, everyone can see the guts of the project. In this particular case, project management is broken out as a separate section at the bottom of the grid.

The next step is to have each person add his or her contribution to each part of the project. Having everyone in the room at the same time allows cross-disciplinary discussion and takes into account various ramifications that would be more difficult for people to do alone.

Figure 10.2 shows the results of the estimating done for each part by each participant. The numbers listed represent days.

Translating this grid into a program like Microsoft Project is relatively simple. You can assign the specific resources, set the

	Prj Mgmt	Design	Web Dev	Tech	Prod Artist	Q/A
Initial Page Review						
Development						
Login						
Password						
Administration						
Administrator						
Supervisor						
Identify Administrator						
Quality Assurance						
Review						
Home Page						
SSL						
Code Upgrade						
Review						
Security Audit						
Project Reviews						
Project Management						

Figure 10.1 Sample form (blank).

	Prj Mgmt	Design	Web Dev	Tech	Prod Artist	Q/A
Initial Page Review	0.25	0.25	0.25	0.25	0.25	0.25
Development						
Login		3	1	0.5	1.25	0.5
Password			0.3	3		0.5
Administration						
Administrator		1.3	4	2	0.5	
Supervisor		1.3	1	2	0.5	
Identify Administrator		1.4	0.3	0.5	0.5	
Quality Assurance						1
Review	0.25	0.25	0.25	0.25	0.25	0.25
Home Page		3	1.5	0.5	1.25	0.5
SSL			2.5	5		0.5
Code Upgrade			1	10		1
Review	0.25	0.25	0.25	0.25	0.25	0.25
Security Audit		1.5	1	1		
Project Reviews	0.25	0.25	0.25	0.25	0.25	0.25
Project Management	7	2		4		

Figure 10.2 Sample form (completed).

dependencies between steps, and assign dollar rates to the resources (usually people) used. M$ Project can then roll up all this information and give you a project cost.

■ DOCUMENTATION

After you have done all of your up-front planning, the net result should be a number of documents. Collectively, they should provide a road map that will guide you toward a living website.

➤ Functional Specification

This document should be a work product of the joint application development (JAD) session. It should contain the sum knowledge of how your site will function, as well as all of the items that you and your client or user agreed on. This is a detailed nontechnical document—it is concerned with the "what" issues of your site.

➤ Technical Specification

This "how" document is typically written by your systems staff *after* the functional specification is accepted or any changes are agreed to.

Part of the process of writing a functional specification is having it reviewed by the technical staff and getting feedback and modifications with respect to what is feasible and can be technically achieved within the desired scope of the project. Ideally, most of these issues will also have been discussed and negotiated as part of the JAD session, but a thorough technical review of the functional spec is critical.

The Technical Specification will contain all of the details of how the site will be technically implemented, including desktop platforms and browsers-supported software design methodologies and approaches, multimedia elements, server middleware and programming languages, databases, back-end technology, architectural models, server configurations, web hosting, and networking.

➤ Creative Brief

This is the road map to the visual brand and impression of the website. It is created by your design staff and is usually the result of the visual style reviewed and accepted by the client/user. The creative brief may go through several iterations if the users don't like what your graphic designers have created for the site. Most designers try to set a limit on the number of these iterations. Additional (or endless) efforts to come up with a visual theme that satisfies the users are charged as extra work.

➤ Information Architecture

This unit is usually built after the functional specification is agreed on. The information architects will model the functional flow of the website (see the section on information architecture in Chapter 5). The flow is represented through a series of diagrams called schematics or flow diagrams. These sometimes are modeled in HTML without the graphics and put through usability testing and focus groups to determine the best and most effective layouts of the functionality on each screen.

➤ Project Plan

The Functional Specification defines the "what"; the Technical Specification defines the "how"; and the Project Plan defines the "when," "who," and "how much." The most popular tool for creating a project plan is Microsoft Project, which allows you to take the task analysis that was presumably created when you performed your project estimate. Details as to what resources will be assigned to each task, what dependencies exist between steps, and the rates and start dates all get incorporated into the Project Plan.

When the plan is successfully completed, it will provide a complete picture of the entire project, as well as a method for being able to track the progress of the project and be aware of potential problems (e.g., bottlenecks) by having the project plan identify the project's critical path.

All of these documents become the actual "instruction manual" that the various groups will use for building the website.

■ SERVICE LEVEL AGREEMENTS

Service-level agreements (SLAs) are very important when making deals with vendors and (in large organizations) when setting up interdepartmental processes within a company. An SLA can be either a legal or an organizational artifact. SLAs, when they are well constructed, keep you from getting screwed.

By quantifying the expected performance of a service provider, you can subsequently measure that performance. If you aren't getting what you are supposed to be getting, the SLA has been broken, and you can have some recourse. This may sound pretty obvious, but you might be surprised at how many companies, from huge corporations to little bitty shops, have paid huge set-up fees and recurring fees but still received terrible service. You would certainly be surprised at how many of these abused firms had no recourse because the terms of service, stated in the SLA, were either vague or nonexistent.

The less direct control you will have over a process, the more carefully you need to craft your SLA. We always see cheesy ads in in-flight magazines, in which a PhD guy with a horrible comb-over says, "In business, you don't get what you deserve, you get what you negotiate." We are not suggesting you sign up for this guy's seminars, but that statement is true. If you are going to depend on another company or organization to run your business, then you need to spell out exactly what you expect and it has got to be something that can be measured. Phrases like "Party will make reasonable effort to respond to issues as soon as they are reported" are very bad.

The reason this is so crucial is that it is very hard for courts of law and for senior executives to evaluate who is right or wrong with e-commerce. Words like "reasonable," and "best effort," and "quality" may mean something in traditional industries that everyone is familiar with. With e-commerce, what is ridiculous and unforgivable to us (e.g., MS Hotmail, purchased for $400 million—yes, that is correct— went down on Thanksgiving Day, 1999, for several days) may seem perfectly OK, not only to a federal court, but also to millions of users who don't know any better. (If consumers knew the reasons why these huge overvalued systems go down, it would turn their hair gray and the stock market would crash instantly. We heard about a major site's going down because it ran out of hard-drive space on a critical system. The site stayed down for a couple of days while the management of this company went through its bureaucratic procurement process. Finally, a fed-up developer ran out to Frye's—a cool computer equipment warehouse store—and bought the hard-drive himself.) The only way to keep everyone honest is to figure out how to quantify and measure—and, of course, to define—serious consequences for failing to honor the terms of an SLA.

The thing to keep in mind is that SLAs need to be simple. Not everyone has the same idea of "reasonable" where technology is involved, and not everyone (like the courts, or your boss) will understand a complex SLA. The other thing to confirm is that you have an easy way to measure and document your service provider's performance.

A classic example occurs when you outsource the management of a website to a vendor. You expect the site to be up all the time. But, recognizing the forces of chaos and entropy, you allow that a site may be down .1 percent of the time. So, now you have agreed on 99.9 percent uptime over each month. Good. Now what if the site is up, but it's really *really* slow—so slow that no one can use it. Is it still up? Not really. So you need to define "up." Let's say that, for this particular site, if it takes more than four seconds for a page to be returned after a user clicks on a link, it is "unacceptable" and the site is then functionally down. The vendor may say, "Well, we can't help it if a user has a slow connection. The nature of the Internet is that sometimes it gets all clogged up and slow. Trust us. We want this to be really fast, and we want your business to succeed. Let's just get these negotiations done and start making you lots of eMoney!"

If someone gives you a spiel like this, you would be wise to run away, like the Monty Python guys ran from that little rabbit in *The Holy Grail.* Seriously, what you need to do is quantify all the pieces of performance on an internet site into two things that affect website performance: (1) the server performance and (2) the network performance.

➤ The Server Performance

This is how long it takes the web server to respond to a request, once the request is received. This doesn't take the Internet into account at all. It only measures the time from when it got the request from the Internet to when it sends the response back to the user. It doesn't count the time it took for the user's request to get to the server, or the time needed for the resulting page to travel from the web server back out over the Internet to the user. The place to see the server performance is in the web traffic reports. If you have outsourced the whole site, then you might not have access to the web reports. It would be very smart to have access to these reports on demand, and there should be penalties for not providing them. It may sound paranoid, but remember what Andy Grove (Intel Chairman) called his best-selling book: *Only the Paranoid Survive!*

➤ The Network Performance

This is the time it takes for information (requests for pages, or the pages themselves) to travel through the Internet between a user's system and your website. Website operators can't help a user who has a bad connection to the Internet (except ISPs!), but you can make sure that your website has the best possible connectivity. One user may have a very fast connection to your site, and another might have a slow one, but the more robust your website's connectivity, the better chance you have of serving all your users well.

In the early days of the WWW, it was difficult to measure network performance accurately. Today, services such as Keynote and Web-Metrics make it their business to set up virtual users in major cities all over the world, connecting them through the major ISPs. You can pay these services to connect to a Universal Resource Locator (URL) every few minutes from every location, and deliver reports on the overall performance of both the network and the server. These companies are the best way to measure against website performance SLAs.[1] It is valuable to have such an objective third-party audit. Remember: If you are outsourcing your website, agree beforehand on a third party to do the measurements.

Website performance and uptime is just one thing that can be agreed-on and measured in an SLA. There may be many other kinds of services that often need to be addressed. SLAs can (and usually should) work in two directions. If you are responsible for running a website for a larger organization, you will find SLAs very handy there, too. For example, if the Sales and Marketing department is constantly requesting that you change the pricing or marketing messages on the site, you may get swamped with editing the site and uploading changes to the HTML or the database. The Sales people may have an unrealistic expectation as to how much effort is required to do this maintenance. Frustration will result on both sides. An SLA, in a case like this, can act like a mini-partnership agreement. In it, you can state things like: "The web team will make changes to pricing and certain marketing data, daily. Changes must be proofread and submitted to the web team, by Sales, before noon every day, in order for those changes to appear on the site by 7:00 A.M. on the next business day. Emergency changes shall be submitted by Sales via email, and will be implemented and uploaded within four hours. . . . " You get the idea. In this case, you would want the Sales and Web managers to sign the agreement. Then there can be no misunderstanding about the level of service each party expects from the other.

Chapter 11

Development to Launch and Beyond

In the euphoria of having completed most of the work of an e-commerce project, people often race to the finish line and miss the last critical steps that can deliver either a smooth launch or an explosion on the pad. This chapter takes you through the planning, internal and external communication, testing, quality assurance, and validation steps, and the final launch strategies that will increase your likelihood of success.

■ WEB DEVELOPMENT

Whether you are building a website from scratch, adding major new sections to an existing website, or merely making ongoing changes to the content on your site, the process by which all of this material moves from inception to a live site is pretty much the same. In the web development world, this concept is termed "promotion."

Materials being produced for a website go through three distinctly different states: (1) development, (2) staging, and (3) production. Different activities occur at each state. You can have more states, depending on your approval process and how complex your technical requirements are. The bottom line here is that you never want to go directly from the developer's sandbox to the live environment. Promotion puts a process in place that brings order, ensures quality, and maximizes the productive use of your staff.

➤ Development

This is the first phase of website creation. All material being developed—content, copy, design, programming, or HTML—starts out in Development. This is where these materials are built. They may exist in an incomplete or nonworking state, or they may appear ready for production. All of this material is usually segregated onto separate servers that are pegged solely for development. This step is important because later steps in the development process need to be kept separate, and the tasks being performed must not be interrupted by materials being changed, deleted, or modified, which often occurs when things are being developed.

➤ Staging

When the producers of the materials for the website are satisfied that their stuff is complete to the best of their ability and knowledge, it is ready to be moved or promoted to what is called "staging" or, in some circles, "user acceptance testing." Staging should involve a completely separate set of servers, so that these processes can go on apart from any other ongoing development. The staging server setup should be identical to the "live" hosted web environment that the public accesses, with the exception that it cannot be accessed from the outside. In this way, the testers can examine the site in its entirety as though it were live, without hanging your dirty laundry in public—at least until you are ready.

The staging phase is where the Quality Assurance (QA) folks perform exhaustive testing on all new material (to make sure that it works according to the specifications) and identify things like missing links, graphics, text, or other missing or broken content. If problems are identified, the proposed materials may be rejected and sent back to the developers for correction. After the corrections are made, the materials are sent back to staging and the testing begins again.

User acceptance testing is also a potential step during the staging phase, depending on how your group is organized. In some organizations, materials that have been tested successfully will be forwarded to certain individuals or users—often from the user side of the house—for their final approval. After they "sign off" on them, the new web materials are promoted (moved) to production.

➤ Production

This is the final stop in the web development process. After content has been developed, tested, and approved, it is moved to the production servers and is then available to the public.

One item is worth mentioning. Having separate states—development, staging, and production—usually means having separate physical servers or groups of servers, depending on the complexity of the systems. For example, if your site uses both NT and Unix-based servers in production, each type will need to be replicated for use in development and staging as well.

In most shops, the physical task of moving content from one state to another is done by the operations staff (their role is described in Chapter 5), and may be automated either through the use of commercial web content management systems or through some document workflow management systems, or—as is most often the case at any firm of any size—a set of thrown-together perl scripts and batch files that only one or two system administrators can understand.

The important concept here is: Protect the integrity of your production environment (including your web hardware and the software/content you put on it) to make sure that changes are not made directly to a live site, since this will be visible to the public. The problem with building directly to a live site is that, more often than not, you will introduce an "oops" factor (untested materials that go directly into production are invariably laced with problems). However many states you decide you want to have between development and the live site, you have to establish playpens where your workers can perform their jobs without worrying about or dealing with other groups stepping on them. In addition, you need to create a quality control process so that what you put on your live site will end up being not only of the highest professional caliber, but will represent your firm in the way that it should be represented to the public.

■ DEPLOYMENT

If they have them at all, most web companies don't schedule their launch parties until at least a month or so after the "launch." You and some of your staff may crawl toward a bottle of strong whiskey directly after (and in extreme cases, before) all systems are go, but that's more of a medical condition than a party. No one ever has time to plan a party around a launch. Much like NASA's Space Shuttle launches, there is a target time, but no one ever really knows whether a launch is going to happen until a few minutes before it does. It would be pretty funny to send out a party invitation that said, "Please come to mybusiness.com's launch party. We think it will be at 7:00 P.M. at the Techno Bar, but we're not sure. It depends on whether the database server arrives today and whether we can find Alan to load up the operating system. If you see Alan, by the way, tell him to call the office!" But that's what it would look like if you tried to make a launch party coincide with an actual launch. If anyone has the time to be doing prelaunch launch-party planning, he or she should probably be fired.

Launching a new website, overhauling an old one, or even launching a new part of a website is nerve-racking in any organization, no matter how many times the team has been through the same process.[1] Even after the switch is flipped and new visitors begin to arrive, everyone holds their breath to see if anything crashes or slows to a grinding halt. Everyone continues to check and double-check every bit of functionality to be totally certain that the launch has been a success. Every hiccup sends staff running to investigate and fix it. Sometimes, the worst fears are realized and there is a crisis to deal with. There's no avoiding it; there is no such thing as a perfect launch. Don't even hope for one. It's like pitching a perfect game, or more like winning the lottery. It doesn't happen. It's not possible to predict every glitch that may be discovered leading up to a launch, but there are some basic concepts that can help you to avoid a complete mess.

The first concern involves the project plan. Just because you said six weeks ago that your application would be ready for launch tomorrow, doesn't mean it is ready. A project plan is a living document and it needs to be maintained vigilantly. The faster you can react to changing conditions or assumptions, the better chance you have of meeting your deadlines. The project plan also needs to be sane to begin with. Monolithic projects that try to deliver everything all at once are virtually impossible to deploy. It is always better to launch something simple, with quality and manageability, and add more functionality later. The best project plan is one that calls for small, bite-sized launches. Even then, you will have your hands full, so give yourself a chance to succeed by setting achievable goals, and be prepared to cut unnecessary pieces when you are down to the wire.

Testing is paramount. You should have a complete working version of your new site, subsite, or feature well in advance of its launch to real users. Ideally, you'll want to allow several weeks to test, fix bugs, and get comfortable with any new business processes that give ongoing support to your new stuff. You can't do enough testing. If you are two weeks away from launch and you haven't seen a working system, you are in for a very rough ride. That doesn't mean you will necessarily fail abjectly, but you are definitely not going to have adequate time to be 100 percent confident.

It helps a great deal to have all of your content and design completed well ahead of time. Content constantly changes on a website, but having your content in a 99 percent completed state will cut down the organizational noise as the developers and operations people get ready to go live. The point is: The more you can get out of the way ahead of time, the fewer things you have to worry about. You can then focus on the actual launch activities, which are complex and largely technical.

Don't ever leave sections under construction or have placeholders of any kind when you launch. Placeholders are fine to use when you're developing websites, but you can't expose your users to them under any circumstances. If something is not finished, don't put it up on your site and don't have any links to it. Nothing screams "Unprofessional moron!" more plainly than "Under construction" and "Coming soon" pages. It is unforgivable to encourage a user to click on, link to go somewhere, and then not have anything there except a message saying that there's nothing there. It's like having a room full of doors that open to brick walls. If you and your team can't manage the complexity of changing navigation buttons and hyperlinks again and again as you are developing new and changing functionality, you may as well hang it up, because that's what running a website is all about.

A "soft launch" is useful as a method of minimizing risk. With a soft launch, you make a site (or subsite) available to the public but do not advertise its existence. This gives you an opportunity to go live and work out potential problems without exposing these problems to your entire user base. The soft launch is becoming the preferred method of bringing new sites up. When management feels that everything is ready, only then is it time to advertise that the site is open for business. For example, if a new version of a site is launching to replace an old version, you might soft-launch new.3clicksaway.com (there is nothing there, by the way; it's just an example!) and ask some friends and a few customers to try it out. At some point, you just replace the old www.3clicksaway.com with the new one.

In the end, you need to let the Ops people do their thing. They are responsible for technically operating your site, and they are the folks who are going to flip the switch. Operations typically plans, coordinates, and manages the launch activities. Ops people need to be accountable for the success of a launch, but management needs to listen to them about the state of "readiness." If your Ops people say it isn't ready to go, don't go. It's essential that you and your Operations staff see eye-to-eye in terms of your expectations of quality and consistency. If you don't directly manage Operations, you need an SLA BEFORE your launch.

Make sure you know exactly how things are going to go, once you are live. A web manager's worst nightmare is to realize, after launch, that there is not enough to maintain something, moving forward. To retreat from functionality—that is, to roll out some functionality to users and then be forced to remove it—is one of the worst things you can do in e-commerce. It is confusing and embarrassing, and it damages your credibility. Adding is great, taking away is bad. Adding too much salt to your food makes it inedible, and you can't take the salt away. Only do what you can handle, moving forward. For example, imagine you are running a site that sells forks, and part of your site is called "Industry News." You go live with three great articles that your summer interns wrote about exciting silverware topics, such as new developments in spoon production in the Far East. But the day after the launch, you realize that you never arranged a way to get more content. Maybe you didn't even consider how you would maintain the content once you got it. You can't do enough thinking, worrying, checking, and double-checking. How does each piece of functionality and content affect your day-to-day operations? Is everything accounted for? If you are doing a good job, you should feel somewhat paranoid. This is a good thing. When you are satisfied that you have the answers to *all* of these questions, you are ready to complete your countdown to launch. Never before.

■ TRAFFIC ANALYSIS, REPORTING, AND METRICS

Without information to tell you quantifiably how your business is performing, you are driving blind and without a dashboard. You will either crash or go nowhere fast. As we have discussed in so many ways in this book, it is absolutely essential to identify unambiguous, measurable criteria for evaluating success. Just as in any competitive business (we would say, *even more so than in any other*), in e-commerce the ability to turn on a dime is richly rewarded. Lack of this ability can be punished by a cruel and public death. Being able to respond to change is obviously dependent on having fresh and relevant information.

In e-commerce, knowing your numbers is just as important as in any other kind of business. What are your numbers for sales data, inventory, accounts payable, accounts receivable, assets, liabilities, and so on? We can't stress enough the importance of keeping track of all critical business factors, especially the tools you use for e-commerce. They are no different from the tools a conventional business uses. But it goes without saying that websites are substantially different from conventional channels and therefore they require special tools for collecting web data, generating reports, and analyzing the information.

Hits reports, web log reports, web reports, web statistics, usage summaries, traffic analyses—there are many names for these reports, and there are many tools that provide them. Probably the most popular product out there is WebTrends. It's a good product, but, for very busy sites with many web servers, it is not very attractive. For big sites, and especially for people who want to report on many large sites at once, Accrue is a better product. Its charts and graphs aren't as pretty as those at WebTrends, but it is faster and easier to manage. For most sites, given similar prices and give or take a few whistles and bells, most of the web analysis tools are pretty similar. They periodically collect and store data from web servers (usually, directly from the web server log files), they crunch the data into a database, and then they provide customizable summary and detail reports from those data. These tools, which, for simplicity's sake, we will refer to as "traffic analysis tools" are the basic dashboard for a website.

This is where web managers get their "hits" and "page-views" reports. It's important to understand the difference between the two. Hits are actually not very meaningful statistics by themselves. To say, "We had a million hits yesterday!" is actually not that exciting a statement. A hit is counted any time anyone downloads anything from a website. In the old days, before more sophisticated tools were available, hits were sometimes the only way to look at the popularity of a site, but it wasn't very accurate. Because of the way HTML works, a single user viewing a single simple web page might account for anywhere between 1 and 100 (or more!) hits. Unqualified hits are probably more interesting to the Operations people, who worry about the servers and how many hits they can physically handle. They don't tell you much about how your business is going. Page views are a little more interesting. Not surprisingly, they tell you how many pages have been viewed from your site.

But page views by themselves, although they are more accurate than plain old hits, don't tell you that much either. You need more context. What we want to know is:

➤ How many users visited today? How many times did they visit?

➤ Of those who visited, how many have been here before and how many were first-time visitors?

➤ How were they referred to our site (that is, did they click on a link from another site, a search engine, a banner ad, or did they just type in the URL)?

➤ Which ISPs did users come from? What country?

➤ Which web browsers are they using?

➤ What times of day were the most popular and least popular for visitors?

➤ How much time did users spend on our site?

➤ How many pages did each user view?

➤ Which pages were the most popular and least popular?

➤ For pages that we want users to visit (e.g., the page where they buy something), what were the popular paths to get there?

We want to know these statistics daily, monthly, and yearly.

With tables, pie charts, and graphs, these are the questions that we expect to have answered by our traffic analysis tools. More importantly, we can slice and dice the data to ask more complex questions, such as: For all visitors who use Netscape's Communicator, how many were referred from site X? With cookies, we can answer even deeper questions with our tools, such as: For all visitors who were referred from site X after midnight, how many bought our Model 5 widgets?

Cookies are a much maligned technology. In the simplest sense, cookies are a way to tag visitors when they arrive at your site, so that their actions can be tracked. Cookies, when used properly, are completely safe and secure. For a while, there was much public outcry concerning invasion of privacy, Big Brotherism, and so on. The fact is, cookies are very useful and they allow websites to provide richer experiences for their users. They also allow sites to better assess what users are doing. From the point of view of traffic analysis, cookies can be used to answer all kinds of questions, and they can (and should) be completely anonymous. So the user with cookie XJD432 came from Yahoo! and bought a toaster from you. Is this invasive? Studies show that most users are comfortable with this. And if they aren't, they can turn off their cookies. If that happens, some of your traffic won't be analyzable in the granular way you want it to be, but that's OK. Web reporting should be about trends and tendencies, not about zeroing in on specific users and exploiting them. A small percentage of users will complain no matter what, but you should not be bothered. The value of the information obtained through cookies is too great to be sacrificed to please a paranoid minority.

Web traffic information tells you who your users are and where they came from, but it also tells you how effective your media campaigns and search engine listings are. If you are paying a popular website for banner ad space, and none of the users/referrals are buying, you will react by moving those media to a more effective site—one that you think better matches your target—and you can review your data after a week and see whether you were right.

Traffic analysis tools tell you what users like and what they don't like about your site. If you have a great tool on your site, but no one is using it, maybe it's because it sucks, but maybe it's because no one can find it. This indicates that you need to look for improvements in your user interface and navigation, to make the links to the tool more prominent.

One thing to remember is that traffic analysis isn't usually plug-and-play. You can get the basic statistics pretty easily, but getting more sophisticated reports typically requires some special configuration and may even require you to reprogram some components of your site. So, when you set out to build a new site or add functionality to an existing one, always ask yourself what information you expect or need to get out of it. Try to write out on a piece of paper the daily reports you want to get about the new site and how you will use that information. This will help you and your developers to create a site that gives back actionable information.

Another thing to remember: Traffic analysis is always an engineering challenge for high-volume websites. If you have thousands of visitors per day, you will start to fill up hard drives with precious data. We once had a situation where a website had so much traffic that the logfiles couldn't be analyzed fast enough. It took more than a day to analyze one day's traffic. The solution was to buy bigger hardware and more efficient software. It's a great problem to have, but don't underestimate the expense and complexity of managing your precious web data.

If you are just starting out and you don't expect huge traffic up front, most ISPs include reporting in their commercial web hosting packages. If you are hosting your own server, a few sites out there can accommodate uploading your log and running reports online. This is pretty nifty, and it's also a good example of an ASP.

Notes

CHAPTER 2

1. U.S. Department of Commerce report: "The Emerging Digital Economy."

2. In case you don't know, "Six Degrees of Kevin Bacon" is a drinking game in which the drinkers give each other the names of any actor and have to associate him/her with Kevin Bacon. The name of the game is *Six Degrees of Separation,* by John Guare, which is actually based on the sociological assertion that all people are separated in acquaintance by no more than six people.

3. Some people might say the most successful site is AOL, but AOL isn't a website. AOL's unspoken mission is to keep its users away from the WWW altogether, and it tries to keep all of its content within its proprietary network. We'll talk about that more in a later section.

4. Some tools, like email, are not strictly content, but the focus is content. Yahoo! is not a search engine, either. Search engines go out on the Internet and search for things. Yahoo! is more like the Yellow Pages of the Internet. It lets you search or browse its directory. The actual WWW search engine at Yahoo! is powered by google.com and was added only a couple of years ago.

5. From "Sesame Street."

6. Media Metrix (http://www.mediametrix.com) is the Nielsen rating system of the online world.

7. Notice how many cool domain names CNet registered: search.com, download.com, ftp.com. They were ahead of their time.

8. One of the ironies of the "technically advanced" web is that many of its sophisticated-looking sites actually take your order and send it to an order taker, who then has to manually rekey your information

into a back-office order entry system. The problem is that it takes a lot of work, as well as changes in cultural attitudes, to integrate the web with the traditional systems of a big company.

 9. In sales terminology—using McDonald's as an example—an up-sell is: "You want fries with that?" or "Do you want to SuperSize it?" (an opportunity to upgrade your meal). A hypothetical example of a cross-sell would be if the cashier said: "Did you know that McDonald's can wash your car for $5?" A cross-sell is in progress when you are presented with a relevant, but not necessarily directly related, purchasing opportunity.

10. Many of the companies that have implemented sales or service chat functionality on the web do a good job with the technology and a lousy job with their people management. If you have a "contact us" feature on your website, you are inviting communication. You need to do some forecasting on how many emails you expect to receive and how long it will take to respond (and staff accordingly) to meet the anticipated demand. If you implement a real-time chat functionality, you must ensure that any customer who clicks on "chat now" *can* chat now; that you have enough people ready to manage the demand immediately. *Now* means NOW, and customer expectations of immediacy on the web are serious. Many sites fail by mismanaging the people side of the technology and underestimating the demand that will be generated.

11. There was a time, a few years ago, when "push" became an absolute buzzword bacchanal. Push was going to change the world, take over the Internet, and solve the chicken-or-egg quandary. So, what is push? There is not 100 percent agreement on the definition. In general, it refers to technologies in which one party sends content proactively to another party, not just after being requested. In general, the web is referred to as being a "pull" environment. The user points a browser somewhere and then "pulls" down the content he or she is interested in. In push, the content driven to the user is based on some previously established criteria. The absolute king of push was a company called Pointcast, which went from being the darling of the industry to being out of business in three years.

12. An interesting, high-profile exception is Egghead, now Egghead .com. Egghead was a major presence, but not a profitable presence, in retail software in the United States. As software became less and less of a specialized purchase, Egghead began to lose ground to Staples, Wal-Mart, and similar stores. More than a year ago, Egghead pulled out of all of its bricks and mortar as well as its emerging "clicks

and mortar" strategy, and went for an internet pure play. After a few quarters of understandably difficult transition, Egghead emerged as a profitable dot.com e-tailer.

13. An article entitled "The Epic Story of The Well," in *Wired* magazine, is an amazing account of an early noncommercial web community. It includes an account of how Tom Mandel, a member of the Well community, literally bid his fellow members goodbye as he died online.

14. Community, content, and commerce are at the heart of many sites. This means, for example, that a medical supply company sponsors (i.e., pays to place ad banners near) a community of women talking about what kind of car seat to buy for their kids. These communities are always anonymous. Are all the opinions expressed in the message boards and chats the opinions of concerned citizens and fellow parents, or of paid shills from the media company or the advertiser? Hard to say. If a community member trashes the products produced by the sponsoring multinational mega corporation, and the criticism is fair and well documented, does that posting stay on the community site? Also hard to say. The Internet has enabled fascinating new business models, to be sure, but it has also created loads of opportunity to seriously and dangerously stretch the limits of journalistic editorial integrity. Caveat emptor.

15. Only the real old-timers will remember that Yahoo!'s original URL was http://yahoo.stanford.edu/.

16. Naturally, the nature of the current employer of most of this book's authors has nothing at all to do with this viewpoint.

17. Actually, almost every major investment bank has recently gone casual and abandoned the dress-up game, possibly in an attempt to appear to be "regular people," like the new internet billionaires whom they serve. What are they going to do with all those cufflinks and suspenders?

18. By the way, our friend didn't buy the bat. It was, ironically, a gift from one of his vendors. If you meet him, say, "Shalom, Habibi!" This may spare you a beating.

19. SAP is the second largest software company in the world. It does big ERP systems.

20. Our money is on the giants.

21. Technically, some exchanges, like the New York Stock Exchange and most of the commodity rings, are not automated. They still have people who run around shouting strange commands to one another and giving secret hand signals, and they write things on little slips of

paper. They clang a bell at the end of the day. This is all going away in the next few years.

22. By the way, don't ever be embarrassed to ask about TLAs (three-letter acronyms). They are the bane of technological existence, and hardly anyone can ever remember—or agree on—what they stand for. Companies often make up their own esoteric abbreviations for things that have nothing to do with the industry at large. If some gearhead (or gearhead wanna-be) uses an acronym and you don't know what it refers to, ASK! Be confident. You might even get to enjoy watching the speaker squirm as he or she realizes that he or she doesn't know either!

23. This kind of custom, large-scale outsourcing is the domain of fat old-guard giants such as EDS and IBM. Many big companies like to outsource applications to these giants when they don't have the required "core competencies" to manage them, or they don't care to develop the skills needed because they don't view them as strategic. In the e-commerce world, technology skills are strategic, so think twice before making the "easy" call to outsource. In the end, large-scale outsourcing of custom solutions rarely provides net savings.

24. For more on Service Level Agreements, see Chapter 10.

25. Scuba = Self-Contained Underwater Breathing Apparatus.

26. Don't forget all of the bad press that AOL got, a few years ago, when it switched over from timed to flat-rate service. AOL had so many new customers that its network was swamped, and users screamed bloody murder about getting nothing but busy signals when they tried to connect. Even the politicians started to get involved, which tells you how pervasive the problem was, since politicians tend to be totally clueless when it comes to the web and the Internet.

27. Sometimes the connection between the ISP and the consumer or business is called the "final mile."

28. "Clouds" are what we call very large and complex networks. Clouds are usually used on network diagrams to represent the Internet. Connections go into one end of this fuzzy cloud and come out from another.

29. UUNet is owned by MCI Worldcom.

30. You will notice that websites often have to create special instructions "for AOL users." AOL doesn't always follow internet standards, but because it has a large enough user base, website operators are frequently forced to cater to its idiosyncrasies.

31. Except for internet access itself. You pay for that. You *can* get dial-up access for free in some situations, but, with internet access, you usually do "get what you pay for."

32. Brad Stone, "Coping with the Internet," *Newsweek* Special Issue: Computers and the Family, Winter 1997, p. 15.

33. "The New Wired World," *Newsweek,* September 20, 1999, pp. 40–78.

34. It is interesting to note that the XXX industry has spawned a lucrative "counter-industry" that sells software products like Net Nanny and Cyber Patrol to help parents keep their children from viewing inappropriate content.

35. Translated into English: "Women, women, women, I love you all!"

36. This is the technology that makes it safe for you to send and receive information such as credit card numbers over the Internet by using difficult-to-decipher encryption technology.

37. There isn't any room for them in legitimate e-commerce either. Never make the user do any work that you cannot do. If there is a way to provide functionality without forcing the user to download and install special software—and there almost always is a way, 99 percent of the time—do the extra work and handle the extra complexity, to provide a seamless experience and instant gratification for your users. If you aren't willing to go the extra mile, your competitors will.

38. A notable exception to this is the I-mode phones being provided by Docomo, a spin-off of NTT in Japan. I-mode, wireless internet phones are based on a different set of technologies. These phones can browse standard web pages. They are still phones with small screens, and they can't handle the complex graphics of most internet sites, but they are opening up wide possibilities. By the end of the first quarter of 2000, Japan had more than 6,000 I-mode enhanced websites.

CHAPTER 4

1. Naturally, his idea of "my expense" was flying to the "States" and using up some frequent-flyer mileage.

2. Instead of getting resumes from remote parts of your region, you'll now be contacted by individuals and agencies located in India, Eastern Europe, and Russia.

3. Depending on how much their employees are abused . . .

4. Section 1706 of the Tax Reform Act of 1986 removed the "safe harbor" that generally exempted consultants and engineers from the tests that the IRS uses to determine independent contractorship. The government contended that a lot of consultants weren't paying taxes (it was also a closed-door deal by former Senator Daniel Patrick Moynihan of New York, to favor large consulting practices). These tests include things like maintaining an office, a corporation, multiple clients, and so on. If a consultant acts too much like an employee, the IRS could construe that it is a de facto employee and is therefore liable for back taxes, benefits, penalties, and so on.

CHAPTER 5

1. The distribution problems with lemonade on the Net are manifold. We don't recommend adopting this business except as a silly example to be used in books like this.

2. Beware: Large consulting firms and web shops make a practice of hiring inexperienced staff (often just out of college) and letting them learn on the clients' time and money. Always check resumes and ask questions about relevant experience when working with consulting firms and head shops.

3. This is a great story. ICQ is a chat program that students and geeks use to chat over the net. It's a nice tool, but it's not something that can't be duplicated quickly with a few million dollars. Anyway, ICQ was the most popular chat tool, and a few million users were playing with it on a weekly basis. So, AOL bought this company of less than 20 people for $300 million. How could AOL justify this cost? It's pretty funny actually. They guessed that several million users who spent hours online every week had to be worth a lot, but, two years later, they still haven't made a cent from them. The punch line is that the young punks from Mirabilis would have been overjoyed with $10 million.

4. The section on Quality Assurance (QA) later in this chapter describes ways to avoid these kinds of careless errors.

5. Not to be confused with the popular abbreviation for Internet Protocol.

6. One of the things that is keeping pirated movies from running completely rampant is that they have huge files. The content of a DVD takes up gigabytes—thousands of megabytes. It might take an

average user 15 to 20 hours to download a movie over a standard modem connection, assuming the connection could be kept up that long. As the availability of so-called "broadband" (in the form of cable modems and satellite and DSL services) expands to homes, the traffic in perfect, digital, pirated copies of films will become widespread. By 2003, the film and music businesses are going to be very, very different because of this technology.

7. Ironically, this now sounds a lot like something from the Dilbert *Mission Statement Generator.* Take a look at http://www.peanuts.com /comics/dilbert/career/bin/ms2.cgi. It might prove useful in your next proposal.

CHAPTER 6

1. OPM: Other people's money.

CHAPTER 7

1. Most of this book was written collaboratively, but we, the authors, were in Manhattan, Monsey, San Diego, London, Frankfurt, Majorca, Reykjavik, Jerusalem, and Dublin. Rarely were we located in the same place. We used email to send sections for review and editing, and our project plan was kept up-to-date on a special web page, www.3clicksaway.com.

CHAPTER 8

1. Scient and Viant sound alike, and that's not a coincidence. Scient was formed by some senior people who left Viant in 1998.

CHAPTER 9

1. "Cover your @$&."
2. Running the numbers: Doing all of the painstaking financial calculations needed to arrive at a business decision.
3. A Gantt chart is the most popular type of graph used to visually represent the dependencies of different tasks in a project, and the project's milestones.

4. One colleague used to say (with admiration) that his CIO was so sharp at people management that he could call a meeting, magically have the final call to action be what he wanted to begin with, and have everyone leave the meeting convinced that the decision was their own idea. He used to say that he could sleep with your wife and have you think it was *your* idea and you would even *thank* him for it.

CHAPTER 10

1. If you don't have a few hundred bucks a month to spend on their services, there are some lower-end alternatives, such as Web Garage, which will also give you a "load time" for pages.

CHAPTER 11

1. From a certain point of view, there is no such thing as a launch, because to run a website is to be forever in "launch mode." There is always something new to roll out, something to change, something to freak out about.

Glossary

Above the fold A concept taken from the world of print newspapers. It refers to the part of a site that is visible without scrolling. The space on a website that is above the fold is more valuable than that below the fold because it receives more traffic. Above the fold advertisements are commensurately more expensive.

ADSL Stands for A-symmetrical Digital Subscriber Line. This is the most common type of DSL sold to business and consumers by ISPs. It is A-symmetrical because the "upstream" bandwidth is lower than the downstream. For example, a customer might have a download speed of 800Kbit/sec, but an upload speed of only 300Kbit/sec. In most cases this is not a significant issue for users because they are much more likely to be downloading large files (such as video content) than they are to be uploading it. What is cool about DSL is that it uses the existing copper wire telephone infrastructure to transport data from your home or office, so to set up DSL in a new area, no new cables need to be run from the telephone companies to the homes and offices (this is known as the "final mile"). Another benefit of the technology is that voice and data can run simultaneously across the same copper wire.

Advertising inventory In web terms, it is the amount of advertising impressions available during a given period of time. Inventory is a function of time, traffic, and the number of advertising units available per page.

Applet A kind of Java program that can appear inside of a web page. Java is a rich programming language (HTML is not) and so applets can be used to give web pages special capabilities.

ASP 1) Application Service Provider—a new kind of business related to outsourcing. An ASP provides remote access to an application and allows its customer to subscribe and use it without having the headache of managing it. Hotmail is an example of a very simple ASP, where the application is email.

2) Active Server Pages—A Microsoft technology that provides a framework for developing interactive web pages, allowing a developer to connect to back end services such as databases and other application. Because of Microsoft's competing definition for "ASP," some people in the Application Service Provider business have considered changing their acronym to ASM for Application Service Manager.

Authentication The process of verifying the identity of a user. This can be as simple as a short password, or as complex as a biometric test such as a thumbprint or retina-scan. The key to authentication is ensuring that someone is who they claim to be.

Availability With information systems, "availability" has a special meaning. It refers to the percentage of time during which a system is up and running. Another word for availability is "up time." Most commercial websites have a goal of 99.9 percent up time.

Back end A rather used and abused term. If the website is what the users connect to, then the back end is what is behind the web systems. These are systems such as accounting systems, user databases, and order management systems. These are sometimes referred to as legacy systems, which is a funny way that web people have of talking about the systems that were there (working very well, thank you very much) before the web came into being. One of the missions of the web, is to take all these terrific back end business systems and make them available to the public.

Banner ad The most ubiquitous form of online advertising. In most cases, it appears as a thin stripe at the top of a website. They are usually placed at the top of a page, above the site's main navigation, but can appear just about anywhere: on the bottom, in the middle of the page and so on. When clicked, the banner will hyperlink to another location on the WWW.

Banner wrap Essentially, a banner wrap is a banner ad at the top of a page that extends down the left or right hand side creating an upside down "L" shaped area.

Below the fold See "Above the fold."

Bricks-and-mortar The way that most web people refer to the offline world. Bricks-and-mortar is a reference to the fact that traditional business world is bound to physical locations built of bricks-and-mortar. Among techie people this term is sometimes used in a derogatory way, although less so since NASDAQ has come back to Earth and proven that the traditional world will not be gone by 2002.

BBS—Bulletin board service This is the primordial internet community, and they still exist. A BBS is a text-only system accessed through a terminal emulator such as telnet. BBS members send messages to each other, chat, post announcements, exchange files and ideas. BBSs are the precursers to AOL and CompuServe.

Buttons These are tiny graphics that appear on a web page.

Cache A cache is technical term for a temporary storage place. Caches are very useful and appear all over the Internet. The purpose of a cache is to avoid unnecessary trips across a crowded network or to avoid overloading a system. For example, your web browser normally keeps files in its cache so that it doesn't have to keep downloading the same image over and over again from a website. We would say that it *caches* these files on your hard drive in a temporary directory. In order to make sure that you are not getting stale content, it regularly will purge the cache and reload all the files you want to look at. The length of time that an item should be cached before it is considered "stale" is called the "time to live" (TTL).

CMO—(Chief Marketing Officer) The new snazzy term for the head of marketing. Internet companies seem to like this title.

CGI—(Common Gateway Interface) This is the oldest way to create interactive web pages. The first interactive websites were all done with CGI. It allows a web server to talk directly to a program, so instead of serving a static HTML page (one that is already written), the web server can talk to a program that builds a page "on the fly" and pipes it back to the web server who serves it to the user. This may sound like a lot of technical huey, but don't worry. The main thing to remember is that CGI is old and except in certain circumstances it is best to avoid using CGI because it is slower, less scalable, and less stable than the more modern techniques which involve special web server interfaces (APIs).

CIO—(Chief Information Officer) This executive takes responsibility for development and operations of the company's information systems. Until about 10 years ago, most information systems at most companies were used primarily by the CFO organization and IT managers reported to the CFO. Since information technology has moved well beyond accounting software, the CIO has become a critical role in all large companies and this person is expected not only to manage IT, but to promote an overall technology vision. See also: "CTO."

Clicks and mortar A combination of a website with an existing bricks-and-mortar business. In the end of 1999 it became popular, particularly for traditional companies with lots of entrenched overhead, to talk about the value of mixing together the 24/7 availability and self service immediacy of the web with the high touch, easier to brand environment of the classical clicks and mortar world. Also called: "Click and Bricks."

Click through Click through, or more typically click-through percentage, refers to the percentage of people that click on an online advertisement, a section of a site, and so on. It is an important metric to examine when looking at the effectiveness of ads or site navigation.

Community (See Communities section in Chapter 2) A "real" community in the "real" world has a natural analog in the online world. It is a group of people who share something in common and communicate and work together in a rewarding way. From a commercial point of view, to be the host of a dedicated community of users is the holy grail of e-commerce. In the web world, "community" was the big buzzword of 1995. The first online communities were newsgroups and bulletin boards (see: BBS) where techies with common interests could get together on a professional or personal level to share their ideas, their lives, and files such as images, documents and programs. The mainstream popularity of noninternet communities such as AOL and its competitors (remember AOL's offering didn't include full internet access until much later) got web people very excited about using web browsers and other software to create user-friendly communities. As e-commerce has come into its own, communities have taken on another dimension. eBay.com, for instance, as well as being the biggest consumer action site, can be viewed as a very successful community of merchants and consumers who work together, earn a livelihood together, and get to know one another beyond their virtual workplace. What makes eBay successful is the commitment of its community who essentially pay a tax to "live" there.

Cookie An invention of Netscape that was instantly adopted by the Internet community as a standard in 1995. Cookies are tiny bits of text or files that let web servers store small pieces of information on the users hard drive. This allows websites to remember who it's users are, from click to click and from visit to visit. There has been much ado about cookies and the bottom line is this: like any good technology, if it is used responsibly it is extremely valuable, and if not, it can be dangerous. There is nothing evil about cookies by themselves. The underlying protocol of the WWW-http- was designed to be totally stateless, meaning a web server would not know who you are or what you did from one click to the next. This made functionality like shopping carts very hard to do. Cookies extend the http protocol to allow for the indication of the state or disposition of the user. There are other solutions to the stateless problem, but they are all fragile, very complicated and cannot go for very long before they lose track of the user.

Cost per click A web advertising pricing scheme where a website establishes a per click fee, rather than a cost per thousand impressions structure. In this scenario, the advertisers pay for every actual click from a user. All impressions that do not generate clicks are free.

CPM In the web world, CPM or "cost per milla" means the cost for 1,000 impressions.

Creative brief A document delivered to a creative team that outlines the marketing goals, the target customers, the products and any special brand issues. The creative team uses this brief as their guidebook and reference to come up with a concept and design for a website or an advertisement. A creative brief is to a designer what a business requirements document is to a software developer.

CRM — (Customer Relationship Management/Marketing) A broad category of systems that are used to electronically manage customer contact and transaction histories. The goal of such systems is the first commandment of business: "Know Thy Customer." Since customer contact and transactions can occur through many channels (such as telephone, retail stores, website, and email), CRM systems have the job of collecting data from many disparate systems, organizing that data and simultaneously providing it to other systems and to people in the form of reports.

CTO — (Chief Technology Officer) This role usually only appears in technology companies. Usually, a CTO is the executive responsible for product development and for the product strategy from a technology perspective. You can think of it as the head of R&D or the head of engineering. Typically, in small firms, the CTO is also the CIO. CTOs tend to be more focused on the products that get sold to customers, and CIOs tend to be more focused on using technology to run the business. Often, the line between CTO and CIO gets very fuzzy.

CYA — Cover your "derriere" Example: "That memo I wrote to my boss about the risks of this project was strictly CYA. I am confident that we can do it, but if anything goes wrong, I can say, 'I told you that might happen!'"

Data warehouse A specialized computer database for holding vast amounts of information in ways that are easy and efficient to retrieve. Often these are referred to as OLAP (online analytical processing) databases.

Data mining Using specialized computer software tools for analyzing subtleties and relationships in the vast amounts of data held in data warehouses.

Destination sites Sometimes used interchangeably with "portal." These
are generally large, high traffic sites with a wide array of features and functions.

Dial-up Internet access via a modem over a regular phone line. The maximum speed attainable with this technology is generally 56K per second. This is far and away the most common way for people to access the Internet. Dial-up is effectively the opposite of "high bandwidth" or "broadband" access.

Digerati a.k.a. Nick Negroponte. This term is used to refer to those members of the intellectual internet community who are prone to pontificating about the future of online life, wearing black, and spending a vast majority of their time at conferences attended exclusively by people who wear black and pontificate about the future of online life.

DSL See "ADSL."

Dynamic Content that is driven by a database that is created for presentation on-the-fly. The opposite of "hard coded" or "static."

Encryption The use of encryption dates back to ancient warfare. Encryption is a way of protecting data by converting it into seemingly meaningless pieces. The unrecognizable (encrypted) data can only be returned to their original form (decrypted) by using a special key. Since the Internet is a public place, data can not be safely transmitted unless it is protected by strong encryption. There are several popular types of encryption and many companies that specialize in them.

Fat pipe A slang term for a high-speed or "broadband" connection to the Internet or between any two computers.

Firewall A piece of software (usually with its own dedicated hardware) that enforces policies about who is allowed to connect to a given system. Firewalls protect sites from unauthorized access, and allow administrators to organize complicated access policies in a manageable way.

Front end The user presentation layer of a site. The branding, look and feel, and user accessible features and functions of a site. See "Middleware" and "Back end."

Hard launch A launch of a new site or new section of a site that is accompanied by marketing support, intended to drive traffic. The last stage in an internet project. See "Soft launch."

HTML—(Hyper Text Mark-up Language) This is the language that defines the layout of web pages. HTML consists of content (mainly text and images) along with tags which are used to "mark up" the content. Tags are bracketed "statements" that tell a browser how it should present a given piece of content. For example, the <p tag tells the browser to start a new paragraph. For a quick look at HTML, open any web page in your web browser, go to the View menu, and select "Source." This will show you the HTML source code for the web page that is currently displayed in your browser.

HTTP—(Hyper Text Transport Protocol) The application protocol of the WWW. Web browsers and websites use http to request and transfer HTML documents (web pages), images and any other type of file as well as user input such as credit card numbers. HTTP is a relatively simple protocol, and the popularity of the WWW has led to the dominance of HTTP as the preferred application protocol for many nonweb applications.

HTTPS—(Secure Hyper Text Transport Protocol) Just like HTTP except it adds encryption so that everything that is transferred is protected. See "Encryption" and "SSL."

Information architecture In the world of front end design this refers to the navigational schema, the navigational choices, not the "look and feel" of a website. In the world of software and system development this refers to the high level blueprint for how data flows through a system.

Impressions An impression is essentially a pair of "eyeballs." One impression means that an ad was delivered (or downloaded) to one web browser one time.

Initial public offering The initial sale of shares of stock to the public. The IPO craze has been a major feature of the dot.com explosion creating the capital that has allowed companies like Amazon.com to become a major global brand in just a few years.

Interstitial ads Special web ads that are spawned into a separate window by your web browser.

ISP Internet Service Provider.

JAVA A technology platform and a programming language. Sun Microsystems created Java and owns the license, but the technology and even the source code for Java is freely distributed to the public. As a result, many companies compete to provide Java products. This openness is believed to be responsible for its rapid acceptance and huge success. Java has become the standard programming language and platform for many IT shops for a variety of reasons. It is platform-independent (which means that once a Java application is developed it can run inside almost any operating system with few or no changes). Java is an internet-centric language. It was built to be run in a distributed, networked environment. As a programming language, Java fits nicely into the Object Oriented (OO) model which is a methodology for developing software that has been almost universally embraced by the academic and commercial world. It is worth noting that Java was originally created to run in tiny computers inside of household appliances. Since the consumer appliances world wasn't ready for this level of sophistication, the Sun people decided that they would see if it would fly in the world of business applications and the Internet.

K size, weight This refers to the amount of data that a banner ad will use in order to be transmitted to a user's web browser. The "K" refers to thousands of data bytes.

Kluge Techie slang for a cobbled together, messy, technical solution.

Latency Delay. Often used in reference to the unpredictable and largely unavoidable "internet latency" which occurs to a greater or a lesser extent anytime information is moved across the public internet.

Live environment The web servers and websites they host that are accessible by the public. The opposite of a "test," "staging," or "development" environment.

MarCom Marketing/Communication.

Matrix organization An often unavoidable but complicated organizational structure in which employees have usually two bosses. Common matrices have employees reporting to a product head and a geographic head, or to the e-commerce head and a product head. The inherently multidisciplinary nature of web work tends to breed matrix organizations.

Mcommerce "Mobile" commerce. eCommerce using cell phones, beepers, wireless modems, and so on.

Media spend The part of an advertising budget expended on media (space, time, or impressions) as opposed to the product of the advertisement or "creative" itself.

Netizens Early adopters of the World Wide Web and the Internet. Citizens of the web.

North Sioux City, South Dakota Former site of the corporate headquarters of Gateway, Inc. and location of some of their large manufacturing facilities, as well as the site where two of the authors of this book learned some tough and useful e-commerce lessons.

Offline Work or processes conducted while disconnected from the Internet.

Online 1) On the Internet. 2) Functioning (e.g., "The server is back online").

On the beach/on the bench A consultant who is not billing hours. Consultants will do anything to avoid being "on the beach."

PERL—(Practical Extraction and Reporting Language) A common tool for building web CGI scripts. See "CGI."

Personalization A word used to describe a wide array of technologies that customize the features and content of website based on a user profile. Easy examples of personalization can be found in the customizable home pages of all the major portal/directory sites such as Excite and Yahoo!

Pipe A connection to the Internet or between two or more computers. Synonymous with "line."

Pop-up An area of a site, or most often an advertisement that appears in a separate browser window on top of the main browser. These "pop-up" windows, as they are often called, are most often found during special marketing promotions or as the entry into online marketing surveys. They are powerful and attract a lot of user attention but users tend to find them very annoying. Use with caution.

Portal A website that aggregates a variety of features, functions and, in some cases, other sites under a common brand with unified navigation.

Producer In the web world, particularly the web agency world, a project manager who is focused on managing the creation of a website's look and feel, the programming of the front end, and the integration of content.

Production Term used to refer to the live or publicly available environment. A site that is up or online is said to be in "production."

Promotion Term used to describe the process of moving a site or application from the development environment to the staging environment, or from the staging environment to the live or production environment.

Pull Content that users actively request or search for themselves. See "Push."

Push An internet buzz word that has died down to a whisper but may always reemerge. The concept here is that content is "pushed" to the user through email or customized website or other mechanism rather than the user being forced to search for or "pull" their own material. All of the daily newsletters, daily update emails that are offered by many sites are examples of push content. All the "my" sites like my.yahoo.com are examples of push content in the form of a personalized website.

Site map Essentially an index that exposes the overall structure of all the sections of a site. There are two camps in the world about the inclusion of a site map on the site itself. It is our general opinion that if you need to put up a site map for users to find what they are looking for, it is probably a sign of navigation problems.

SLA—(Service Level Agreement) A critical component of any contract between you and an outsourced (or even internal to a company) service provider. A good SLA should define in exquisite and excruciating detail the exact expectations for uptime, performance, response time when issues arise, and so on. Properly negotiated SLAs mean life or death online, particular in areas such as outsourced internet hosting.

Soft launch Whenever time allows, a very good idea. In a soft launch, a new site, or new section of a site is promoted to the "live" or "production" environment but without any marketing support. Real customers who happen to "discover" the site are welcome to use it but no attempt is made to drive people to it. This is a part of the testing quality assurance process before the balloons and brass bands herald the arrival of your new site to the public at large.

Spam Unsolicited email. Don't do it. Only communicate with customers via email if you have their permission to do so. Spam can get you deep in hot water with your customers.

SSL — (Secure Socket Layer) A type of encryption. A key technology in e-commerce used extensively for transmitting personal information such as credit card data.

Staging The term that refers to the point in the development of an application when it's being readied for promotion into the publicly accessible environment.

Static The opposite of "dynamic." In the online world usually refers to content that is not database driven, but instead "hard coded," or unchanging.

Stickiness This is a term that refers to how likely a given site or area of a site is to attract repeat visits. Sticky applications are things like web email or stock trackers because people return every day, sometimes several times a day. Stickiness builds page views, particularly important to advertising driven sites, but is important for any e-commerce business. The more a customer returns, the more likely they are to transact, the more times your brand is presented to them.

T1 An internet connection that enables the transmission of 1.544 megabits per second. The basic "broadband" connection typically used by businesses.

Test environment To ensure quality, developers will always establish a simulation or test environment before promoting their work to a publicly accessible place. As much as possible the test environment attempts to simulate the exact hardware and software configuration of the live environment to catch problems before they are noticed by customers.

TLA Three letter acronym.

Unit What web media people like to call ads.

URL — (Universal Resource Locator) A web address.

Viral marketing Marketing schemes that self perpetuate. An easy example are sites that give a user free space to post personal photographs. Users point their friends to the site to see their pictures, who then decide to post their own pictures, and tell another set of friends to view them, and on and on. The idea here is that a viral marketing campaign can spread with the same dynamics as a viral infection, working its way through a population with exponential increases in participation as the "campaign" is passed from one person to another.

Virtual 1) Not physically bounded, not bricks-and-mortar as in a "virtual office" where employees work together in an integrated electronic environment even though they may be separated by oceans in the real world. 2) Used clumsily to refer to anything online.

VR—(Virtual Reality) A rather imprecise term used to refer to the creation of immersive electronic environments that are perceived to the user to be "virtually real." True "VR" usually involves the use of a helmet or goggles. There are an increasing number of real useful VR applications but they are not found on the web. For a large variety of reasons, true VR internet experiences are some way off.

Visual noise A software ergonomics/design term that refers to cluttered and confusing graphics. The key to web design is: simple is good, simple is better.

WAP—(Wireless Application Protocol) The data transfer structure used in mobile internet devices.

Webcast A live online broadcast.

WML—(Wireless Mark-Up Language) The WAP version of the PC-based internet HTML. This is the language that instructs a mobile device how to display wireless internet data to the user.

Index

About the Authors

MICHAEL DRAPKIN

Michael Drapkin took his first programming course at a local Los Angeles university in 1975, using punched cards. A gifted musician, Drapkin attended the Eastman School of Music while continuing his computer education at the University of Rochester. Upon graduation, he moved to Manhattan to pursue a career as a symphony orchestra musician. Instead of supporting himself by waiting tables, he programmed computers while auditioning for symphony positions

Rather than retiring to orchestra life, Drapkin returned to New York City at the dawn of the PC era where he made a career shift to workstation software developer. He began a ten-year journey in technology consulting for major corporations. In 1993, after the birth of his twin daughters, he moved to Wall Street. He spent over four years at Lehman Brothers, overseeing the firm's deployment of client/server technology for its retail practice, including its first installation of a company-wide data warehouse for brokerage client business intelligence.

With the rise of the New Economy, he left Lehman Brothers as a vice president at the end of 1997 and joined Avalanche—a leading Silicon Alley/new media firm—as director of technology where he also acted as senior technologist for its sister firm Razorfish. At Avalanche he not only led technology, but client, project and business management as well. In mid-1998 a former Lehman senior manager recruited him to become chief technology officer of DMS Corp., a quarter billion dollar multinational publicly traded firm in the courier industry.

At the end of 1998, Michael founded Drapkin Technology (www.drapkintechnology.com), a senior-level business, technology, and management consultancy for web-centric businesses. As principal of the firm, he consults to numerous dot-coms and Fortune 1000 firms on all aspects of e-commerce—from how to cut profitable deals with vendors, to how to effectively deploy the latest technology, to how to manage to profitability.

Drapkin is chair of eCommerce Management for Columbia University's Advanced Information Technology Management program at their school of continuing education and teaches a course on Reengineering for Web, Internet & E-Commerce. He is also a visiting lecturer on e-commerce at The Graham School of the University of Chicago.

His articles have appeared in numerous trade periodicals, including the *New York Times, Information Week, and Electronic Musician* magazine. He has been quoted in *Fortune, Wired, PC Week, Chicago Tribune, Philadelphia Inquirer* and numerous other publications and on camera with CNBC and CNET. He also is a regular public speaker throughout the metropolitan New York area and at major business and e-commerce conferences, including PC Expo and eVenture World. He is in demand as a moderator for e-commerce panels, moderating panels for Akamai, Linkshare and other firms and conferences. He is the author of books on both music and computers including *The OS/2 Presentation Manager Mentor* (1996), also with John Wiley and Sons, and *Symphonic Repertoire for the Bass Clarinet* (Roncorp, Inc., 1979), which has become the definitive work of its genre worldwide.

JON LOWY

Jon Lowy began his career in the Spring of 1995, as a technician and one of the first hires at IDT (International Discount Telecommunications, NASDAQ:IDTC) in their ISP division. IDT was the first company to offer dial-up internet access nationally at a flat rate. While serving as a customer support technician, often handling more than 50 incidents per day, he also worked as IDT's webmaster, postmaster, and operator of the company's IRC support channel.

After three months on the job, Jon independently developed and implemented an automated email support system that significantly improved the firm's responsiveness to customers. He built the entire system using free software downloaded from the Internet. He was then moved to the firm's development team where he became the product manager for IDT's dial-up internet access software. While continuing as product manager, Jon designed a web-based videoconferencing application.

In 1996, he was headhunted by Cambridge Technology Partners to run information systems at Violy, Byorum & Partners, a boutique investment bank in midtown Manhattan.

Daniel Marovitz lured Jon away to the Great Plains of South Dakota in 1997 where he was Chief eCommerce Architect for Gateway. Jon guided gateway.com through two complete website overhauls, heading up architecture, development and operations. The site has often been ranked the fastest PC site on the Internet (Keynote Business 40 Index).

By mid-2000, Jon had left Gateway for Deutsche Bank in London, to once again team with Daniel. Jon is Director of Internet Architecture for Deutsche's online investment banking division, eGCI. eGCI is charged with developing online trading and research systems for retail and institutional clients on a worldwide basis.

Jon is a founder and the architect of Softwax.com, a web-based peer-to-peer system that allows communities of users to share files safely and conveniently.

DANIEL MAROVITZ

Daniel Marovitz grew up with PCs and the Internet and has been online since the age of 10. In the early 1980s, his father, Dr. William Marovitz, became involved in the dawn of commercial online services, working with Lexus/Nexus, BRS, and CompuServe, among others.

Upon graduating from Cornell University in 1994 with a degree in Spanish Literature and Japanese Studies, Daniel joined Gateway 2000 (then headquartered in North Sioux City, South Dakota) as a Japanese marketing analyst. In less than three months, Daniel was sent to Tokyo as Gateway's first employee in Japan. He managed Gateway's distribution and marketing relationship with Nissho Iwai, one of the 10 largest companies in the world.

Daniel was part of the team that led to the establishment of the local Gateway subsidiary, Gateway Japan. At the time, with 272 employees on opening day, it was the largest foreign-capitalized start-up in the history of Japan. As the head of marketing for the new entity, Daniel managed advertising, media, public relations, and Gateway Japan's early web efforts.

When he returned to the United States in 1996, Daniel worked for the president of Gateway. His first task was to plan and develop the company's global intranet system. Within a few months, Daniel gained responsibility for all of the company's public-facing "dot-com" sites. Over the next two years, Gateway.com's contribution to overall sales increased from 4 percent to 35 percent. Daily online revenue exceeded $1.3 million.

In early 1999, Daniel joined iVillage, the online Women's Network and one of the 30 most trafficked sites on the Internet, as the Vice President of Commerce. His responsibilities included oversight of all of iVillage's transactional business with the mission to build e-commerce businesses that leveraged the more than 2 million active members of the iVillage network.

In January 2000, Daniel accepted his current position as a Managing Director and Chief Executive Officer of the eGCI group at Deutsche Bank. eGCI is charged with developing and implementing online products for Deutsche Bank's investment and commercial bank on a worldwide basis.

A frequent speaker on the subject of the Internet, Daniel has addressed audiences at the United Nations (in Thailand), the Japanese Parliament, Shop.org, Retail.net, Financial Times, The Economist, and Ziff-Davis conferences.